BASIC CONCEPTS
OF
PSYCHOANALYTIC
PSYCHIATRY

BASIC CONCEPTS

OF

PSYCHOANALYTIC

PSYCHIATRY

Elizabeth R. Zetzel, M.D.
and
W. W. Meissner, M.D.

BASIC BOOKS, INC., PUBLISHERS   NEW YORK

PREFACE

On November 22, 1970, Dr. Elizabeth Zetzel suddenly and tragically died. Her death was felt as a severe and acute loss by the psychoanalytic community in the Boston area and by many others to whom her clinical and teaching influence extended.

Dr. Zetzel's unexpected death put the completion of this book in doubt. In view of the fact that her influence was so central in its preparation and that she died before its completion, it would be useful to put down some of the specifics of the origins of this text. My own association with Dr. Zetzel extended over several years. I knew her first as teacher and seminar leader at the Boston Psychoanalytic Institute and the Massachusetts Mental Health Center. I came to know her best as a control supervisor for one of my analytic cases. During the course of this association Dr. Zetzel suggested that we collaborate in the preparation of the present work.

For several years Dr. Zetzel conducted a seminar and a course of public lectures at the Massachusetts Mental Health Center. The content of these lectures had to do with an introductory exposition of Freud's development of some basic psychoanalytic concepts. Her lectures became an important aspect of the teaching program at the hospital and gained an enthusiastic public among the resident psychiatrists and other personnel in training from surrounding Boston institutions.

Dr. Zetzel suggested that we try to transform the basic skeleton of these lectures into a book which she intended to serve as a clear, correct, informative, and intellectually challenging introduction to the basic concepts of psychoanalysis. She hoped it would serve as a high level introduction to psychoanalytic thinking for psychiatric residents, medical students, psychiatric social workers, and others. She hoped to build on a presumed general grasp of analytic ideas and to present a coherent and integrated account of the psychoanalytic perspective.

With these objectives in mind, I undertook to rewrite, revise, and expand her lectures. The material was reorganized and reformulated, but the basic orientation, emphasis, and approach of her lectures were preserved. Chapter by chapter, Dr. Zetzel would read, comment, criticize, suggest material to be added or subtracted, question, discuss, and review. The result is a version which bears the stamp of her unique approach to psychoanalysis in both its theory and its practice. The process of collaborative rewriting and revision extended through the first thirteen chapters. At the time of her death, the last three chapters were in her hands; she had read and commented on them, but had not been able to put her thoughts and comments in writing. These last chapters were rewritten in accord with her expressed evaluations—but without the benefit of her detailed criticism. I am grateful to Dr. Paul Myerson for his critical evaluation and suggestions for these chapters.

Despite Dr. Zetzel's untimely death, the book to my mind achieves some of her own cherished objectives. It reflects the clarity and precision of her thought and her own depth of clinical experience and insight. It also reflects her penetrating view of psychoanalytic theory and its possibilities for serving the broader needs of psychiatry in understanding and treating mental illness. But most of all, and perhaps more significantly, it represents her commitment to and investment in the teaching of young psychiatrists—a commitment to which she dedicated the major portion of the time and energy of her life. I firmly hope, then, that this book will stand as a fitting memorial to the basic commitment that so characterized her rich and productive life and that it fulfills the expectations and objectives for which she intended it.

W. W. MEISSNER, M.D.

CONTENTS

BASIC CONCEPTS
OF
PSYCHOANALYTIC
PSYCHIATRY

Introduction

The term psychoanalysis refers to a theory of personality structure and function, application of this theory to other branches of knowledge, and finally, to a specific psychotherapeutic technique. This body of knowledge is based on and derived from the fundamental psychological discoveries made by Sigmund Freud.

This definition, given in the Constitution and Bylaws of the International Psychoanalytical Association, indicates in the first place that psychoanalysis is a comprehensive psychology which must therefore include within its conceptual framework both healthy and pathological aspects of psychic structure and function. It suggests in addition that this body of knowledge may be usefully applied to other disciplines. Nonetheless, it clearly emphasizes the fact that the technique of clinical psychoanalysis is a very specific therapeutic method.

Freud first developed psychoanalysis as a therapeutic tool in the treatment of patients whose presenting symptomatology was hysterical. From the outset, however, he clearly regarded the knowledge he was obtaining as applicable in a much wider area. As early as 1895 he said, for example:

I am plagued with two ambitions: to see how the theory of mental functioning takes shape if quantitative considerations, a sort of economics of nerve force, are introduced into it, and secondly, to extract from psychopathology what may be of benefit to normal psychology. Actually a satisfactory general theory of neuropsychotic disturbances is impossible if it cannot be brought into association with clear assumptions about normal mental processes.[1]

This statement introduces two of the major basic assumptions which remain integral to psychoanalytic theory. "A sort of economics of nerve force" implies, first, that the mind possesses dynamic properties. Such properties, in addition, are considered to have quantitative, i.e., economic, attributes. Such general statements suggest that from the outset Freud made a distinction between his discoveries in respect to the content or meaning of mental life and the more abstract assumptions which constitute its basic conceptual framework.

Theory in Psychoanalysis

Every scientific field has to face the problem of the relation between theory and practice, or the application of theory. This involves problems in the validation of scientific theories. For psychoanalysis, the problem is compounded by the lack of purely objective data and the difficulties in achieving repeatability of observations. All social sciences, and particularly those that deal with individual human responses, share these difficulties in some degree.

Psychoanalytic concepts involve several stages in the process of their development. First, the basic clinical material derived classically from the psychoanalytic situation must be collected. Second, this clinical knowledge must be correlated and compared, thus serving as the basis for specific theoretical formulations which are based on the content or meaning of the material. Finally, such content-derived formulations may serve as the basis for further and more abstract theoretical elaborations. These comprise general concepts of an abstract nature which pertain to the qualities, functioning, and general nature of the mental apparatus.

Zetzel has put this basic distinction in the following terms:

The development of psychoanalytic knowledge has from the outset been concerned with even deeper and more penetrating investigation into the specific content of the unconscious mind, the nature of unconscious fantasies, the various mechanisms by means of which unconscious impulses are modified and controlled, the specific situations, both external and internal, which can be related to the development of the ego and the sense of reality. The correlation and comparison of the findings of different workers in respect to these problems has been a main preoccupation of psychoanalytic research. It would probably be correct to say that the general body of knowledge derived from these investigations into the content of the unconscious mind has in a number of respects reached a stage where certain formulations of a general nature have been embodied within our theoretical framework. . . . In addition, however, to this type of theoretical formulation one must also consider another group of deductions which have been proposed as the basis for a framework of general theory. This aspect of theory is not concerned primarily with the specific content of the unconscious mind, but rather with abstract conceptual formulations which could account for the infinite complexities of other findings of a more specific meaningful nature.[2]

Freud's approach in the *Interpretation of Dreams* (1900) offers a good model for this dichotomy in analytic thinking. In the early chapters Freud concerns himself with a basically clinical approach to the dream material. He elucidates the associations to dream material, the resistances related to them, the latent or symbolic meaning of the dream content, and the mechanisms by which the latent meaning is distorted and disguised and expressed in the manifest dream content. In the famous seventh chapter, however, he shifts his position and moves to a different theoretical level. He presents his now famous model of the mental apparatus and his conception of how it functions. Basing his formulation on the preceding material and the generalizable observations that he was able to make, he presents a synthetic view of the psychic apparatus and its functioning that would account for his meaningful findings. He is no longer concerned with the meaningful content of unconscious wishes or conflicts, but focuses on an approach to the psychic apparatus as a structure for modifying and controlling instinctual energies regardless of their source and meaning.

Psychoanalytic knowledge has from the outset been obtained by what might be called a dual, or two-pronged approach: a more specifically clinical approach and a more general cultural approach. The findings of psychoanalysis, particularly in regard to content, have been closely linked with the use of the specific psychoanalytic technique. This technique, as we will see in later chapters, has enabled psychoanalysis to achieve a broad and deep understanding of the neuroses and the less serious character disorders. Despite less successful therapeutic results, this same technique also provided Freud and his early followers with much information particularly relevant to content in respect to more serious psychological disorders. During this same period of early discovery Freud applied his method of investigation to a wide spectrum of psychic phenomena—dreams, the psychopathology of everyday life, literature, and even mythology. These and other studies of common human experience were all based on the assumption that what had been discovered in the investigation of neurotic patients was not limited to a special form of mental disorder, but in fact could be identified as characteristic of a wide range of human action and experience. The content and thought processes of the unconscious mind which could be identified in neurotics were also operating in *all* human beings. The specific clinical technique developed and used in the treatment of neurotic patients was thus from the outset combined with investigations of a broader and more general nature.

The dual method of approach, the specifically clinical and the more general, may be applied to the development, structure, and function of the human mind in both its healthy and its disturbed forms. Duality is a basic aspect of psychoanalytic methodology and remains an integral part of psychoanalytic orientation and thinking. The correlation and comparison of the findings of these two approaches is very clear when we are dealing with content. Material that derives from similar levels of instinctual development can be easily correlated so that the respective approaches become mutually supportive and complementary.

Development

Beyond these basic approaches to the data of psychoanalysis lies the more difficult step of integrating the valid content obtained by these endeavors into a coherent and consistent conceptualization of the human psyche and its functioning. Both the specific content and the conceptual formulations of psychoanalysis have been widely applied in the field of psychiatry, an area with which psychoanalysis is closely allied. It has not, however, always been easy to integrate the conclusions of psychoanalysis with knowledge in the field of descriptive general psychiatry. Earlier attempts to integrate analytic principles with descriptive diagnostic categories led to a classification of mental illness based on developmental phases indicated by instinctual content. Such attempts have by and large not been very satisfactory.

The recent publication of the *Minutes of the Vienna Psychoanalytic Society* have revealed the degree to which Freud himself, and some of his early colleagues, recognized the problems integral to an approach which confined itself to instinctual content. In a number of discussions Freud referred certain problems to the area of ego psychology, which had not yet been studied. By 1911, when he published *The Two Principles of Mental Functioning,* he made a distinction which will be consonant with the approach to psychoanalytic psychiatry in this volume. He made a clear differentiation between problems attributable to failures in respect to instinctual development and problems attributable to developmental inhibitions of the ego, with particular reference to the development of the reality principle. This paper, which will be discussed in more detail in a later chapter, serves to illustrate the degree to which psychoanalysis has from the outset been both a developmental and structural psychology.

Heinz Werner defined developmental psychology as "a discipline which investigates the characteristics common to any behavior in the process of progression or regression in order to establish both the common patterns of each developmental level and the relationship between these levels that is the direction of mental development." [3] David Rapaport has clearly demonstrated the degree to which psychoanalysis meets this criterion. In an earlier contribution on the topic, "Symptom Formation and Character Formation," the following statement was made:

Our developmental hypothesis includes by definition both progressive and regressive potentiality at all times. This statement applies both to instinctual development and to the structured ego-superego system. It is a cardinal feature of psychic life that every important maturational challenge presents highly significant regressive threats.[4]

The developmental perspective, then, with its implicit recognition of the potentiality for progressive achievements and regressive impairments, provides the fundamental point of view—the basic assumption and orientation—by which the complexities of the psychoanalytic view of personality structure and functioning can be most clearly and organically grasped. The developmental process, including the vicissitudes of instinctual development and the attainments of ego development, as well as their complex interaction, forms the basic structure—the skeleton— of this book.

The view of psychoanalytic theory and concepts that we shall present in these pages takes as its basic presumption the conviction that the understanding of the developmental process—with its inherent potentialities for progressive adaptation as well as regressive retrenchment—is essential to the understanding of the other basic metapsychological assumptions of psychoanalytic theory. The integration of the dynamic, the economic, the structural, and the adaptational points of view becomes meaningful and comprehensible in relation to the developmental hypothesis and the developmental process. Moreover, this integral understanding secondarily provides the basis on which the rationale for treatment can be established. As we shall see, the basic developmental issue of whether the patient's psychopathology represents a regressive return to less mature levels of functioning and development is fundamental to determining the usefulness of specific therapeutic approaches.

It will be our objective, then, to show a double development. We will try to trace the essential conceptual steps by which Freud developed and modified his basic concepts that established the core of psychoanalysis as a systematic theory of psychopathology and as a general theory of human personality development and structure. Along that path we will follow the development of Freud's views from a primarily dynamic to an increasingly structural conceptualization of the psychic apparatus. We shall also trace the emergence of his concept of the ego as it gained in strength and stature in psychic functioning. The second process we shall delineate is that of the development of the psyche itself— particularly with an eye to integrating the patterns of instinctual development with the achievements of ego development. The conjunction and overlap of this double developmental path will lead us inexorably to the important post-Freudian ramifications—particularly in the area of ego psychology. For this latter development of psychoanalytic understanding is perhaps the most important and productive extension and enrichment of Freud's own progressing views. The most significant achievements of contemporary psychoanalytic ego psychology have been specifically in the deepening and extending of our understanding of human development.

[I]

Psychoanalysis and Contemporary Psychiatry

This book purposes to outline an approach to contemporary psychoanalytic theory within which psychiatric diagnosis and methods of treatment other than that of traditional psychoanalysis may be understood and applied. Although most of the concepts with which we shall be dealing were originally derived from the findings of clinical psychoanalysis, other methods of investigation have made and are making substantial contributions. For example, longitudinal studies of childhood development have made increasingly important contributions to our body of knowledge. In this and other areas, analytically trained observers have been led to employ a wide variety of investigative and research methods. And on the clinical side, psychoanalytic knowledge has been heavily utilized in the treatment of patients in a broad spectrum of therapeutic approaches.

The "As-If" Hypothesis

In addition to its immediate value for psychiatry and psychotherapy, it is important to recognize that contemporary psychoanalysis is to be regarded as a comprehensive developmental psychology. It can thus be expected not only to explain psychological disturbances and maladaptation but also to illumine the major criteria for mental health and mature emotional development. It should be remembered also that Freud's first major contribution was not directly in the area of clinical psychiatry. It was rather in the study of dreaming—a process that is common to all human beings. Freud started his career, in a sense, with a major contribution to general human psychology.

Freud's study of the meaning and process of dreaming offers an interesting illustration of the impact on psychoanalytic thinking of the development of new techniques and methods of observation. In the last few years, dreaming activity has become an area of intense interest, not only for psychoanalysts, but for experimental psychologists and neurophysiologists. The development of new techniques and approaches has contributed new knowledge which has inevitably led to a review and reconsideration of some of Freud's initial theories about dreaming and sleep. Briefly, it may be said that insofar as a dream is remembered and reported to a therapist or analyst, we have as yet found very little reason for making any significant changes in Freud's original interpretations. As one psychoanalytically sophisticated invesigator of dreams has indicated, all Freud's statements in respect to the meaning of dreams remain quite valid with one limitation—that they refer primarily to dreams occurring during a particular stage of sleep, i.e., the REM state. Those familiar with Freud's *Interpretation of Dreams* may recall the fact that Freud tried to separate his discussion of the dream as a reported experience from the psychology of sleep. He was not always able to maintain this distinction—as, for example, in his hypothesis that the motivation for dreaming was the preservation of sleep. This hypothesis may be validly applied to dreaming during the REM state. It may not, however, be relevant to what occurs during other periods of the sleep cycle.

The advance in the study of dreaming processes indicates the fact that many if not most of Freud's original observations retain a certain degree of validity. It should be clear, however, that any and all of his findings are subject to re-evaluation in the light of advancing experimental knowledge which indicates that the relevance of his findings may not be what he had originally suggested. As he himself, however, wrote to Fliess as early as 1890:

I have no inclination at all to keep the domain of the psychological floating as it were in the air without any organic foundation, but I have no knowledge beyond that conviction so I have to conduct myself as if I had only the psychological before me.[5]

In attempting, therefore, to correlate Freud's findings with contemporary scientific knowledge, we would be taking steps which Freud himself would certainly have wished to take if the techniques and approaches had been available to him. At the same time, however, it is important to recognize the fact that our understanding of the physical structures and functioning of the mind has not yet reached a point at which we can explain away the psychological dimension of the mental apparatus.

In general, therefore, it is crucial not to forget the considerations which led Freud to construct his "as-if" hypothesis. Psychological findings must eventually be compatible with definitive physiological knowledge. The fact, for example, that we now regard the dream as safeguarding only one stage of sleep indicates that Freud knew more about the dream as a psychological experience than he did about sleep, which we now know to be composed of a complex cycle of different patterns of cerebral functioning.

Use of Psychoanalytic Concepts

Many propositions originally derived from psychoanalysis are familiar not only to medical students, young doctors, and beginning psychiatrists but also to a great many reasonably well-informed and well-read laymen. It is a common experience to hear references to the oedipal situation, transference, and the psychopathology of everyday life. Psychologically sophisticated individuals are seldom averse to interpreting the behavior, including the slips and errors, of their friends, relatives, and acquaintances. Not only psychiatrists but individuals in many fields like to describe their colleagues or friends as "anal retentive" or "passive aggressive" or as "oral" or "narcissistic" individuals.

Such statements are based on the familiar content of psychoanalytic reconstructions. Few people, however, are aware of all that is being taken for granted in such psychological statements and interpretations. It is partly for this reason that it seems appropriate to present the basic concepts of contemporary psychoanalytic theory in relation to their underlying hypotheses. This means in brief that it is important to make the differentiation between concept and content. It contrast to content, with which most of us are familiar, concept concerns the more abstract or general basic assumptions which originally determined our understanding of such statements. Understanding of concept should throw light on the theoretical implications of material or content which at first glance often appears to be so evident that we tend to ignore its important and often still controversial implications.

A brief example may be given to illustrate this point. A psychologically sophisticated patient reported a dream to his analyst, prefacing his statement with the somewhat complacent remark, "This was clearly an oedipal dream." The dream took place in his parents' bedroom in a childhood summer home. His former girl friend, with whom he had broken some weeks before, was lying on his mother's bed. She told him something he already knew, that she was now engaged to another man. "I didn't mind at all," said the patient, "but anyhow the whole scene belongs to the distant past." The patient went on to say how glad he was that his former girl friend was now engaged. He had no regrets whatever, nor, he implied, was he any longer concerned about his jealousy of his mother's relationship with his father. When the analyst mildly mentioned the complete lack of affect both in the dream and the associations, the patient's mood abruptly shifted. Although he himself had broken the rather long and complicated affair with the former girl friend, he had by no means anticipated that she would find a replacement so soon. He was in fact furious about it. He didn't like the man she had chosen and he had really expected her to remain faithful to him, even though he had broken with her.

As he went on talking he became more and more aware of current important feelings which had been successfully disguised in the manifest dream statement, "I didn't mind at all." By placing the dream in the parental bedroom he had made a further successful disguise. It was as if the dream said, "I don't mind at all about this girl, and anyhow if I did it wouldn't mean anything because the whole thing refers to something which happened years ago when I had 'an oedipal conflict.' "

This dream may be utilized to illustrate several of the statements made in the opening remarks. First, pat interpretations that a dream or a symptomatic act has an oedipal meaning are common. They are so general that they have often little if any real impact or significance at the time they are made. Second, this very fact may facilitate, as in the given case, defenses against current situations which are arousing more immediate feelings. Third, we must recognize that the patient may in fact have been quite correct in calling this dream oedipal. However, in order to understand its true significance at the time it was dreamed, we would need to know a great deal more about the basic concepts of psychoanalysis.

For example, it became abundantly clear even in this one hour that the patient had not been aware of his affective response to the announcement of the engagement. He had clearly repressed his anger and disappointment. This repression was purposive in that he had succeeded in avoiding a painful, possibly anxiety-provoking impulse in respect to his anger at the rival who had displaced him. Why had he done this? On the face of the evidence, we can't give a direct answer. We could, however, make an educated guess. The fact that the dream is located in the parental bedroom now becomes more significant. We might suggest that his repression of anger in the current situation gives us some clue as to the defenses he had established against rivalry at a much earlier period of his life.

Basic Concepts

What basic concepts have we used in making this tentative formulation? First, we are assuming that the mind possesses dynamic energy. Such energy can be seen in this brief clinical example acting in two very different ways. In setting up the repression of anger and jealousy so that he didn't mind at all, the subject was using energy to establish and maintain a defense. Second, the anger and jealousy itself, which implied aggressive feelings toward a rival, also involved dynamic energy. Next, we can see that this dynamic energy has certain peculiar characteristics. This man was not, for example, genuinely jealous of the girl's fiancé in the sense that he wanted her back. It was the situation—namely, her engagement—which had reproduced a triangular conflict. In the setting of his analysis, this trangular situation became important as a displacement or transference. Feelings of jealousy and fear of his own aggression which had been substantially repressed in the past could now be permitted partially to reappear in a disguised and much less intense form. In writing this off as an oedipal dream and not recognizing that affect and impulses were re-emerging in the current situation, the patient was making an attempt to reinstate the original defense. This displacement and the related re-emergence of past conflicts in current situations may be explained by a general hypothesis. The mind's dynamic energy has quantitative aspects. It can be shifted and displaced so that past conflicts may be revived in a new setting. This is one of the basic concepts of psychoanalytic theory. Without it we could neither understand nor interpret transference neuroses.

It is important to keep in mind that psychoanalytic psychiatry has not reached its definitive formulation, but that it is an open-ended process of scientific inquiry which must constantly seek to understand and integrate the continuing input of clinical data that our patients present to us. It is a continual process of reflecting on the content of clinical material to penetrate its inner meaning and generalizable significance and to integrate this level of generalizable insight into a more abstract conceptualization of psychic structure and function. There is a continual dialectic between content and concept, between analysis and synthesis— weaving back and forth in an ongoing process of mutual regulation between clinically based meaning and theoretical formulation and understanding. Part of our knowledge derives from and rests on fruitful but as yet unproven hypotheses. These relatively conceptual levels of the theory must be distinguished from the impressive body of clinical knowledge which has been repeatedly observed and confirmed in our clinical experience. Most of this knowledge is now regarded as relatively uncontroversial. The problem of validation in psychoanalysis, therefore, lies more at the level of concept than at the level of content.

The above clinical example not only illustrates certain of the basic concepts of contemporary psychoanalytic theory—it is also illustrative of the fact that psychoanalytic psychiatry has been mainly derived from the findings of traditional psychoanalysis. These findings, however, include not only the results of successful analysis but also the knowledge which has been gained through therapeutic failures. The contemporary Freudian would thus agree that traditional analysis is no longer regarded as the sole or even the best therapeutic technique for every type of mental disorder. He will often agree that the establishment and utilization of a sound relationship between doctor and patient may be a primary goal in some forms of therapy. He would, nevertheless, explain his therapeutic techniques in the light of his understanding of contemporary psychoanalysis. He would in addition still maintain that traditional psychoanalytic techniques, based on interpretation of the transference neurosis, remain the treatment of choice for a wide range of clinical conditions. Contemporary psychoanalytic theory and practice thus recognize the need for technical modification in many cases and in many types of clinic disorder. Nevertheless, it maintains the continued validity of the findings which led to Freud's original formulations. In comparison, some of the divergent groups, self-styled as neo-Freudians, have a very different attitude. Interpersonal relations and external adaptation have been emphasized at the expense of the repressed unconscious. The techniques based on this theoretical approach necessarily differ considerably from that of traditional psychoanalysis.

Psychoanalysis and Dynamic Psychiatry

After World War II psychoanalysis as an approach to the understanding and treatment of mental disorder became exceedingly popular in this country. On the one hand, as already noted, diagnostic formulations based on the content of individual symptoms have represented a widespread application of psychoanalytic theory. The term "dynamic psychiatry," however, has also been widely used to include not only the findings of traditional psychoanalysis, but also approaches which emphasize a dynamic approach to interpersonal relations. It is thus essential to be specific as to how psychoanalytic psychiatry compares to other approaches which are not based on all the major theoretical assumptions of contemporary psychoanalytic theory.

It was not by chance that we illustrated the importance of recognizing the underlying significance of basic concepts by reference to an example of a defense against ego-alien internal impulses. The dynamic and economic hypotheses which were briefly discussed in relation to this clinical example are the two assumptions basic to psychoanalytic theory which are most frequently minimized, if not neglected, by other schools of dynamic psychiatry. It is thus essential to recognize that the concept of psychic energy is as basic to contemporary psychoanalytic theory as it was at the time when Freud formulated his first theoretical proposition, namely, the concept of repression. Although the theory of instinct remains controversial, and although in addition repression is no longer regarded as the major basic assumption of psychoanalysis, the shift has been mainly one of emphasis. Neither the concept of a dynamic process of repression nor the continued dynamic impact of that which has been repressed has been in any way bypassed or excluded by the increase of knowledge obtained through wider and more varied experience.

Freud's Approach

The position of contemporary psychoanalytic psychiatry still remains somewhat problematic for many reasons. Psychoanalytic knowledge originally developed by means of what might be described as a dual, or two-pronged, approach. Freud made his first clinical discoveries in the treatment of patients suffering from hysterical symptoms. The group of patients described in his *Studies On Hysteria* impress most contemporary psychiatrists, however, as at best borderline, if not actually psychotic. Through the study of these very sick patients, however, Freud discovered many of the processes now understood as characteristic of primitive primary process thinking. The investigation of these patients also revealed content and memories of a sexual nature which led Freud over a period of years to the discovery of infantile sexuality, with particular reference to the oedipal situation. As already noted, it was during this same period of early discovery that Freud applied a similar method of investigation to the interpretation of dreams, the psychopathology of everyday life, to mythology, and to art. Of special importance was the fact that his own self-analysis was largely based on his interpretation of his own dreams.

In these and other studies, Freud made an important basic assumption to the effect that the infantile sexual material revealed in the investigation of hysterics was not exclusive to a special form of neurotic illness. The process of repression and in essence the content of the repressed unconscious were found to be very similar in the minds of all the individuals Freud studied. The specific technique gradually developed in the treatment of neurotic patients was thus combined from the outset with investigations of a more general nature. Such a course led to the gradual emergence of a developmental approach to the structure and function of the human mind, both healthy and pathological.

As Freud's investigations continued, he gradually extrapolated the now familiar stages of early sexual development. With other pioneer analysts, findings relevant to content, that is, material indicative of different levels of instinctual development, were related to different types of psychological disturbances. Several attempts have thus been made to classify mental illness in terms of psychoanalytic instinct theory. On the whole these efforts have not been altogether satisfactory.

Limits of Psychoanalytic Technique

If one reflects a little it is not hard to see why this should be the case. Insofar as the different levels of instinctual development are experienced by all maturing individuals, it is not surprising that symptoms or character traits reflective of different levels of such development should be met in a wide variety of clinical conditions. The findings of psychoanalysis, in addition, have been mainly obtained through the use of psychoanalytic technique. Over the passage of time it has become increasingly clear that this technique cannot be utilized without significant modification in the treatment of serious character disorders, borderline states, or psychotic illness. Psychoanalytic understanding of the neuroses, including the less serious neurotic character disorders, is far wider than the understanding so far obtained in respect to the genesis and nature of more serious disorders.

Moreover, increased knowledge, both from analytic and from objective observation, indicates the extreme importance for future mental health of the preverbal period of life. We thus have come to recognize that the very patients about whom we would like to know most are those who are as a rule able to tell us least. We may thus have to accept a paradoxical situation. It is psychoanalysis which has helped us to become aware of the extreme importance of the earliest months and years of life. But it is just here that psychoanalysis may have to accept the limitations of its own method of investigation, namely, psychoanalytic technique, and turn to other methods of investigation to find better answers. It has already been noted here, for example, that there are currently a number of longitudinal studies of families and children, beginning with prenatal care and following the child through to later periods of development. Such studies are using psychoanalytic understanding. They are not, however, using psychoanalytic techniques as the primary tool of investigation. In several of these studies, however, some of the children observed as infants have later been taken into therapeutic psychoanalysis. Such investigations offer the possibility of integrating objective observations of the developing infant with the reconstructions of the therapeutic psychoanalyst. As such studies accumulate and are compared, it will be increasingly possible to reach a greatly enriched understanding of the relationship between analysis and other approaches to child development.

One difficulty, therefore, in developing a really satisfactory psychoanalytic psychiatry derives from the limitations of our major tool of investigation, that is, the traditional psychoanalytic technique. Application of this technique remains the treatment of choice for patients whose major problems are attributable to repression and related defenses. This constellation of neurotic defenses formed the basis for Freud's original theory of neurosis. Patients whose pathology is more severe may use repression in a variety of ways, but they do not, as a rule, rely on it as a major defense. They utilize other mechanisms of a more primitive kind —denial, isolation, and projection, for example. To deal effectively with such primitive defenses the basic psychoanalytic technique must be modified and adapted.

To some extent psychoanalysts themselves have been responsible for the continuing tendency to apply psychoanalysis or closely related techniques in the treatment of patients for whom this form of treatment is definitely contraindicated. The distinction of content from concept is particularly useful and important in this context. For example, psychoanalysts regard the oedipal situation as a crucial conflict in childhood development. Failure to resolve this central conflict is a major predisposing cause for the development in adult life of the more analyzable forms of neurosis. This includes both hysterical and obsessional neuroses. For a long time, therefore, there was a widespread tendency to accept symptomatic evidence that a patient has an unresolved attachment to the parent of the opposite sex as indicating the presence of an unresolved oedipal conflict. The implication is then drawn that the patient has an analyzable neurosis. Unfortunately this is often not the case. There are many patients in whom the manifest symptoms suggest an unresolved oedipal conflict and attachment, but who at the same time have a severely disturbed character structure. Beneath the more manifest oedipal attachment, the character structure may be more primitive and reflect earlier developmental levels than would be expected in neurotic characters. Such neurotically appearing patients may in fact be "as-if" personalities, borderline personalities, or even schizophrenic. The content of the symptom cannot be accepted as a sufficient basis or as evidence for a diagnostic formulation.

The whole area of diagnosis has become increasingly complex and difficult as our knowledge of the structure and organization of personality has developed. Correlative with our increasing awareness of developmental aspects, there has emerged a body of knowledge that deals not primarily with content and conflict, but which pertains to the form, organization, structure, and functioning of the mental apparatus. This whole area of psychoanalytic understanding comes under the rubric of ego psychology. Ego psychology was initiated during Freud's later career, particularly in his formulation of the structural model of the psychic apparatus. More and more, considerations of the structure and function of the ego have come into play in the evaluation and diagnosis of patients. This has been particularly true in attempts to assess patients for psychoanalytic treatment. Levels of ego development must be taken into account. The degree of ego integration is important as well as the capacity of the ego to internalize and apply its energies in the service of further growth. Correlative to the ego's inner structure, its capacity for object relations has become an increasingly important aspect of overall assessment. Unless the patient is capable of entering into a meaningful alliance with the analyst, of internalizing something from the analytic situation, of undergoing significant development and change, analytic efforts are liable to frustration.

Specific and General Theories

As we have already indicated, Freud also explored the dreams of other people—normal people in addition to his own patients. He examined the slips and errors of everyday life, and he delved into literature and mythology. His explorations into these areas, in addition to his clinical work, led him in the direction of two kinds of theoretical formulation. The first consisted of those formulations which were based on and closely related to empirical clinical observations, especially those which he had obtained in the analytic situation. The theory which he derived from these specifically clinical observations forms what may be called the "specific psychoanalytic theory." This clinically derived and clinically directed theory remains a body of knowledge which we have not been able to find ways of confirming outside of the clinical situation. The derivation of evidence and the formulation of concepts—as well as their confirmation and validation—are so closely involved in the clinical setting and the analytic method that they cannot be disengaged from the clinical frame of reference without significant distortion. The content of repression, for example, was first formulated on the basis of observations of resistance in the clinical setting. The understanding of the various forms of resistance and of the different types of material against which the various forms of resistance are directed is based on information that comes directly from clinical experience. The verification and validation of such formulations have been based almost exclusively on the repeated observations of different analysts with different patients in different parts of the world and in different cultures. The fact that they have independently reached similar or at least compatible conclusions offers some support for these formulations. It should be noted, however, that mere repeatability of observations is neither strictly achievable, nor is it the sole basis of analytic verification.

Validation of specific theory is unlikely to include to a significant degree methods other than clinical. To give one brief example of this type of validation: at the outset of World War I psychoanalysis as a recognized movement had been established for several years. The First International Congress had been held in 1908. When World War I started in 1914 the most important pioneer analysts in the world were located on different sides in the war and had little if any means of communication during the four war years. It is of considerable historical interest that a small volume entitled *The Psychoanalysis of the War Neuroses* was published soon after the end of World War I. This contained papers by Freud, Abraham, Jones, Ferenczi, and others who had examined and treated war neurotics in their own countries during the war years. Their findings and explanations of the psychopathology of some of the traumatic war neuroses were highly compatible and often almost identical.

This is the kind of verification which derives from the application of a clinical method leading to the development of specific psychoanalytic theory.

A related type of validation is contingent on what might otherwise be described as a significant drawback among practicing analysts, namely, their tendency to be highly selective in respect to their reading of analytic literature. For example, in a paper reviewing Melanie Klein's contribution presented to the American Psychoanalytic Association in 1953, Zetzel reached the conclusion that in essence mastery of ambivalence in the early mother/child relationship was a crucial feature of separation and loss appropriately symbolized by the weaning process. She concluded that "More than anything else, the term 'depressive position' is unfortunate. . . . The concept under some more suitable name may well prove of considerable importance in our growing knowledge of the development of object relations." In an almost contemporaneous paper Dr. Winnicott, who had not seen Zetzel's contribution, reached an identical conclusion: "The term 'depressive position' is a bad name for a normal process. My own suggestion is that it should be called 'the stage of concern.' "

In *Childhood and Society,* published several years earlier, Erik Erikson had made the following statement: "The firm establishment of enduring patterns for the solution of the nuclear conflict of basic trust vs. basic mistrust is the first task of the ego." It is of some theoretical interest to note the compatibility between Zetzel's and Winnicott's approach to the depressive position, and Erikson's concept of basic trust. The common emphasis on the importance of the mother/child relationship should be noted as independent contemporary consensus of the growing importance of this aspect of early psychological development. The fact, however, that none of these authors included in their bibliographies the relevant contributions of the others illustrates the frequent lack of communication which is an important feature of some psychoanalytic literature.

Repeated experiences of this type do tend to act as one form of validation mainly limited to specific psychoanalytic theory. In contrast, Rapaport has suggested that general psychoanalytic theory should, over the course of time, be testable by methods other than those from which the initial evidence was obtained. Insofar as this is accomplished, one could then say that psychoanalytic theory has been brought into line with other scientific theories and methods. Findings which have resulted in formulation of a hypothesis are tested, in the course of scientific validation, by methods other than those from which the original suggestion derives.

Extensions of Analytic Theory

The specific psychoanalytic theory has given rise to a number of more general deductions which have permitted the extension of analytic ideas to broader areas of extra-analytic observation. Freud based this broader perspective on his analysis of dreams and on extra-analytic material like the famous Schreber case. But in more recent years the attempts to extend analytic thinking into general psychoanalytic theory have been made on a much more objective and systematic basis. Approaches to the verification of the general theory have also been made in terms of the elaboration of specific hypotheses derived from the general theory and the attempt to verify these hypotheses on experimental grounds.

One of the most significant areas in which this extension has occurred is the whole question of the developmental hypothesis, including both instinctual development and the development of ego functions. Originally the developmental concept was based on material derived from the treatment of adults, but in more recent years there has also been a fair amount of experience from the treatment of children. Such children, however, are sick children. If we are concerned with forming a general developmental hypothesis, basing such a general hypothesis on data entirely derived from the treatment of disturbed persons has certain built-in limitations. Consequently, a great deal of effort has been channeled in recent years into attempts to set up studies on a more objective basis which would include not only pathological development but also normal development.

Another area which is currently of extreme importance is that of the study of dreaming. This is of special interest since it is so closely related to the material on which Freud based some of his earliest thinking about the human mind and out of which he formed his early theoretical view of the nature and function of the mental apparatus. Ever since Aserinsky and Kleitman's observations of rapid eye movements in certain phases of sleep in the early 1950's, there has been a flurry of experimental and physiological investigation of the components of the dreaming process. Techniques are available for the more objective study of these processes—techniques that were unknown in Freud's time when he was engaged in his pioneering studies of dreaming. The *Interpretation of Dreams* (1900) remains as a monument to his efforts and to his genius. But we now have techniques which allow us to recognize that sleep is not a homogeneous state, and that it must be distinguished from the dreaming state which shows strikingly different patterns of central activation and integration of mental processes. We have learned that mental activity goes on throughout the hours of the night, but that the activity of dreaming seems to occur more cyclically at regular intervals throughout the night. It is not at all clear what the meaning of such differences may be, but there is evidence to suggest that the various states of activation are associated with characteristic kinds of mental activity. Freud's original discussion of dreaming activity may have embraced a variety of kinds of mental organization which more advanced techniques allow us to dissect and study more carefully. This whole approach has only begun to make an impact on analytic thinking, but even so it has substantially advanced our knowledge of dream processes.

Another area of experimental work which is quite removed from analytic observation but nonetheless of intense analytic interest is the study of sensory deprivation and its effects on the mental functioning of human beings. One of the striking effects of sensory deprivation is a shift in the organization of thought processes from mature, logical and realistically based kinds of thought organization to much more subjective, disorganized, fluid, and primitive forms of thinking. Freud had described these respective patterns of thought organization as primary and secondary process thinking. This was one of the key formulations in his famous chapter on the organization and functioning of the mind in the *Interpretation of Dreams*. Studies of the effects of sensory deprivation give us a much clearer idea of what the effects of sensory input on the organization of thinking might be and how different forms of input and their absence influence inner processes.

Another broad and important area that has opened up to experimental exploration is the study of cognitive processes and their organization —not only in themselves but also as they are influenced by motives and emotional factors. A whole area of cognitive theory has grown up which is built out of concepts of attention cathexis, cognitive controls, cognitive styles, etc. Ever since Hartmann's conceptualization of a conflict-free sphere of ego functions, a great deal more attention has been paid to the operation of ego functions independently of drive-derivatives and independently of their involvement in intrapsychic conflict. This has allowed much more active investigation of such functions, and cognitive functions have been a primary and important target. Such investigations have raised a whole new series of problems and questions.

. One of the pressing questions in the area of cognitive processes is how cognitive controls and cognitive styles relate to and interact with the more traditional defense mechanisms which are specifically rooted in conflict and also contribute to the organization of the ego and utilize specific ego functions.

Metapsychological Assumptions

All of this comes under the heading of the general psychoanalytic theory. We have previously discussed some aspects of the specific theory. Both of these theoretical domains can be integrated at the most abstract theoretical level in terms of certain basic assumptions which allow us to understand both general and specific aspects of the theory. These assumptions are called "metapsychological assumptions." Metapsychology is a much misunderstood and needlessly confused area of psychoanalytic thinking. It is intended to express the basic assumptions about the human mind which underlie other parts of the theory. From the study of resistances, for example, we can arrive at the concept of repression. Implicit in the concept of repression is the assumption that the human mind possesses certain dynamic properties. That assumption is a metapsychological assumption. We are not simply saying that repression is an active and dynamic process, but we are further stating inductively that the human mind has an *inherent* dynamic capacity which is a part of its nature and which underlies many of the psychological phenomena that we can observe in our patients and in human behavior generally.

In a similar way we can say that the human mind has adaptive capacities. We shall see that the adaptive hypothesis, like the dynamic hypothesis, can be looked at in different ways. Adaptation can be viewed from an internal perspective or from an external one. There is a difference between adaptation to the outside world and internal adaptation which involves the adaptive use of one's own inner capacities, energies, wishes, and strivings. We have become more and more aware as our experience has deepened that internal adaptation and external adaptation do not necessarily go hand in hand. Sometimes individuals who have shown a remarkable capacity for external adaptation—for accomplishing, performing, and effectively and efficiently managing external affairs —also make it apparent that they have missed out on accomplishing certain important developmental tasks and thus have a diminished capacity for internal adaptation.

We have been discussing the distinction between a general psychoanalytic theory, which shows little relation to or dependence on the clinical situation, and a specific psychoanalytic theory which depends closely on and is directly derived from clinical material. It was Rapaport who had suggested that methodological analysis should establish this distinction between the general and specific theories. He felt that in time the general theory, in contradistinction to the specific theory, could be spelled out in terms of testable hypotheses and subjected to verification by experimental methods. Thus hypotheses would be tested by methods quite different from those by which the original evidence was obtained. Psychoanalytic theory could then be brought into closer approximation and integration with the broader body of psychological theory and evidence. Testing by methods other than those from which the hypotheses derive provides independent verification of the validity of the hypotheses in question and thus puts them on a much firmer scientific footing.

The difficulty and complexity of this process, however, suggests that we are still at—and may for some time remain at—a stage in the development of the theory in which verification in certain areas rests on the same methods from which the hypotheses were derived. This has particular reference to the specific psychoanalytic theory. In the specific theory, the meaning or content or interpretation of the material remains directly dependent on findings derived from clinical methods. But with increasing clarity, the specific theory is being separated from the more general propositions which compose the general theory and which offer the promise—now or in the future—of verification by methods other than those which determined the initial reconstruction. The more general and abstract such propositions become, the greater should be the possibility of objective verification.

For this very reason, the formulation of more general and metapsychological assumptions becomes more than a theoretical exercise. Even if general assumptions cannot be assumed to have inductive validity, they nonetheless serve an important heuristic function in the development of our understanding. The inductive process remains open and even the most basic assumptions must remain open to constant review and re-evaluation in the light of new data and new information. It is important to differentiate between new findings which enrich or modify our understanding within the clinical theory and new findings which would seriously challenge a basic theoretical assumption.

We have sometimes given the analogy of making a distinction between the frame which can be compared to the metapsychological assumptions, and the picture within the frame which is more concerned with specific clinical theory. We may find frequent reference to changes within the picture. We have been too optimistic about certain groups of patients, and on the other hand too pessimistic about others. We may find that our understanding of different periods of childhood development becomes modified with greater clinical experience. This often influences our interpretation of the picture; it does not necessarily modify the basic framework within which we work. Conversely, there are those who say that psychoanalytic instinct theory is a concept which had a certain heuristic value when it was originally formulated but that it has now been outdated. This, if it were proved true, would influence both the dynamic and economic hypotheses which have already been referred to as two of our current basic metapsychological assumptions. Experimentation and new evidence can change the specific meaning of certain hypotheses without necessarily changing any major basic theoretical assumptions. They may, however, introduce new and important theoretical assumptions, as we will illustrate in later chapters.

In summary, the conceptual framework of contemporary psychoanalytic psychiatry has been mainly derived from the findings of clinical psychoanalysis. General psychoanalytic theory has from the outset had many features which fostered the development of a general psychology which could include not only pathology but normal development, language, literature, and many other disciplines. The application of psychoanalysis to psychiatry has been more problematical for several reasons. In the first place, the technique of psychoanalysis is not therapeutic in the approach to many types of disturbed behavior and symptomatology. In the second place, the content of symptoms has become increasingly recognized as an inadequate guide to the overall pathology of many patients. Psychoanalytic psychiatry is still at an incomplete stage of development. We know more about the meaning of symptoms and more about the type of developmental failure characteristic of certain illnesses than we do about the causes. Nevertheless, insofar as psychoanalytic theory can provide us with a comprehensive set of basic assumptions within which we can understand both mental health and mental illness, it is important that we should trace each of these basic assumptions in order to understand their relevance to our evaluation and treatment of patients suffering from the whole range of mental disorder.

[2]

Understanding Anxiety

There is no problem that the clinical psychiatrist meets more regularly or more pressingly than anxiety. It is almost a universal manifestation of mental disorder and illness. The approach to anxiety, therefore, provides an important avenue for grasping some of the basic intents and perspectives of a psychology. We shall attempt to examine the problem of anxiety from the point of view of clinical psychoanalysis to clarify some of the differences in emphasis and theoretical divergences between the psychoanalytic approach to anxiety and other closely related approaches.

Clinical Psychoanalysis and Dynamic Psychiatry

In the first chapter we raised a number of points having to do with the relationship between clinical psychoanalysis and dynamic psychiatry. We discussed the derivation of the conceptual framework of contemporary psychoanalytic psychiatry, both from the findings of clinical psychoanalysis on one hand and, more broadly, from the application of an analytic approach to nonclinical materials—literature, mythology, dreams, art, the psychopathology of everyday life, etc. The development of psychoanalytic psychiatry has not yet reached the point of forming a satisfactory theoretical framework within which all the manifestations of mental illness can be understood. We also pointed out the important distinction of the two areas of psychoanalytic theory—the general theory of psychoanalysis and the specific theory. The former deals primarily with concepts and enunciates a general concept of the nature, development, structure, and functioning of the mental apparatus. The specific theory deals more directly with content and is derived mainly from the clinical practice of psychoanalysis. Finally we discussed the application of both the general and specific theories to general psychiatry and psychotherapy.

26

In the light of such discussions, it becomes quite evident that the psychiatrist who understands and accepts contemporary psychoanalytic theory no longer need limit his clinical work to the techniques of traditional psychoanalysis. The therapeutic techniques that might be recommended for the treatment of different patients are subject to a wide range of variation. Thus clinical techniques and approaches which at first glance seem to resemble closely the techniques and approaches employed by therapists of a variety of theoretical persuasions may also be employed by the so-called classical analyst. Therapeutic techniques must be adapted to the needs and capacity of the patient, as well as to the structural characteristics of his personality. However, there are still basic differences between the theoretical approach of the contemporary psychoanalyst and the conceptual orientation of other more eclectic approaches. The psychoanalyst, for example, remains convinced that the traditional technique of the analysis of the transference neurosis remains the treatment of choice for a relatively wide range of neurotic conditions. One of our objectives in the present work is to clarify the differences in these clinical approaches and to bring into focus the underlying theoretical significance of these differences.

As previously suggested, the term "dynamic psychiatry" has been used in a broader sense to include not only psychoanalytic psychiatry but also schools of thought which focus primarily on the dynamic interaction between persons—appropriately labeled "interpersonal psychiatry." The interpersonal approach, following the lead of Harry Stack Sullivan, moves the interpersonal interactions between the individual and the significant others in his environment into the center of the clinical picture. Interpersonal relations and their vicissitudes thus take precedence over intrapsychic conflicts and their vicissitudes. The traditional psychoanalytic approach, however, tries to keep the focus on intrapsychic conflicts and the mental processes and forces that give rise to them. The psychoanalytic and the interpersonal approaches, therefore, in a sense look in different directions. This by no means implies that they are therefore contradictory or essentially divergent in their theoretical formulations.

The essential findings of psychoanalysis involve a major theoretical premise—that the mind possesses inherently dynamic properties and capacities. This is the dynamic hypothesis, one of the basic metapsychological assumptions that underlie psychoanalytic formulations about the nature and function of the mind. This dynamic quality of the mind gives rise to and expresses itself in instinctual impulses which provide some of the basic sources of energy for psychic functions. The same dynamic properties are also responsible for the intrapsychic responses to instinctual derivatives, for example, the mechanisms of defense which the ego sets up to oppose instinctual impulses and to protect itself from unwanted, dangerous, or forbidden wishes. An essential part of the clinical process of psychoanalysis involves a controlled regression which allows the development of the transference neurosis, and the re-emergence in the transference neurosis of the wishes and fantasies against which the defenses had originally been established. Thus the transference assumes a central importance for psychoanalytic practice as well as theory. Transference is intimately bound up in the question of object relations, and the course of therapy depends on the working through of transference issues and the establishing of more realistic object relations —with the therapist at first, and with other significant objects consequently. This is discussed more at length in Chapter 16.

The contemporary psychoanalyst by no means ignores the crucial importance of object relations; rather they are a central and significant aspect of his approach. Psychoanalytic understanding, however, includes much more than a review of or a modification of interpersonal relations through the medium of a therapeutic relation established with the therapist. It also includes a reopening process which brings to the surface in a fresh and revived form the original conflicts which had been dismissed and repressed by intrapsychic responses. It can thus be seen that the interpersonal dimension of human interaction is not, strictly speaking, opposed to psychoanalytic thinking. Rather it forms an extension and a development of object-relations theory within psychoanalysis. It can thus be viewed as a special subdivision of psychoanalytic theory which can readily be integrated with the basic assumptions of psychoanalysis. If we approached clinical material exclusively from an interpersonal perspective, however, we would be limiting our understanding of the patient's difficulties and what they involve. It is equally valid to say that if we were to limit our perspective to the intrapsychic aspects of the patient's problems, we would be limiting our understanding in another direction.

A Clinical Case

Rather than trying to pursue the theoretical differences and parallels of these various approaches, it will perhaps be more useful and illuminating to examine a brief clinical history. This will give us an opportunity to see some of the possible implications of an interpretation of the case based on an exclusively interpersonal approach. Then we can compare the results of the interpersonal formulation with the results of a more traditionally psychoanalytic approach to intrapsychic conflicts and mechanisms.

The case was one in which a young man suffered from an acute anxiety state which responded quite well to a relatively brief course of analytically based interpretive psychotherapy. This young man came in a state of acute anxiety which was of quite recent origin. He expressed the fear that he was losing his mind, that he was becoming psychotic and would require admission to a mental hospital. His presenting symptoms had been preceded by mounting anxiety, but this had become totally disabling within the previous few days. The anxiety became unbearable after he learned from friends that a common acquaintance had just had a mental breakdown and had to be hospitalized.

The patient was a rather friendly and cooperative young man and showed considerable capacity for psychological insight. As he discussed his problem, it became clear that the precipitating events of his acute and disabling anxiety had to do with the recent taking on of new responsibilities. He was the youngest of three brothers and was employed in the family business with his father and his oldest brother. He had recently taken the important step of buying a new house for his family. He and his wife had two little boys. Buying the new house represented a major undertaking for him, involving added financial burdens and responsibility. He was taking on these new financial responsibilities at a time when his economic situation, although reasonably secure, was also subject to certain risks.

The patient had always been a somewhat passive person, and had been quite dependent on his father and on his older brothers from early childhood. He had always had a happy and rather friendly disposition. At the same time he had been subject to considerable anxiety from time to time, particularly in circumstances where he was forced to function more independently. He would become quite anxious when, for example, he had to take trips alone or, during his service in the navy, when he had to be alone on sentry duty. Under these circumstances he would feel overwhelmed with a feeling of panic. He would be afraid that he couldn't handle the responsibilities that were imposed on him. The resulting feelings of anxiety were quite intense and sometimes were accompanied by feelings of unreality.

In discussing these circumstances, it became quite clear—and the patient was able to recognize and understand this—that his fear of a mental breakdown and possible hospitalization represented a disguised expression of an inner wish to avoid responsibility and to retreat into a situation where, instead of being an active husband and father, he would again become a helpless and dependent child. This wish to become helpless and dependent was quite alien to his conscious goals and ambitions. His marital relationship was quite satisfying and satisfactory. He saw himself as desiring to take a mature and responsible part in the life of his community. He responded quite readily to this interpretation of this aspect of his anxiety symptoms, and the anxiety gradually diminished. Nevertheless, he continued to complain of a number of fears which generally had to do with the assumption of added responsibility and the possible risks involved. In the family business, for example, his work involved relatively long automobile trips throughout the New England area. These trips were for the purpose of seeking out new sales contracts and buying merchandise for the family business. During these trips he would frequently experience a great deal of anxiety while he was driving from home toward his destination. When he was driving back toward home, however, there was seldom any anxiety or considerably less. At the time when his acute anxiety symptoms, for which he sought treatment, had developed, his father had been due to go away for the winter, leaving the patient and his older brother in charge of the business.

How can we explain this patient's anxiety in terms of its dynamic meaning? Could we explain it in terms of interpersonal factors without including the intrapsychic defenses which had in fact determined his definitive character structure and his tendency toward phobic anxiety? It is our position that consideration of only the interpersonal aspects of the case would only provide a partial picture. At this point, perhaps a few additional facts might be helpful. As we mentioned, the patient was the youngest of three brothers. He could remember that as a child he revered his older brother. He could also remember that at times he had angry and hostile feelings toward this same brother. On one or two occasions he had tried to stand up to this older brother, but hadn't been able to make it stick. He retreated into a passive and compliant attitude. At that time, when he first became aware of his rivalrous feelings toward his brother, he felt that the latter was older and stronger—too strong for the patient to overcome. He surrendered in any attempts at open rivalry with the brother, and instead formed a strong passive and positive identification with him. He went to the same college as his brother, joined in the same extracurricular activities and, in general, found himself following closely in his brother's footsteps. After his discharge from the navy, he went into the family business—but only with reluctance. He did so partly out of a sense of duty and a feeling of obligation toward his father, and partly because of his fear of striking out on his own. There was also a practical reason, that the family business offered him the best available opportunity to achieve in a relatively short time enough economic security to support his family. This included, as we have seen, buying a new house.

Understanding the Patient's Anxiety

In the light of the available information, how might we understand this patient's acute anxiety symptoms? If we were to consider the problem on the level of interpersonal processes, we might say that this was a young man who had always relied on dependent relationships with older men in dealing with stressful situations. The purchase of a new house represented for him a decisive step toward independence and maturity. In view of his predominantly passive and dependent personality structure, this step inevitably aroused his anxiety. In other words, we could account for the patient's anxiety by seeing it in the context of environmental factors—buying the house and what that might have signified to him—without going very deeply into the intrapsychic aspects of the problem. We could focus our attention on the interpersonal relationship between the patient and his brother. We could use as the basis of our explanation the fact that his need to comply with his brother and to remain dependent on him had been a basic determinant in his relationships with others both in his childhood and in his adult life. Finally, we could conclude that it was inevitable that each step toward independence and maturity would arouse anxiety because his inner feelings of inadequacy and dependency were threatened. The explanation in terms of interpersonal aspects of the patient's life situation would seem to serve as an adequate basis for understanding the symptoms that he presented.

Let us look further, however, into the actual situation as it gradually emerged in the course of treatment. During the father's long winter vacation in the South, the patient and the oldest brother were left in charge of the family business. During this time he and his brother were responsible not only for management of the business, but also for seeking out new contracts in other parts of the area. The patient was the one who in fact made all of these trips seeking new business. The question came up as to why the patient was the one who had to make these trips and not the brother. The brother was older, he was the senior partner, and, as the patient had originally described him, he was painted as a stronger, more dominant, and forceful character. Why, then, was it that he didn't make some, if not all, of the business trips? In exploring this question, it came out that in fact the patient was a much more capable businessman than his older brother. The brother was extremely passive and functioned rather inadequately in the business world. He had a great deal of difficulty in making new business contacts and in negotiating actively for the firm, and his attempts to get new business usually were failures. In the father's absence, then, the situation was one in which the patient not only had to carry out his usual job more actively, but in addition he had to assume a position in which he had to adopt a more senior role in respect to his much older brother.

How are we going to explain the anxiety that gave rise to the patient's acute symptoms? Can we base our explanation solely on the patient's passivity, his dependence, and his fear of independence? What about the fact that he was in fact stronger and more successful than his older brother? The interpersonal factors do not quite cover this inner dimension of his relation to the brother. We shall have to look more deeply into the significance of his actually stronger position in relation to the brother who had represented such a threat in the past. We have already suggested that the patient felt a strong rivalry with the brother, and at one time with the father as well. We can begin to see his apparent passivity as representing an intrapsychic defense which was mobilized in the face of a perceived danger. If he had expressed overt aggression against his brother in early childhood, he would have had to face a dangerous external threat. Consequently, the stirring of aggression gave rise to a signal of an internal danger. He responded to this danger signal by a defensive retreat into passivity and apparent compliance. The present circumstances of his adult life, however, placed him in the position of surpassing his brother in reality. It was a matter not only of his own interest, but also of his brother's interest, that he should be able to succeed as an active competitor in the business world— something his brother could not do. The demands of external reality involved active competition by which he would have to demonstrate his superior strength and capacity, superior specifically to his brother.

What did this mean in terms of the patient's past experience? What were the internal dangers which successful rivalry with his brother might have meant during the period when his personality was being shaped by these defensive needs? His competitiveness and aggression were by no means threatening to him in the current situation—they were in fact a means for attaining personal goals and satisfactions. But such aggression had been dangerous and threatening to him as a child. The unconscious meaning of aggression, stemming from his childhood, persisted and in terms of his original defenses remained unchanged. Consequently, he was caught in a difficult dilemma. The expression of aggression which was demanded by the present external reality represented at the same time an internal threat. In response to this internal threat, he remobilized the defensive tendency toward passive retreat which he had utilized so successfully in the past. In childhood this passive and compliant behavior had served a useful function and had avoided disastrous effects. In fact, it had in certain ways fostered a good identification with the brother which he had been able to employ in the service of a number of positive ends. But in the current situation, by way of contrast, a similar response would have been inappropriate and maladaptive. He could no longer prolong his identification with the brother and he could no longer remain dependent on him—the brother was in fact now the more dependent person.

An Integrated Approach

This case history—brief though it may be—gives us a good illustration of the differences between intrapsychic and interpersonal dynamics. There are several approaches which we could take to this material which would be misleading. Any one of these approaches could have a partial validity, but each would not allow us to understand the inner or fuller meaning of the patient's symptoms. If we were to adopt an approach which would merely look at the immediate situation as anxiety provoking because of the kind of person the patient was, we would explain it in terms of his being a passive and dependent person caught in a stressful situation. But this does not embrace the whole picture. If we were to adopt the opposite approach and indulge in a too hasty search into the deeper meanings of his conflict, that would be equally unsatisfactory. If we were to adopt either of these partial approaches, we would run the risk of bypassing the complex and delicate interaction of interpersonal and intrapsychic factors that contribute to the patient's anxiety state.

Seen only in an interpersonal perspective, the patient's preoccupation with which he presented, namely, the fear of a mental breakdown and possible hospitalization, can be seen as revealing a distorted wish. It represents a compromise between his wish for passive dependency and at the same time provides a suitable punishment for having the wish. Under the pressure of the present real circumstances, he could put himself in a passive and dependent position only by breaking down and by getting himself admitted to a mental hospital. The explanation in terms of his passivity and dependency, however, seems superficial and to that extent inadequate in that it fails to give us any insight into the patient's dependency needs. Why should he, in fact, have had to resort to and cling to such a dependent and inadequate position? What was the real threat in his assuming greater responsibility?

From another point of view, it would be all too easy for one to adopt an overly enthusiastic and presumably analytic position. We might, thus, bypass the current reality situation and the patient's conflicts in the adult world, including his intense rivalry and disappointment with his brother. We could plunge into interpretations that might be made on the basis of the material which he presented in the very first hour. We might say that the material suggested latent homosexual trends in a man who was passively dependent on his brother and who consequently decompensated in circumstances in which he had to demonstrate a heterosexual masculinity that he did not in fact possess. If the explanation seems farfetched, the fact remains that frequently enough such interpretations have been given on the basis of even less material. The fact remains that, even though he was quite passive and dependent, our patient was in no sense homosexual. He was extremely happily married and had no problems in the area of sexual potency or adjustment. His wife was a very loving, warm, and feminine woman who had sufficient strength to take a supportive and somewhat maternal role when this was necessary. She remained nonetheless essentially feminine in her relationship to her husband. She respected his ability and competence. She encouraged him in his efforts to take on greater responsibility and achieve a mature adulthood. He was a successful and happy father, and was on terms of good friendship with both men and women. In a word, he was not a disturbed, latent homosexual, however deep certain of his problems in the area of dependency might have been.

As we have seen, it was not his dependence that was causing him so much difficulty. Rather it was the demonstration and display of his capacity for independence and competence that was causing trouble. Going back over his material, we found that it was precisely in situations in which he had been confronted with his own competence and capabilities—when he discovered that he could carry out sentry duty adequately, when he found he could do errands for his mother satisfactorily, etc.—it was in these situations of demonstrated competence that his anxiety developed. We could gain an understanding of the dynamic processes that underlay his immediate acute anxiety only by a careful review of his development and by an understanding of the kinds of relationships which had made it necessary for him to utilize certain kinds of defenses. These inner processes could not be fully or adequately understood without studying and understanding the reality area within which the anxiety was experienced. The anxiety in the current situation was not centered around his passive dependence on his brother, nor was it centered on his rivalry with his brother, nor on his homosexual impulses toward his brother—even though these may have been an important part of his relationship to his brother at some past period. The anxiety was centered in the area of current reality—and it was in terms of this current reality that the intrapsychic forces were arrayed against each other. At the same time, the current reality could not be adequately understood in itself without reference to intrapsychic conflicts and their developmental contexts.

We are intent on capturing, in the consideration of this relatively straightforward case, the intermeshing and interaction of current reality with intrapsychic dynamics and with residual infantile conflicts. An analogy can be found in the process of dreaming. The manifest content of a dream and its preconscious latent meaning are influenced by current external reality to no small degree. An interpretation, however, which is cast in terms of reality influences is neither more comprehensive nor more illuminating than an interpretation in terms of deeper, unconscious, or symbolic meanings which ignore current implications. The complex interrelations between external and internal, between past and present, constitute a central core of our considerations in this work. Our primary purpose at this point, however, is to illustrate some of the pitfalls that can come about as a result of a lack of understanding or even an excessively limited perspective on the complex interrelationships that are involved in dynamic psychiatry based on the fundamental principles of contemporary psychoanalytic theory.

The danger in such partial perspectives is that one or other of the basic metapsychological assumptions of the psychoanalytic theory may be emphasized to the neglect of others. In the case we have been discussing, a selective focusing on the intrapsychic factors which determined the patient's anxiety state would provide an emphasis on the dynamic hypothesis. It would bring into our explanation the dynamic nature of the inner mental processes and the dynamic interplay of force and counterforce in the patient's psyche. It would highlight the role of repression in relation to the patient's need to defend himself from the threat of aggressive impulses. If we were to direct our attention exclusively to the external and interpersonal aspects of the case, we would be bringing into focus the adaptive aspects of the patient's symptoms. We would be emphasizing the adaptive hypothesis to the detriment of the dynamic hypothesis. But a complete and adequate understanding of the case material tries to neither minimize nor sacrifice any of the basic assumptions. They are all equally important to a fuller understanding of the development, structure, and functioning of the human mind. It is just as incorrect to emphasize the dynamic and intrapsychic at the expense of the adaptive as it is to stress the adaptive and interpersonal to the exclusion of intrapsychic dynamic factors.

We can begin to appreciate in the case of our patient how inadequate it would have been if we had tried to deal with this very pleasant young man's problem on the basis of what he presented to us at first sight— his passive and dependent facade. His ability to recognize and respond readily to the passive wishes underlying his fears of an acute breakdown might have made it possible for him to deal with his immediate acute anxieties rather effectively. But we can seriously inquire whether conscious recognition at this level would have helped him as time went on —as he continued to find himself confronted with reality situations that demanded that he be more active, more successful, more competitive, more aggressive, more mature, and more masculine. He would continually be forced to deal with the basic conflicts involved in becoming stronger and more successful than his older brother who represented the major rival in his childhood neurosis. Would it be reasonable to expect him to be able to modify his own attitudes toward his brother and toward himself without some exploration into his past, into the roots of his basic conflicts and defenses as well as into their continuation and prolongation in his adult life? Whatever level of functioning he might have attained as a result of a more superficial analysis, there would have been minimal change, if any, in his basic attitudes and feelings about himself and his ability to function as man, as husband, as father —and as brother.

This patient's history and symptomatology provide us with a good illustration of the importance of an understanding of both the current reality situation and the relevant early conflicts and the manner in which they interact in the production of the patient's difficulty. It is worth noting, however, that the exploration of these aspects was attended with some difficulty. When we first began to explore the possible significance of the patient's relationship with his brother, his memories of their early association were quite partial and selective. As he became aware of the anger that he felt when he began to recognize his brother's inadequacy and passivity, he showed himself to be very reluctant indeed to review or revive his own past experiences. He seemed hesitant or unwilling to try to understand the nature of the threat in the current situation. All that he could remember about his relationship with his brother, in the beginning of his attempts to recall the past, was his love of the brother, his admiration for him, and his wish to be like him. It was only after repeated attempts, after the understanding of a few dreams, after repeated efforts to correlate his past and present experience, that he was able to remember the early feelings of anger toward his brother. It was these feelings that he had had to repress because they were so threatening to him. It was these feelings that turned his relations with his brother into situations of danger.

Resistance and Repression

The considerable reluctance that this patient demonstrated in reviving past memories was the same reluctance that Freud had discovered in his own patients and that he had called "resistance." The patient's resistance expressed itself in his inability and unwillingness to look behind or beyond the facade of current events and recognize the continued significance of his past experiences. The resistance and the linking of past experiences with current realities was the crux of our therapeutic work. It was only when he began to remember the real anger that he had felt in childhood that he was able to begin to test and re-explore the current situation with some degree of genuine reality testing. It was only then that he was able to compare and to appreciate the difference between past and present.

The resistance shown by this young man in regard to a very specific yet important conflict experienced in the past illustrates the empirical fact to which Freud referred in making his first theoretical step. He suggested that the resistance that one met clinically in trying to pursue the work of exploration into the past and into its continued meaning in the present must be attributed to some general process in the mind. He inferred a dynamic process in the mind which rendered those memories, thoughts, conflicts, and feelings which were unacceptable to the conscious feelings and thoughts of the individual inaccessible to conscious introspection. Such thoughts and feelings were subject to a process of repression. The resistance which was found in clinical practice could thus be formulated in terms of a more general and more basic concept —that of repression as a dynamic process and property of the mental apparatus.

But our intention in the present chapter was not merely to show that behind the patient's symptoms there was at work a dynamic principle of repression. We also have tried to make it clear that the understanding of the patient's problem was considerably more complex. The intrapsychic and dynamic aspects of it must be seen in the context of the patient's current reality situation. Conversely, the significance of the current reality cannot be understood until we have brought the intrapsychic and dynamic aspects into focus. The latter cannot adequately be grasped unless we can see them in their appropriate developmental perspective. Thus our approach to the clinical material, on both a practical and a theoretical level, must reach out and embrace multiple levels of analysis and must see the clinical material in an integral fashion from the combined perspectives of all of the basic assumptions about the nature and functioning of the mind. To the degree that we fail in this task, we limit our own understanding and run the immediate risk of misunderstanding the patient's problem. To this extent, we run the unforgivable risk of preventing the patient from understanding himself and of finding his way out of his difficulty.

Reminding ourselves of this broader and more general framework of our clinical and theoretical concerns, we will focus in the subsequent two chapters more specifically on repression itself. We shall consider it as a dynamic mental process. As such it will be fundamental and central to our other considerations of the basic concepts of psychoanalysis, in both their theoretical and clinical dimensions.

[3]

Repression: Theoretical Origins of the Concept

In the last chapter we presented a case history of an anxiety state in order to illustrate several points. We emphasized the differences between an approach based on interpersonal dynamics and an approach from the point of view of intrapsychic dynamics. We also made the point that an understanding couched exclusively in terms of one or the other approach to the clinical material would have left us with a partial and inadequate account of the case. Rather, the material must be seen in terms of the multiple basic assumptions that we can make about the nature and function of the human mind, and in terms of the way in which they are related and intermeshed in a given case.

If our approach to this particular patient had only taken into account his passive and dependent character structure and his fear of maturity and responsibility, it would have provided us with a basis for treatment that would have been only partially successful. Briefly, we might have utilized his capacity for a positive therapeutic relationship to increase his capacity for tolerating and at least partially mastering these anxieties. Not infrequently, we find that such an approach is sufficient to give certain patients enough support to enable them to deal with immediate situational crises or periods of developmental stress. In the case of our patient, however, it became quite clear after a relatively short period of treatment that the major problem that was interfering with his well-being could not be explained on an exclusively interpersonal basis. It became necessary from the therapeutic viewpoint to help the patient to see the difference between external reality and its adaptive challenges on the one hand, and the continuation on the other hand of an internal reality, derived from the past, in which the expression of activity, aggression, or rivalry was still perceived as threatening and dangerous.

Repression

The same patient had also manifested a considerable resistance to any attempts to uncover the memories associated with his earlier competitive wishes and aggressive impulses. The dynamic process which determines such empirical resistances is repression. Repression is the active and dynamic process which prevents certain mental contents from reaching consciousness, and being available for introspective recall. Repression is thus a direct illustration of the dynamic hypothesis which is one of the major basic assumptions of contemporary psychoanalytic theory. We would now like to focus on repression specifically. We will attempt in the present chapter to trace some of the theoretical foundations of the concept of repression and to consider some of the methodological implications of its derivation.

In his more or less personal account of the history of the psychoanalytic movement, written about 1914, Freud made the following statement:

The theory of repression is the corner-stone on which the whole structure of psychoanalysis rests. It is the most essential part of it; and yet it is nothing but a theoretical formulation of a phenomenon which may be observed as often as one pleases if one undertakes an analysis of a neurotic without resorting to hypnosis. In such cases one comes across a resistance which opposes the work of analysis and in order to frustrate it pleads a failure of memory. The use of hypnosis was bound to hide this resistance; the history of psychoanalysis proper, therefore, only begins with the new technique that dispenses with hypnosis. The theoretical consideration of the fact that this resistance coincides with an amnesia leads inevitably to the view of unconscious mental activity which is peculiar to psychoanalysis and which, too, distinguishes it quite clearly from philosophical speculations about the unconscious.[6]

Freud makes three important points in this statement. First, he points to the empirical and clinical evidences on which he bases his inference that resistance is a purposive and dynamic intrapsychic process. Second, he indicates that a theoretical concept was formulated to account for the empirical findings, namely, the concept of repression. Third, he also makes reference to the content or meaning of that which is repressed. He is thus clearly separating the evidence from which the theory is derived and the theory itself. He is also referring implicitly to the distinction between content and concept in respect to repression.

At the time of this writing, Freud clearly has in mind that the repression is mainly composed of forgotten past experiences. If you will refer back to our case presentation in the last chapter, however, you will note that we did not emphasize the patient's memories at all except insofar as they related to his early aggressive and competitive wishes. There is more of an emphasis on unconscious processes than on content as such. It must be remembered, however, that the dynamic theory of the mind was developed in the first instance as a result of Freud's recognition of the clinical fact of resistance—with special emphasis on the point of view that the repressed content consisted of memories.

Development of the Psychoanalytic Technique

It should be noted that the whole development which was so central to the further progression of analytic thinking rested on Freud's use of a new technique. It is so often the case in the history of science that new advances and new discoveries come as the result of the development of new techniques of investigation. Even as the telescope revolutionized astronomy and the microscope biology, Freud's development of his new technique of free association was to prove a turning point for psychoanalysis, as well as for psychological science in general. He and Breuer had begun their investigations by using the technique of hypnosis. The results of the hypnotic technique, as we shall see, were not very satisfying. It was Freud who began to experiment with other mehods of dealing with his patients and trying to get at the root of their problems.

It makes a fascinating study in the history of the development of psychoanalysis to trace the convoluted path by which Freud groped his way from the hypnotic method toward the definitive method of free association. It was only gradually in the light of his clinical experience that he began to modify his technique and little by little divested himself of the residues of the hypnotic method. Only slowly did he relinquish the hypnotic technique. And then he resorted to a method of putting pressure on the patient's forehead as a method of suggestion. It was really only in the case of Fraulein Elizabeth von R. (1892–1893) that Freud finally stopped using hypnosis altogether and relied on the pressure technique. He used the pressure technique for some time and with considerable confidence—even though he was quite aware that it was only a device for deceiving the patient's defenses.

As his technique was modified, he began to become increasingly aware of patients' resistances and how they manifested themselves. His emphasis on working against the resistance by the use of suggestion, questioning, urging, persuading, and arguing remained a prominent aspect of his thinking during this period of transition. It took several years before Freud began to move away from his pressure technique and its implied suggestion toward an increasing emphasis on the relaxation of the patient's censorship and the free and spontaneous expression of the patient's associations. By about 1900, however, with the publication of the *Interpretation of Dreams,* the free association technique seems to have come into its own. He describes the associative technique in the following terms:

This involves some psychological preparation of the patient. We must aim at bringing about two changes in him: an increase in the attention he pays to his own psychical perceptions, and the elimination of the criticism by which he normally sifts the thoughts that occur to him. In order that he may be able to concentrate his attention on his self-observation, it is an advantage for him to lie in a restful attitude and shut his eyes. It is necessary to insist explicitly on his renouncing all criticism of the thoughts that he perceives. We therefore tell him that the success of the psychoanalysis depends on his noticing and reporting whatever comes into his head and not being misled, for instance, into suppressing an idea because it strikes him as unimportant or irrelevant or because it seems to him meaningless. He must adopt a completely impartial attitude to what occurs to him, since it is precisely his critical attitude which is responsible for his being unable in the ordinary course of things, to achieve the desired unraveling of his dream or obsessional idea or whatever it may be.[7]

By this time closing the eyes was the only residue of the prior technique, and in a few years even this was dropped. Free association thus became the definitive technique of psychoanalysis.

The development of the technique of free association was of the greatest significance for Freud's thinking and for the development of psychoanalysis. With it he began to see more and more clearly the nature of the patient's resistances—without the contamination of hypnosis and with a minimizing of suggestion from the analyst. But there was also an important development in Freud himself. Concurrently with these technical developments, he began to undertake his own self-analysis. He began to apply the method of free association to his own thoughts, experiences, dreams, etc. He began to find resistances within himself that paralleled the resistances of his patients. Thus Freud came, arduously and slowly, to a dual appreciation of the dynamic properties of the mind and the role of the unconscious in mental processes. He saw these elements at work not only extrinsically in the observation of his patients in their attempts to free associate, but also intrinsically in his own increasing self-awareness and the experience of his own inner resistances. Consequently, when Freud comments that the psychoanalytic view of the unconscious is quite distinct from philosophical speculations about it, he speaks not only from theoretical persuasion but from an inner conviction based on his own subjective experience.

Freud's Antecedents

Freud's differentiation of the psychoanalytic concept of the unconscious and philosophical views of it suggests that the idea of unconscious mental processes had not originated with Freud. There had indeed been thoughts and speculations about an unconscious part of the mind long before Freud began his work. It will serve us well at this point to step back from Freud's momentous discovery to try to place it in its historical perspective. We shall try to recapitulate the important historical influences that came to bear on Freud's thinking as he took the significant steps toward the development of his first model of the psychic apparatus.

A number of important developments in the study of mental processes, both in their pathological manifestations and in their more normal functioning, had entered on the scene by the time Freud began his work with mental patients. These developments had in various ways and in various degrees a considerable influence on the emergence of Freud's own ideas and on the early development of psychoanalysis. Their influence, although less pronounced, can be traced in psychoanalytic thinking even today.

One of the most important influences on general psychiatry in Freud's time was the emergence of a systematic approach to descriptive psychiatry. This was the work, almost single-handedly, of Emil Kraepelin. It is important to realize that Kraepelin and Freud were contemporaries, as was the third great founder of modern psychiatry, Eugen Bleuler. Freud was born in 1856, Kraepelin in 1855, and Bleuler in 1857. In the years during which Freud was struggling toward his penetrating insights into the dynamic properties of the mind, Kraepelin was hard at work bringing some order into the chaos of psychiatric thinking. He bridged the gap between medicine and psychiatry, and brought a more organized, systematic, and scientific approach to the study of mental illnesses. He based his classifications of mental diseases on painstaking observations of many cases. His work was built on the unremitting and comprehensive collection of data and detailed recording. He strove for objectivity and accuracy—an emphasis which was badly needed and valuable, but which also, like hypnosis, precluded a view into the inner dynamic workings of the disturbed mind.

In any case, Kraepelin's efforts culminated in his rather elaborate classificatory system. The central idea of his system was that patterns of symptom-complexes could be identified and their coherence and consistency established. These symptom-complexes represented disease entities, much as physical symptom-complexes or syndromes in medicine are regarded as separate disease processes. The presumption was that once such complexes or syndromes had been established and defined one could search behind each for a specific cause or set of causes. Nosology and etiology were in principle correlative. Kraepelin's work was, in a sense, the culmination and highest achievement of an old order in psychiatry. His work capped and closed the development of descriptive psychiatry—and his influence persists in countless ways even today. But with Bleuler—and particularly with Freud—the new era of dynamic psychiatry was ushered in.

Bleuler's historic work on schizophrenia was both an extension of Kraepelinian psychiatry and a revolt against it. His work was deeply influenced by Freud's emerging views. He put thinking on schizophrenia on a new footing. He broke away from Kraepelin's concern with description and classification. He made it clear that schizophrenic patients did not suffer from a loss of affect, but that they displayed quite powerful emotions. He also brought the thought disorder, particularly the loosening of associations, into the center of these disturbances. He described autistic thinking, which he saw to be more influenced by emotions than by external realities. The combined influence of Kraepelin and Bleuler formed an atmosphere of scientific study and observation of mental illnesses. More significantly they gave shape to a concept of mental disorders as disease processes which could be studied, observed, analyzed, and understood in scientific terms, like medical diseases. But even more important, they brought the persuasion or conviction that such diseases could not only be understood, but that they could even be cured. This was the climate of psychiatric interest and direction in which Freud's more dynamic understanding of mental processes came to life.

Along with the Germanic developments in descriptive psychiatry, the French school in the latter half of the nineteenth century began to move toward a better understanding of neuroses under the leadership of Charcot, Bernheim, and Janet. Interest in and use of hypnotism—or mesmerism as it was known in the wake of Mesmer's magnetism—had developed to a considerable degree. The method was evolving toward a form of psychotherapy. Along with hypnosis, suggestion was the main therapeutic technique. Posthypnotic suggestion was particularly in favor as a method of treatment of mental disorders. By the use of posthypnotic suggestion Bernheim had been able to demonstrate quite clearly that it was possible for a patient to have an idea in his mind of which he was not at all conscious.

Using the technique of posthypnotic suggestion, Bernheim was able to show not only that unconscious ideas could persist in the mind, but that they could influence the patient's actions and behavior—even while he remained completely unaware of their existence or influence. He also showed that such ideas could be made conscious if the therapist persisted in searching them out. Demonstrations of posthypnotic suggestion and its effects are familiar to most people. A hypnotized patient can be told to carry out some action or to experience some thought or feeling at a given time interval or in response to a given stimulus after the hypnotic trance is ended. He is then awakened from the trance and subsequently carries out the suggested action. If one were to inquire why he was doing the action or why he was reacting in a certain way, he might admit that he had no idea or reason for it, or he might try to rationalize it in some way, but he would not remember that it was suggested under hypnosis. He would only know that he had experienced the need to perform the action. If one were to persist, however, the memory of the induced suggestion could be recovered. In .this way it could be demonstrated that the memory had in fact been retained in the mind, but in an unconscious manner. It was left to Freud to discover the nature of the resistance that kept such ideas out of consciousness.

There were also broader influences at work in the culture at large and in other areas of scientific endeavor. Natural science had made and was making giant strides in Freud's time. The scientific world that he grew up in was the world of Newtonian physics, of determinate and determinable causes and effects, all of which could be measured and quantified. The universal laws which were conceived of as governing all natural processes, physical and psychological, animate and inanimate, were the laws of thermodynamics. These basic laws of the nature and forms of energy governed the direction and exchange of energy, thresholds of stimulation and response, principles of inertia, and interactions of cause and effect. This was the world of universal scientific determinism. It was the world in which Freud's early ideas took their shape, and since he was deeply and intimately a man of science and a man of his times, he was inevitably influenced by the climate of thought.

It was the period before Einstein and the revolution of relativity. Freud was in fact to live through the intellectual turmoil and reorganization of the post-Newtonian era which was triggered by Einstein, and we can surmise that his own remarkable capacity to alter and adapt his concepts to the demands of new ideas and new points of view was in no small degree due to the shifting scientific climate around him. The influence of the deterministic and quantitative demands of scientific method on Freud's thinking can be most clearly seen in his *Project for a Scientific Psychology*. He wrote this remarkable document in a burst of energy in 1895, but not long afterward repudiated the whole thing. It was a tour de force by which he hoped to integrate the basic deterministic orientation of natural science, the extant body of neurological knowledge, and what he had learned about the nature and functioning of the mental apparatus.

The work reflects his basic scientific bent as well as the strong influence of Helmholtz's influence on his thinking. Helmholtz's deterministic views dominated the physiology of the time. His influence is reflected in Freud's thoroughgoing determinism, in the central position which he gives to pleasure and pain, in his use of the entropy concept, in his development of the principle of constancy, in the principles of least action, and in the "economic" principle of the conservation of energy. The attempt was not satisfactory and Freud, as we shall see later, gave up his attempt to neurologize or physiologize psychological processes. His giving it up, however, was never total—so that the tension between the physiological and psychological has remained an important aspect not only of Freud's later thinking, but of the continued progress of psychoanalysis.

On a broader intellectual scale, if the nature of the unconscious and the dynamic properties of the mind was properly Freud's discovery, it can also be said that the existence of the unconscious had been a secure intellectual possession for some time before him. For Descartes, subject and consciousness had been synonymous and coextensive: "Cogito ergo sum." Whatever lay beyond consciousness was pure extension, pure object. In the post-Cartesian era, however, that clear and distinct idea became less clear and less distinct. Speculations about unconscious mental processes began around the turn of the sixteenth century, particularly in the romantic tradition. They were viewed as mystical powers which somehow linked man with the forces of the universe or the powers of a divinity. Such ideas were common among the German proponents of *Naturphilosophie* in the early nineteenth century—Goethe was the leading figure of the movement and its primary expression. But even earlier one of the leading figures to propose and give clear expression to the idea of unconscious mental activity had been Leibniz. His doctrine of *petits perceptions*—minute perceptions below the threshold of awareness that had to summate in order to reach consciousness and form our ordinary perceptions—was the basis for an elaborate theory of unconscious mental activity.

The whole body of thought about unconscious mental processes, however, remained a loose element in the scientific and philosophic culture of post-Cartesian and premodern Europe. Its treatment remained fragmentary and highly speculative. It was based on occasional introspection, but the approach was in no way systematic or in any way scientific. Freud was the first to observe unconscious activity in a systematic and scientific way. He was thus the first to see it in a meaningful context and to begin to appreciate the relation between unconscious phenomena and the dynamic operation of the mind. He was able to relate unconscious activity specifically to clinically observed resistances and amnesias and to account for these observations in meaningful terms. He had every right, then, to distinguish the psychoanalytic understanding of the unconscious from what had gone before, even though he owed his intellectual heritage a debt of gratitude.

Another development within psychology that had an influence on Freud was the emergence of associationism. The concept of mental processes as based on associations had developed in post-Cartesian philosophy but also had arisen in the British empirical school. Such ideas were common coin in Freud's time. The failure of his early cathartic method forced on him the view that the traumatic ideas were hidden in the patient's memory. The techniques he employed, from hypnosis on to free association, were calculated to bring the hidden ideas out of the patient's memory. His conviction that the hidden ideas were tied to conscious ones by associative links underlay his thinking and led him in the direction of free association. What Freud added to the extant association psychology of his day was the appreciation that associations were the products of dynamic and wishful activity of the mind rather than of mere mechanical contiguities.

Freud's Integration

All of these influences, however, even though they were extant and active influences in the culture of the time, remained disparate and unrelated. There was little or no cross-communication or cross-fertilization between these various emphases, even though each in its own fashion was concerned with the basic question of how and why the human mind functions as it does. Freud's pioneering effort in the initiation and development of psychoanalysis was that he brought these various areas of human interest and endeavor to a common focus. In a sense, what Freud developed was the first significant interdisciplinary approach to the problem of understanding human behavior and mental processes. He combined in his own thinking the influences derived from different disciplines and areas of interest, integrating certain findings and certain basic principles from each of these areas of knowledge into a new approach which little by little grew into a new discipline.

Freud took in something from each of these approaches. From Kraepelin he adopted a basically scientific or more strictly medical approach to the problems of mental illness. From Charcot and Bernheim he adopted the findings derived from hypnosis and more specifically hypnosis as an approach to the treatment of hysterical patients—a method which was to evolve in Freud's hands into the psychoanalytic method. From the natural sciences he adopted a number of important energic principles which provided the basic theoretical substructure of his developing theory. The most important and pervasive of these principles was the law of determinism which he accepted in the form presented by Helmholtz. From the philosophic tradition he adopted the idea of unconscious mental activity, a vast subcontinent of mental processes beyond and beneath the islands of consciousness that are visible to us. He accepted the idea also that such unconscious activity could have an influence on thinking and behavior, even though it was not directly available to conscious introspection. And from psychology he took the associative method, using its basic theory as a working hypothesis for approaching the problem of unconscious memories and modifying its method, which had been developed in experimental settings, into a technique of clinical investigation and therapy.

We might wonder to ourselves how Freud ever got involved in all of this. What was it that drew him to his investment in these problems and to the searching out of new methods and new ideas? The answer lies in

Freud's own training and background, but also in certain contingencies of his life and circumstances. His background and formal training were scientific and his specialized training was in the area of the neural sciences. He was skilled in the areas of neuropathology, neuroanatomy, and neurophysiology. His earliest publication while still a student was a study of neural structure in the spinal cord of the Petromyzon, a genus of cyclostome. He had thus established the beginnings of a distinguished career as a neurologist. He went on to work in the laboratories of Brücke and Meynert—two of the most distinguished investigators of the era—and published several important works in neurology and neuropathology, including a monograph on cerebral infantile paralysis. His work on aphasia was a landmark in the field. And he became a *Privatdozent* at the University of Vienna in 1885.

New Discoveries

From the point of view of this promising career, it was most unfortunate that economic necessity forced Freud to give up his neurological teaching and research. From the point of view of psychoanalysis and the understanding of the human mind, it was perhaps the most influential decision of the modern era. Freud went into private practice. And he began to find, in dealing with his patients, who presented themselves with a broad range of complaints, that a large proportion of their complaints had no organic basis. The discovery was not new. It had been made by Charcot, by Janet, and for that matter by any practicing physician—particularly those specializing in neurological diseases. Freud's practice included a fair proportion of neurotic patients in whom no organic disease process could be demonstrated. It is not surprising, given Freud's innate curiosity and his scientific background, that he should be puzzled by this phenomenon and stimulated to study these patients more carefully. When he began to make observations that were consistent and meaningful enough to suggest some form of more general process underlying such symptoms, he was led to try to find some scientific basis for such findings.

What were the new findings that captured Freud's interest? They were of several kinds, some of which we have already discussed. In the first place, there were Freud's observations of his neurotic patients. His interest was stimulated by the experience of his good friend and colleague, Josef Breuer, with his now famous patient Anna O. Anna was an unusually intelligent young woman of twenty-one years who had developed a symphony of symptoms in relation to her father's fatal illness. She developed a variety of paralyses and anesthesias, disturbances of vision and speech, anorexia, and a nervous cough. There were also disturbances of consciousness and clearly discernible transitions from one state to another. Breuer treated this patient by the hypnotic method, but during one session she related to Breuer the details of the onset of a new symptom without hypnosis. To Breuer's surprise the symptom disappeared. In subsequent sessions, the patient continued to discuss one symptom after another with similar effects—she dubbed the procedure the "talking cure" or "chimney sweeping." Thus Breuer and Anna O. evolved what has since become known as the cathartic method.

Freud's interest was stimulated by these fascinating findings, and he began to find something similar in his own patients. He and Breuer used hypnosis as a means of accomplishing the chimney sweeping more effectively. Gradually, however, Freud began to make other observations which led him to believe that these findings might not be unique or peculiar to hysterical patients. They might indeed have a wider distribution and consequently broader implications. The resistance that he ran into when he tried to uncover the memories which his hysterical patients had forgotten seemed to present many similarities to resistances to recovering memories that he could recognize in himself and in other more normal people. He began to feel that such resistance was a reflection of a more general process. It was not confined to sick patients or something to be regarded exclusively as a result of a disorder in the patient's thought processes. With this premise in mind he began to investigate common errors, lapses in memory, slips of the tongue, phenomena of misnaming, misremembering, or misidentifying, parapraxes of all sorts, and his investigations confirmed his suspicions. He found principles of mental functioning at work in these common mistakes similar to those he had found at work in the production of his patients' symptoms. He came to call these commonly experienced errors and slips the "psychopathology of everyday life."

From the very beginning of his interest in mental phenomena—as opposed to neurological phenomena—Freud followed parallel lines of investigation. His inquiries were guided by observation and investigation not only of a variety of clinical conditions but also of some important areas of normal mental functioning. The most important of the latter were dreams and the psychopathology of everyday life. His inquiries were parallel not only in the sense that he looked at different areas of human activity, both pathological and normal, but also in a methodological sense. He was not only observing and analyzing the behavior and experiences of others in an objective frame of reference, but he was also caught up in the introspective analysis of his own subjective experiences and thought processes. The difficult and extensive analysis of his own behavior and particularly of his own dreams stands as a monumental piece of careful subjective analysis. But in both subjective and objective approaches, he assiduously applied the associative method.

Resistance

The findings from these various approaches, however divergent their methods and contents, led Freud down a sort of final common path. If we consider first the clinical evidences, we have already noted the resistance that he encountered whenever he tried to uncover forgotten memories. The interest in these forgotten memories and the search for them came about as a result of Breuer's important discovery—that certain hysterical patients, if allowed to talk and ventilate their feelings under hypnosis, finally came to recount forgotten memories which had been traumatic at the time of the occurrence of the events. Two important facts emerged about these memories. First of all, the memories were generally of a specific kind, namely, sexual. They usually had to do with some sort of sexual trauma the patient had supposedly suffered when a child. Second was an observation that Breuer had originally made and which Freud was able to confirm, that if the patients were able to recount such experiences under hypnosis with full emotional release there appeared to be some form of discharge which was followed by relief of the symptoms. Such a release followed by symptomatic relief was called "abreaction." (The traumatic memories which were recovered by this method were primarily sexual, and as Freud continued his investigation of them they seemed to reach further and further back into the patient's life experience.)

As his experience grew, however, Freud began to place less confidence in the hypnotic method. As we have seen he gradually abandoned the methods of hypnosis and suggestion and little by little evolved his associative technique. Along with this he came increasingly to rely on and emphasize his basic theoretical assumption that the law of determinism applied unequivocally to mental phenomena. His development of the free association technique was based on the assumption that if the patient said everything that came into his mind the thoughts that came into consciousness would be determined by the laws of association and would thus be connected. Freud reasoned that the patient's associations would thus lead inevitably and determinately to the forgotten memory.

There were disturbing factors nonetheless. They were apparent in the use of the hypnotic method and were even more apparent in the use of free association. The disturbing factors can be grouped under the heading of resistance. Frequently enough, hysterical patients who were able to recall forgotten experiences under hypnosis would forget these memories again soon after. The memories could only be recovered again if the hypnosis were repeated. Also, with discouraging regularity, the symptomatic improvement after hypnotic sessions and abreaction proved to be only temporary. The patient would either relapse, the old symptoms would return with renewed vigor, or he would develop new symptoms to take the place of the old ones. Some patients did get symptomatic relief and their improved condition persisted, i.e., they remained free of overt hysterical symptoms. Such patients, however, began to show a marked attachment to the therapist and a strong dependence on him. Consequently, they would have to return more and more frequently to maintain their improved status. It looked very much as though the feelings for the therapist had in some way been substituted for the earlier neurotic or hysterical symptoms.

Resistance in Dreams—"My Friend R."

Another important area of discovery for Freud was his research into dreaming and dream content. In approaching the problem of dream interpretation, he made a basic assumption that was a direct application of the principle of psychic determinism. He assumed that dreams have meaning and that the meaning was determined by specific causes. He also assumed that the meaning of dreams could be traced to these determining sources and thus the dream content could be understood. The assumption that dreams have meaning is not surprising or startling to us. In Freud's time the idea was new and revolutionary, at least in scientific and medical circles. Previous investigations that had sought some form of meaning in dreams had tried to relate them to physical sensations or external stimuli that the dreamer might experience in sleep. The content of the dream, from a psychological point of view, was generally regarded as meaningless and confused. The belief in dreams as somehow meaningful belonged to ancient, prophetic, mystical, primitive, religious, or philosophical belief systems, and consequently the idea was looked at askance and with disdain by scientific circles. There were some discordant voices, however, among them the renowned British neurologist, Hughlings Jackson, who had written, "Find out about dreams, and you will find out about insanity."

Freud's assumption was not only that the dream was meaningful, but that its chief internal significance was related to a meaningful psychological event. He started with the manifest or remembered content of the dream and applied the associative method in order to gain access to the latent content which remained hidden. His method rested on the assumption of determinism in psychic events, that the manifest content was determined at least in part by the unconscious latent content of the dream. Freud had been applying this same technique to the analysis of neurotic symptoms in his patients, but what he discovered when he began to associate to his own dreams was in the first instance slightly different from what he had found in his neurotic patients. It will help us at this point to look at one of Freud's dreams. This particular dream is one that Freud describes in which he most clearly refers to the experience of resistance. We shall see how clearly the resistance was manifest and also what kind of meaning was revealed by Freud's associations.

The dream was short and rather simple. Freud dreamed: "My friend R. was my uncle. —I had a great feeling of affection for him." [8] As he himself described it in his *Interpretation of Dreams,* his first reaction on recalling this dream fragment was that it was nonsense and couldn't possibly have any meaning. He didn't think that it was worth trying to associate to it. But he stopped himself short. He realized that he had met a similar attitude in his own patients and that his attitude must be an expression of some resistance to interpreting the dream on his part. His associations led him to the following material.

The dream had occurred at a time when Freud was very concerned as to whether or not he was going to obtain a professorship. He was quite concerned as to whether the fact that he was Jewish might interfere with an appointment for which he felt himself to be qualified in terms of ability and accomplishment. He had known that two of his friends who also were Jewish had not been granted professorships which they had anticipated. One of these men was "my friend R." The other vaguely resembled his uncle in appearance. However, the uncle who had appeared in the dream as "my friend R." was known to him as something of a knave. His associations, moreover, to his friend R. contained a number of references which suggested that he thought of R. as a rather foolish man. As he went on associating to these two figures, he began to recognize the underlying wish that these two friends of his should not have been barred from professorships simply because they were Jewish. They should rather have been barred because of the fact that one of them was a fool and the other a knave. Freud saw, therefore, that the extreme affection expressed in the dream was an effective disguise. The dream, in fact, represented the disguised gratification of an extremely hostile wish—that these two friends should be seen as despicable: one a fool, the other a knave. Of course, since Freud was neither fool, nor knave, he could therefore become a professor.

We can appreciate that such a wish was one that Freud might have repudiated from his conscious thinking. Today we would call it an ego-alien wish—one that was unacceptable to his conscious thinking and to his conscience. The resistance is directed at keeping this unacceptable wish out of consciousness. Previously, in dealing with clinical material, Freud had encountered resistance in his patients to recalling memories which were too painful to be remembered. Now in his own dreams, analysis had repeatedly revealed hidden wishes, which were unacceptable, as well as resistances to their recall. The divergent approaches led to a common conclusion: that which is repressed is in some manner unacceptable to conscious thought. In respect to dreams and the psychopathology of everyday life, Freud emphasized the role of ego-alien wishes; in respect to the neuroses, his main emphasis had been on the existence of repressed memories. As we shall see, these different aspects were later brought together. But at this point in the development of Freud's thinking, the predominant finding was the existence of mental content which was unacceptable to conscious thinking and which was therefore kept out of consciousness by the operation of a dynamic process. Freud's first theoretical formulations were primarily concerned with the explanation of this dynamic process.

The Neurological Approach

With these different observations in hand, Freud's impetus and interest was toward integrating them in terms of some more comprehensive scientific theory. His training, as mentioned, was in neurology and related sciences, and his thinking was organized along neurological lines. It is not surprising then that he should try to find a suitable explanation for his exciting new findings in terms of the scientific base with which he was most familiar and to which he was intellectually committed. Consequently, his first attempts at explanation of these phenomena were cast in an organic framework. The attempt was certainly consistent with his own background and also with the dominant persuasion of contemporary psychiatry. Psychiatric thinking, including that of the dominating figure of Kraepelin, had been committed to the idea of an underlying physical-organic cause for mental disturbances. What Freud tried to do in the first instance was to explain the phenomena of resistance, repression, and unconscious mental activity in terms of what was then known about the structure and function of the brain. He based his theory on available knowledge about the nature and functioning of neurons, and tried to build out of these fundamental building blocks a view of the integration of the central nervous system which would explain the dynamic properties of the mind with which he was dealing clinically.

His attempt is recorded in a series of drafts and finally his brilliant *Project*. Shortly after the attempt Freud repudiated it entirely, or nearly so, and the documents never saw the light in Freud's lifetime. He had sent copies of his work to his close friend Fliess which were fortunately preserved. These were discovered again after Freud's death. The *Project* is an interesting and difficult monograph but one that is of considerable interest in contemporary terms. The interest lies in several aspects of the work. It is important in the first place because it gives a unique insight into Freud's thinking at a time when he was generating his basic theories and struggling with some important basic issues. It provides us with a valuable entrée to the roots in Freud's thinking, since a number of basic ideas which were not to reach more mature expression until much later in his career are clearly identifiable in germinal form in the *Project*. This is particularly true of his views of the ego and its functioning; some of these views have reached fruition only in the post-Freudian developments of ego psychology. Furthermore, the issues concerning the link between psychological processes and neurophysiological processes which Freud raised and formulated in a preliminary way are still live issues in modern psychiatry. Our increasing sophistication in areas of psychological and neurological understanding allows us to approach these problems in fresh ways which give promise of increasing our understanding of the complex relations between CNS activity and mental processes. Freud's original views are still seminal and provocative, and must be regarded as heuristically valuable, if not more.

The "As-If"

But, in Freud's time and from Freud's perspective, the attempt did not succeed. He himself regarded it as a dismal failure and took it as a serious blow to his visions of extending the Helmholtz doctrine to the human mind. As a result, he gave up further attempts to explain his psychological findings in neurological terms. He did not, however, give up on the principle. He continued to maintain the view that ultimately, with an increase of knowledge, it would be possible to ground our understanding of mental processes in the physical activity of the nervous system. For him, to surrender the attempt was difficult. He could not surrender his commitment to physical science and its principles without great reluctance. He wrote to Fliess in September, 1898:

> But I am not in the least in disagreement with you, and have no desire at all to leave the psychology hanging in the air with no organic basis. But, beyond a feeling of conviction [that there must be such a basis], I have nothing, either theoretical or therapeutic, to work on, and so I must behave as if I were confronted by psychological factors only.[9]

The "as-if" represented an extremely important and crucial step in the development of psychoanalytic thinking. Freud was saying, in effect, that he could not satisfactorily explain in neurophysiological terms the conclusions he was reaching about the functioning of the mind. He was by no means renouncing the idea that psychological events could be explained in terms of their organic basis. He was merely postponing this possibility to a later era when greater knowledge might make such a correlation feasible. Until that time, however, the domain of the psychological would have to be approached and understood in terms of specifically psychological postulates, methods, and theories.

With the development of physiological knowledge, there have been repeated attempts to relate psychological, and particularly psychoanalytic, findings to new physiological information and understanding. The concept of stress has been used by a number of psychoanalysts who have tried to reformulate psychoanalytic views in terms of stress theories. There have been attempts to reformulate psychoanalytic theory in terms of reflexes, reformulating anxiety in terms of conditioning and conditioned relfexes, for example. More recently memory mechanisms, mechanisms of repression, cerebral activity in certain forms of attention and cognitive activity, organization of nervous activity in states of emotional arousal, and a number of other important spheres of study have given promise of further development in these areas. But on the whole these attempts remain more suggestive and promising than areas of achieved understanding. Most psychoanalysts still feel that Freud's "as-if" remains a fundamental premise of the analytic frame of reference. We have not yet reached the point where we can even begin to translate what we know about the structure and functioning of the mind into natural science terms. Even though there are areas of research in which the possibility of greater understanding of the links between mental and neural activity are foreseeable, we must still work primarily in terms of the Freudian "as-if." We must base our thinking about mental processes on a hypothetical model of the structure and organization of the mind, rather than on an understanding of anatomical structure or physiological processes.

The Model of the Mind

The question of model making and the use of models in scientific thinking is an extremely important but nonetheless complex and difficult area. Theoretical models are involved in nearly all forms of scientific thinking. Questions about the relation between available evidence and the integration of such evidence in terms of the model, of the relation between the model and scientific thought processes, of the extent to which the model organizes and brings consistency to a body of scientific facts, or the extent to which it leaves certain parts or aspects of the data and available understanding of underlying processes unexplained— these are all questions that plague the process of scientific understanding. Models are of various kinds and have a variety of functions in scientific thinking. One can think of early Empedoclean theory about body humors as a primitive sort of model of the influence of bodily factors on mental functioning. The model assumed that illness could be explained by the production and distribution of the four humors—blood, bile, phlegm, and black bile. Available observations could be related to these hypothetical factors. Similarly the explanation of mental illness in the Middle Ages by appeal to diabolic possession might also be thought of as an animistic theologized model. The formulation of models as explanatory devices is not only a universal characteristic of human thought processes but it is an integral part of any scientific theorizing.

Freud's theorizing and his working model of the mental apparatus went through several stages of development. Throughout his career, he was able to maintain a remarkable openness and flexibility, formulating and reformulating his thinking in the light of new evidences which his clinical experience was constantly providing him. Some years later he would write:

Psychoanalysis is not, like philosophies, a system starting out from a few sharply defined basic concepts, seeking to grasp the whole universe with the help of these and, once it is completed, having no room for fresh discoveries or better understanding. On the contrary, it keeps close to the fact, in its field of study, it seems to solve the immediate problems of observation, gropes its way forward by the help of experience, is always incomplete and always ready to correct or modify its theories.[10]

It was Freud's empirical rootedness and his focusing on the evidential base of his thinking that made him acutely aware of the limitations of his theoretical concepts as well as the functional models on which they were based.

If we look more carefully at Freud's early model of the mental apparatus—the model of the *Project*—we can gain some understanding of what Freud accomplished when he finally surrendered his attempt to formulate psychological findings in terms of a physical model. On one hand, he gave up the attempt to localize mental events exactly in the brain. Nonetheless, in moving to a more psychological model of the mental apparatus, he retained a basic orientation derived from physical science and utilized some of the basic concepts of contemporary natural science in the formulation of his theory and the model of the mind implicit in it. We might reconstruct the logic of his thinking in the following terms. He found that he could not correlate his psychological discoveries with the then available knowledge of physiology. The physicalistic model would not work. Therefore, he had to develop an alternative hypothetical model. He would not renounce, however, his conviction that ultimately science would arrive at a correlation of the mental and the physical. What he hypothesized was not only a model of the mind as purely psychological—the "as-if" he spoke of to Fliess—but also a model of the mind as possessing certain dynamic properties. He postulated as part of the "as-if" that the model of the mind had to be constructed according to the dynamic laws and principles which dominated current physical theories of the distribution and regulation of the flow of energy. Freud's surrendering of his objective of explaining mental life in terms of physiological and neurological processes was more of a compromise than a surrender. What he did not give up was the rooting of his thinking and of his evolving theory in the basic postulates of physical science.

Psychic Determinism

Among the basic postulates that Freud retained in the further development of his thinking, the law of determinism was primary. It provided
him with the rationalization and justification for his method of free association in that according to the principle of determination nothing
could enter the mind haphazardly. Whatever came into consciousness by
way of free association was determined. Freud commented that "Psychoanalysts are marked by a particularly strict belief in the determination of mental life. For them there is nothing trivial, nothing arbitrary
or haphazard. They expect in every case to find sufficient motives." [11]
For the most part during the whole of his career Freud maintained a
rather thoroughgoing determinism—although it seems unlikely that his
use of the notion of psychic determinism was simply a transferal of the
notion of causal determinism from physical science. Freud himself introduced the notion of overdetermination, meaning that a particular
psychic event or set of psychic events could be explained in terms of
more than one set of determining factors. He envisioned a kind of "lay-
ering" of determinations in psychic life which could be seen over and
over again in his patients. The patient's behavior had to be understood
not only in terms of the determining events and motives of his present
circumstances, but also in terms of the determining events and motives
of the past. Such a view of determination is difficult to reconcile with
notions of physical determination and cause-effect relations. Moreover,
the problem of determination in psychoanalysis is made more complex
by reason of the fact that the subject matter of the science does not simply have to do with physical or behavioral events. Rather it involves
human actions and intentions which carry and reflect meaning. Psychic
determinism, therefore, has to do with meanings and the relations of
meanings more than it does with causal relations.

The law of determinism that Freud knew in his early career grew out
of the prevailing scientific view of the world. It was a world view that
was Newtonian in origin and conviction—a world composed of determinate causes and effects which could be measured and mathematically
specified. The great scientific preoccupation of the time was to take the
laws of Newtonian physics and thermodynamics, which governed all
physical processes and the transfer of energies, and apply them to more
complex biological and psychological systems. The belief in these principles was as confident and as self-assured as the reign of England's

Victoria with her far-flung empire. It was only after the turn of the century that Einstein introduced theories of relativity which began to raise problems for the Newtonian world of causal determinism.

Views of determinism have changed in scientific thinking in general, but particularly so in analysis. For Freud, at least in his early approach to psychological problems, determinism was absolute and particular, in the sense that he postulated that every mental event, no matter how trivial, had meaning and was determined. But many analysts today would not apply the principle in this particularistic and mechanical sense, and many would raise serious doubts whether the mental structure can really be adequately viewed in quite the rigidly deterministic manner that Freud had originally suggested. The notion of determinism in psychoanalysis can be conceived in considerably broader and more flexible terms. For example, in his original formulations Freud would have explained every example of the psychopathology of everyday life, every forgetting, as something that could be interpreted like a dream and its relation to a specific unconscious wish as capable of being established. He would have conceived the wish and its related motive as determining the forgetting. Recently, however, Anna Freud has written about the problems of "losing and being lost." She made the point that one might not be able to explain each individual act of losing in terms of its immediate determination. Rather we might have to recognize that in the early development of an individual there might be established a general tendency to lose things which might become part of the individual's character structure. What is central to the consideration of such cases is the general trait, the tendency to lose things, rather than the immediate explanation of every specific loss. Such a notion implies a form of determinism at the level of character formation and development, but it no longer acknowledges the sort of rigid and absolute determinism that dominated Freud's original theoretical efforts.

Constancy

Freud also retained a number of the basic principles and laws of thermodynamics in his thinking. Perhaps the most important of these was the principle of constancy which he derived from the law of inertia. This principle formed one of the basic postulates of the *Project,* though he had referred to it even before that. He called it the principle of neuronal inertia—that when neurons are excited by stimulation they tend to divest themselves of energy and to return to a state of rest. This was related to his view of pleasure and unpleasure. The state of cerebral excitation was related to unpleasure and the state of diminished excitation was related to pleasure. Freud postulated that there was an inherent tendency to keep excitation at a minimum. He changed his views about the principle of constancy very little during his career. He linked it with the pleasure principle and returned to this point several times in later writings to re-emphasize it. In *Beyond the Pleasure Principle* (1920) he wrote:

> The facts which have caused us to believe in the dominance of the pleasure principle in mental life also find expression in the hypothesis that the mental apparatus endeavors to keep the quality of excitation present in it as low as possible or at least to keep it constant. This latter hypothesis is only another way of stating the pleasure principle; for if the work of the mental apparatus is directed towards keeping the quantity of excitation low, then anything that is calculated to increase that quantity is bound to be felt as adverse to the functioning of the apparatus, that is as unpleasurable. The pleasure principle follows from the principle of constancy. . . .[12]

Thus the principle of constancy (inertia) provided one of the major theoretical props of his thinking early in his theorizing, and continued to do so even in later years.

Our understanding of scientific principles has grown greatly since Freud's time. We can see more clearly now the range of applicability of some of the earlier principles and Newtonian laws. In terms of a broader understanding of physical principles, Newtonian laws can be seen as a special case that has limited application. Within the area of proper application the laws are still valid and have value. With regard to psychoanalysis, we have to recognize that Freud based his theoretical thinking on the scientific laws of his time, and that he shared the scientific understanding of these laws that were extant at the time. When we use the language of constancy, entropy, thresholds, etc., we are speaking out of the context in which Freud formulated his original construct of the psychic apparatus. The terms have shown considerable flexibility and have allowed for considerable development in the theory of psychoanalysis. We have thus been able to expand and modify many of Freud's views without making substantial changes in terminology of basic concepts.

Problems

Adherence to these basic postulates, however, has put contemporary psychoanalysis in a difficult and problematic position. A considerable amount of psychoanalytic theory has been built around these postulates, but the question arises whether these physicalistic postulates are the proper or adequate basis on which to erect a comprehensive theory of mental organization and structure. Has the attempt to cling to these postulates given us only a partial understanding of the mental apparatus? Have they actually hampered our advancing understanding of the mind's functioning? Questions are being raised in contemporary psychoanalysis about the relevance of these postulates and whether the basing of theory on physicalistic principles is any longer valid—even heuristically. Not only basic postulates, but also basic theoretical notions, like the notion of psychic energy, are being challenged. Does the idea of psychic energy have any validity or reality at all? Might psychoanalysis have a firmer theoretical footing in other theoretical bases, like information theory or general systems theory?

These are all perplexing and difficult theoretical questions. But their urgency reflects the significance of Freud's crucial decision and the first theoretical steps that he took. Starting from his clinical observations of resistance and unconscious wishes, he was led to several important shifts. He abandoned hypnosis and turned gradually to free association as a method of investigation, and with it he turned to a practical acceptance and application of the principle of determinism in psychic life. When his attempt to articulate an organic basis for psychological processes failed—particularly in regard to the dynamic properties of the mind that he had discovered—he developed a hypothetical construct of the mental apparatus that was based on and presumed a number of basic postulates derived from the natural sciences of his time. In so doing he set psychoanalysis on a theoretical course which it has followed ever since. Whether it can continue on that course, or whether these postulates and the theory derived from them—like the Newtonian physics in which they were born—must now be seen as a special case based on a limited perspective of mental activity remains a moot question. We may need a broader basis for our continuing progress in the understanding of the human mental activity and mental life. These problems are far from solution.

[4]

Repression: Clinical Origins of the Concept

Freud's early theoretical attempts to formulate a model of the psychic apparatus were motivated by his desire to explain the phenomena associated with resistance. His view of mental phenomena, as involving dynamic forces and properties, led him to seek to base his explanation, and the mental model associated with it, on more general specific theories that dealt with energy and force and the laws of their regulation and distribution. Specifically his objective was to explain the clinical phenomena of resistance, as he observed it first in the treatment of his neurotic patients, and second in his investigations of dreams and the psychopathology of everyday life. In his hysterical patients, he discovered an amnesia for specific traumatic experiences which seemed to derive from the individual's early life experience. In the case of dreams and slips and errors, he was able to discern the role of ego-alien wishes which remained for the most part unconscious. Nonetheless, it was the repression of memories which remained in the central focus of Freud's early interest.

Freud vs. Breuer

A number of important findings emerged during the years of collaboration between the older Breuer and the younger Freud. The first finding of significance concerned the nature of the memories which had been repressed and which were recovered originally through hypnosis and later by associative methods—the repressed memories were primarily sexual. The second important finding had to do with the nature of the process, which made these memories unavailable to conscious introspection. The break that took place between Breuer and Freud was at least in part a matter of irresolvable differences in both these areas; they parted ways over the crucial questions of the role of sexuality and of the understanding of how memories became unconscious. It was a fundamental divergence in the approach to both content and concept.

We will first examine the mechanism which makes memories unconscious, since this leads directly to the concept of repression as an active, purposive, and dynamic process. There was a definite transition in Freud's thinking about this matter. He and Breuer agreed, at least in the beginning of their work, that their hysterical patients had been subjected to traumatic sexual experiences. It was also apparent that these traumatic experiences were not available to conscious recollection. They also agreed for a time that the recovery of these forgotten experiences during a hypnotic state resulted in abreaction and consequent symptomatic improvement. Even though the two men were in agreement on these points, their respective points of view and explanations of the process began to drift apart, even while they were working on these problems together.

Breuer had originally advanced the concept of the hypnoid state as the explanation for hysteria. The hypnoid state represented an altered type of consciousness in which part of the mind was split off from the rest in a state of dissociation. Breuer felt that it was because of this splitting of consciousness under the stress of emotional arousal that the normal course of emotional reaction and expression was prevented. In such a hypnoid state, the content of the dissociated part of the mind was isolated from associative links with the rest of consciousness. These links could be re-established through hypnosis. In the *Studies on Hysteria,* Breuer wrote:

The longer we have been occupied with these [hysterical] phenomena the more we have become convinced that the splitting of consciousness . . . is present to a rudimentary degree in every hysteria, and that a tendency to such a dissociation, and with it the emergence of abnormal states of consciousness (which we shall bring together under the term "hypnoid") is the basic phenomenon of this neurosis.[13]

It was Breuer's view that the traumatic experiences had occurred at a time when the patient was in one of these hypnoid, dissociated states. Consequently the traumatic experience had been dissociated, its normal associative links with the rest of conscious activity had been disrupted, and so the content of that dissociated segment was not available to conscious introspection.

If we were to consider Breuer's hypothesis in terms of an analogy, his premise was that the unconscious memories were shut out from the conscious part of the mind—like a closed-off room in the house of the mind. All that was required was that one open the door separating the closed-off room and it would be open to the rest of the house. One had only to re-establish the associative links and the lost memories would be retrieved. Freud seems to have accepted Breuer's hypnoid hypothesis only with reservations. As an explanatory concept it carried little conviction for him. It was based on a clinical state that was merely postulated and never observed, that supposedly occurred at the time of the trauma. To Freud's mind it represented a rather elaborate theory which was based on a meager amount of clinical evidence. Breuer developed the theory in terms of energy transformations and special states of consciousness which were highly organized, and different from normal conscious states, but which persisted in the mind parallel to the latter states. The whole thing was top-heavy and ran against the grain of Freud's more empirical mindedness.

The Defensive Hypothesis

The tension between their points of view is manifested from the beginning of their collaboration. At the beginning of the *Studies,* they describe two varieties of hysteria—dispositional hysteria and psychically acquired hysteria. The former notion was based on the idea of a personality which was somehow disposed to forming hypnoid states. The latter notion of psychically acquired hysteria represented a more reactive approach, implying that the condition could be acquired through the reaction of an individual to external trauma. This was essentially Freud's view, which would gradually evolve toward a view of hysteria as a defensive neurosis based on repression. Freud's halfhearted agreement with Breuer's view did not fade until his analyses of the cases of Lucy and Elizabeth von R. The latter case was crucial, since it marked a definitive change in his technique in which he abandoned hypnosis (see Chapter 3). In treating the same patient, he arrived at a clear-cut formulation of the defense concept. The patient's associations in response to Freud's pressure technique made it abundantly clear that the conflict between her sexual impulses and her moral misgivings were at the root of the problem. The hypnoid hypothesis did not suffice, since the sexual thoughts were originally conscious and had to be excluded from the patient's consciousness. The two sides of the conflict had to coexist in the same system of consciousness. Thus Freud moved toward the basic notion of conflict and the need for defense against repugnant thoughts and wishes as the basic meaning of hysteria. This shift in viewpoint would soon lead to both greater clinical efficacy and greater theoretical explanatory power.

The shift from the hypnoid hypothesis to a defensive hypothesis was extremely important. It also reflected basic differences between the approaches of Breuer and Freud. Breuer had postulated the hypnoid state as a given. Freud moved a step beyond that and suggested that the dissociated state was produced by an activity of the mind. The splitting off of the unconscious portion of the mind was due to an intrapsychic conflict and was based on an active and defensive process in the mind. If we return to the analogy of the house, Freud did not see the process of recovery of the lost memories in such a simple light. It was not to his way of thinking simply a matter of opening the door. The door had been closed as a defensive measure, and it could only be opened in the face of the patient's continuing defense. One had to deal with an active force holding the door shut. And the more one tried to open the door, the greater was the force exerted by the patient's mind in keeping it closed. The more one tried to recover the traumatic experience—as if to force the door open—the more one ran into a block, into resistance.

Freud's thesis of conflict and defense by repression, then, was the first truly dynamic hypothesis about the functioning of the mind. He suggested that repression was a meaningful and dynamic process which was specifically directed against the admission to consciousness of traumatic memories as well as against their retrieval in treatment. Freud commented simply: "Everywhere I seemed to find purpose in resistance and I could not accept the hypothesis that all that had happened was a simple dissociation."

The evidence on which Freud based his dynamic hypothesis of repression and defense did not rest simply on the evidences for resistance that we have already discussed (see above and Chapter 3). Both Breuer and Freud discovered, as they continued to hypnotize their patients, that symptomatic recovery was combined with another and surprising clinical phenomenon: the patients, all hysterical women, began to fall in love with their therapists. The longer the process of hypnosis continued, the more likely they were to develop intense sexualized feelings toward the therapist. As a result of their sexualized attachment to the latter, the patients would return for more and more treatment. They would continue to recover more and more memories without ever seeming to come to an end. They would start by recovering a recent traumatic experience and would experience some symptomatic relief. The relief was more or less transient. They would then recover some further traumatic experience, again with relief of the troubling symptoms. The memories thus recovered reached progressively further and further back into the patients' life histories until finally they reached some very early childhood sexual experience.

From Breuer's point of view all that was happening in hypnosis was that a simple connection or communication was established between two sets of experiences which had been separated from each other. The dissociated experiences had been hidden because they were painful. They continued to cause symptoms just like an unopened abscess—walled off and separated from the rest of the organism—which can produce painful symptoms. Just as the opening of an abscess can relieve the physical pain associated with the accumulation of noxious material and the resulting pressure, so the psychological equivalent of hypnosis could open up the dissociated material and release the dammed up affect associated with the traumatic memories. Freud had accepted this view for a time, but he reasoned that if it were true, it should follow that the recovery of the traumatic memories should be sufficient to resolve the dissociation and allow the release of the dammed up material.

Transference

It was apparent, not only to Freud but to Breuer as well, that the recovery of the traumatic memories was not having its expected effect. Freud's dissatisfaction with the results of treatment and his doubts about the explanatory power of Breuer's hypnoid hypothesis brought him to an alternative attempt at explanation in terms of a dynamic and defensive process. This led of course to the formulation of his dynamic hypothesis. Breuer, however, did not accept the idea of a dynamic process of repression. Moreover, he was considerably troubled by the development of a sexualized attachment to him on the part of his female patients. Breuer was a distinguished physician and a faithful and conservative family man. The experience of having his patients develop such strong sexual feelings for him was a new phenomenon—and one that he found very disturbing. We can understand Breuer's reaction from our contemporary point of view in terms of his countertransference feelings. For Breuer it only meant that these young and attractive women were falling in love with him. They began calling him for extra appointments, began acting in more seductive ways, and even on occasion begged him to divorce his wife. All of this was too upsetting to Breuer. He was unable to divorce himself sufficiently from his own feelings to be able to observe and analyze these phenomena with an objective and scientific eye. And so he fled the field. He broke off his association with Freud and gave up the investigation of hysteria completely.

Freud, however, unlike Breuer, did not fly from his patients' sexualized feelings for him. With surprising empirical rigor, he regarded these feelings as further scientific data provided by his hysterical patients which needed to be integrated and understood. He was thus able to adopt a broader scientific perspective and to see these phenomena in relation to other aspects of his patients' psychic processes.

There were several things going on in Freud's thinking and experience that helped him to gain a deeper understanding of what was happening. For one thing, he was gradually evolving his therapeutic technique. As we have already seen, he abandoned hypnosis for several reasons. First, the recovery of traumatic memories in the altered state of hypnotic consciousness gave some symptomatic relief, but it did not seem to foster the patient's capacity to master and resolve the trauma. Second, Freud, like many others, did not find it appealing to use a method like hypnosis in which the therapist assumes a relatively powerful and influential position in respect to the patient. Third, if—as his observations and Breuer's experience seemed to suggest—there was a tendency for any of these hysterical patients to become attached to the physician, then a method like hypnosis would certainly reinforce the development of a dependent and sexualized attachment of the patient to the therapist. So Freud gradually abandoned the hypnotic technique and depended more and more on the assumption of the operation of determinism in psychic life. By using the free association method he hoped to be able to reach the repressed or dissociated memories without putting the patient into an altered state of consciousness. What he found was that the patient's memories were recovered only after considerable resistance was overcome, and that the memories were primarily sexual, often reaching back to the patient's childhood years.

From the vantage point gained through these shifts in viewpoint—a vantage point Breuer could not share—Freud recognized that the sexual feelings that his patients manifested toward him represented a reliving and a revivification of earlier sexualized feelings that had been associated with the patient's original neurosis. He recognized the sexualized feelings in the therapeutic relationship as an important form of resistance. The sexualized feelings took the place of the previous neurotic symptoms. It was Freud's recognition that the sexualized feelings for him represented a new and disguised form of the original neurosis which led him to form the concept of the "transference neurosis." The transference neurosis was a new and special form of neurosis related specifically to the treatment process, in which the patient's feelings for the therapist were substituted for the earlier neurotic symptoms. By explaining transference in dynamic terms and by regarding the transference neurosis as a specific form of resistance, Freud initiated the technique of transference analysis as we know it today.

The other important development in Freud's experience that helped him to gain a broader perspective on these problems was his own self-analysis. The importance of this aspect of his thinking cannot be overestimated. At the time of these other important developments, Freud was actively engaged in delving into his own past. He was vigorously applying the associative method to his own mental productions—his dreams particularly, but also his slips, errors, lapses of memory, and what not. The result as we have already indicated was that he not only gained a deeper understanding of what was involved in the process of repression, but he also became considerably more aware of the role of infantile sexual thoughts and feelings. It was through Freud's own self-analysis that the way was opened for his understanding of infantile sexuality, the oedipal involvements of the child with its parents, and the origins of transference feelings.

Gradually Freud was able to see that the patient's transference feelings not only served as a resistance in the treatment, but also reflected and revivified earlier levels of the patient's infantile sexual experience. More and more as time went on and he was able to continue to analyze transference feelings, the connection between oedipal sexual feelings and transference feelings became clear to him. By interpreting transference material, he continued to find that his patients were able to recall and report traumatic and often incestuous sexual experiences that had taken place during their childhood years. In the *Preliminary Communication* (1893) he and Breuer had concluded that "Hysterics suffer mainly from reminiscences." [14] Freud gradually reached the conclusion that the reminiscences involved in hysteria were the memories of traumatic incestuous experiences. This led to a clinical generalization: hysteria was caused by childhood sexual experiences, usually incestuous, which were unwanted and traumatic. These were the memories that had to be defended against and which were thus repressed.

Sexual Trauma and Repression

The goal of psychoanalysis was envisioned as the recovery and bringing to consciousness of these repressed memories. It was Freud's early view that the experience of a real sexual trauma in childhood—a childhood seduction—led to repression. The repression affected not only the specific memories but also the feelings experienced at the time of the seduction. This conclusion had some important implications: first that childhood experience can influence adult mental health, and second that specific real experiences could determine the later development of an hysterical illness.

The seduction hypothesis—that sexual trauma in the form of an actual seduction by genital manipulation early in childhood was the primary etiological source of adult hysterical as well as obsessional neurosis—attained a certain solid conviction in Freud's thinking during the years from 1893 through 1897. He cited a number of apparently well-substantiated cases which seemed to support the seduction hypothesis fairly well. Freud even came to refine his theory somewhat. He concluded on the basis of his clinical material that the seduction in hysteria was primarily passive, i.e., that the seduction and genital stimulation was undertaken by an adult and that the child merely submitted to it passively. Freud thought this might explain the predominance of hysteria among females. Conversely he felt that the seduction experience in obsessive-compulsive cases had been active, i.e., that the child had been the active agent in the seduction in these cases. In a fair number of cases, he was able to obtain memories which seemed to have been repressed and which gave further confirmation to his theory. It seemed as though the seduction hypothesis was becoming solidly established.

At the same time Freud was still employing his combined technique of pressure and suggestion with great assurance. His insistence that patients recall the seduction scene brings the role of suggestion in his apparent confirmations of the seduction hypothesis into question. Little by little, as he became more aware of the role of suggestion in his technique, he also began to have doubts about the seduction hypothesis. In September 1897, he wrote to Fliess of his doubts.

Let me tell you straight away the great secret which has been slowly dawning on me in recent months. I no longer believe in my *neurotica*. That is hardly intelligible without an explanation; you yourself found what I told you credible. So I shall start at the beginning and tell you the whole story of how the reasons for rejecting it arose. The first group of factors were the continual disappointment of my attempts to bring my analyses to a real conclusion, the running away of people who for a time had seemed my most favourably inclined patients, the lack of the complete success on which I had counted, and the possibility of explaining my partial successes in other, familiar ways. Then there was the astonishing thing that in every case . . . blame was laid on perverse acts by the father, and realization of the unexpected frequency of hysteria, in every case of which the same thing applied, though it was hardly credible that perverted acts against children were so general. . . . Thirdly, there was the definite realization that there is no "indication of reality" in the unconscious, so that it is impossible to distinguish between truth and emotionally-charged fiction. (This leaves open the possible explanation that sexual phantasy regularly makes use of the theme of the parents.) Fourthly, there was the consideration that even in the most deep-reaching psychoses the unconscious memory does not break through, so that the secret of infantile experiences is not revealed even in the most confused states of delirium. When one thus sees that the unconscious never overcomes the resistance of the conscious, one must abandon the expectation that in treatment the reverse process will take place to the extent that the conscious will fully dominate the unconscious.[15]

Self-Analysis

The interplay of Freud's own self-analysis in this aspect of his thinking was unmistakable. A month later, Freud reported to Fliess that he had become aware of his own libidinal feelings toward his mother. Then on October 15, he wrote:

I have found love of the mother and jealousy of the father in my own case too, and now believe it to be a general phenomenon of early childhood, even if it does not always occur so early as in children who have been made hysterics.[16]

It was in the same letter that Freud stated: "My self-analysis is the most important thing I have in hand, and promises to be of the greatest value to me, when it is finished."

It is apparent in reading through Freud's writings and letters of this period that he was struggling against his own inner resistances to accepting a change in the seduction hypothesis. It was only in terms of his own self-analysis that he became gradually aware of his own oedipal fantasies and wishes. Even more important, his self-analysis brought home to him the realization that the unconscious mind was unable to discriminate between memories of fact and memories of fantasy. The shift from an emphasis on sexual acts as realities to sexual fantasies was a central factor in the development of psychoanalysis. It was important both from a methodological point of view and also from the point of view of the redirection of psychoanalytic interest. Methodologically Freud's changed view had been derived from the subjective data of his own self-analysis. This brought into a significant position in the future development of psychoanalysis the intrapsychic and subjective world of the analyst himself. Freud came to realize that the analyst must overcome the resistances to his own inner conflicts and unconscious strivings before he can recognize and respond to the patient's unconscious. Consequently, this development moved the analyst's subjectivity into the center of the analytic picture. His subjectivity became a functional part of the methodology of psychoanalysis—as an essential means of approaching and reading the patient's unconscious subjectivity. The emphasis fell on the development of the analyst's own subjective awareness through his own training as a necessary part of the preparation for doing the work of psychoanalysis.

The redirection of analytic interest was the other important aspect of this progression in Freud's thinking. It marked the beginning of a new phase in the development of psychoanalysis. Rapaport has emphasized the importance of the shift from reality to fantasy for the development of psychoanalytic ego psychology.[17] He divided the history of ego psychology into four phases. The first phase was the period up to 1897 which saw the development of what was really a prepsychoanalytic theory. The second was the period of development of psychoanalysis proper and extended to 1923. In 1923 the publication of *The Ego and the Id* marked the beginning of the third phase in which Freud's efforts were directed to the development of his ego psychology. The fourth phase came with the publication of Anna Freud's *The Ego and the Mechanisms of Defense* (1937) and Hartmann's *Ego Psychology and the Problem of Adaptation* (1939). Psychoanalysis is still in the last phase.

Abandonment of the Seduction Hypothesis

The abandonment of the seduction hypothesis and the realization that the patient's reports of infantile seduction were not based on real memories but on fantasies marked the beginning of psychoanalysis as such. The importance of reality as a determining factor in the patient's behavior faded into the background. It was not to regain a central position in the theory until Freud returned to the development of an ego psychology years later. The focus of analytic interest turned to the mechanisms by which fantasies were created. Freud was taken up with the exploration of the instincts and their derivatives. Defense was conceived globally in terms of repression. Perhaps more broadly and more significantly, the dynamic hypothesis was cast in terms of instinctual derivatives and instinctual forces. Thus there was a tendency to conceive of even relatively autonomous ego functions in terms of their relation to instinctual drives. The work of the third and fourth phases of the development of psychoanalytic ego psychology has been centered on the problem of trying to determine the extent to which autonomous ego functions are derived from instinctual sources and to what extent they are independent. The issues have yet to be resolved.

The dissolution of the seduction hypothesis might have been seen as a serious setback to Freud's thinking. It had become a firm conviction in his mind and one that he had literally been forcing on his patients. It must have come as a shock when he began to realize that none of his convictions were true—that there was no basis in fact for his theory, that there had never been a seduction. But Freud's road to discovery had been strewn with setbacks and disappointments. Some of the most difficult disappointments, however, proved to be the starting points for his most significant steps forward. He had tried heroically to establish and explain his psychological findings on an organic and physiological basis. But he had failed and gave up the attempt. But this surrender led him to the construction of a more psychological model of the psychic apparatus and the adoption of the basic "as-if" in his approach to mental phenomena. The encounter with transference resistance was another serious setback when he first ran into it. It had defeated Breuer, who had retreated from the field, and it confronted Freud with a difficult clinical problem. Instead of getting over their symptoms and being cured, these patients became increasingly dependent and increasingly insistent on continuing therapy. Freud was able to recognize, however, that this dependence and the transference feelings associated with it formed a meaningful substitution for the original neurosis. The discovery led to the development of the technique of transference analysis and added an important understanding of the contribution of infantile wishes to adult neuroses.

The loss of the seduction hypothesis was a major setback, and a very painful one for Freud at the time. For Freud to admit to Fliess that he no longer believed in his *neurotica* must not have been without difficulty or disappointment. The seductions on which he had staked so much and on whose recovery in the form of memories his whole therapeutic technique depended were simply not real. There were no seductions and no truth in his theory. It would have been an understandable and human response to give up in discouragement. But, once again, as before, what appeared at first as a severe setback became the basis for an important, in fact, crucial, step forward—one which was essential for the emergence of psychoanalysis as based on both a dynamic and a developmental theory.

Freud recognized that the recollections which he had accepted as actual memories were not deliberate fabrications on the part of the patients. But they did not imply that the events which the patients had described as traumatic and unwanted had actually occurred. What they really meant became clear to Freud only gradually—and it was something quite different. They concerned fantasies which related to something the patient had wished for, but which had not in fact occurred. Moreover, the recollection of these experiences, whether fantasied or real, seemed to be important. The material that emerged in the course of the recovery of these so-called memories was of particular importance in the patients' lives.

This realization confronted Freud with a basic question. If the content of a patient's recollection does not correspond to any actual historical events, does that mean that the recollection is without truth? Can one make a useful and meaningful distinction between the recall of factual and historical events and experiences on the one hand, and the recall of inner psychic events or experiences that may have psychological meaning on the other? We could imagine that at this point Freud's mind turned to his understanding of what was responsible for the same mechanism of repression in regard to dreams and the slips and errors of everyday life. His careful analyses of this kind of material had led to an important discovery. In both cases he had found that there were wishes which the subject would not accept and which were therefore repressed. These same wishes had been expressed and gratified in a disguised form in the manifest content of the dream or in the actual slips.

From Reality to Fantasy

As we have seen, the wishes that Freud described were not at first childhood wishes, but rather current adult wishes, like the wish which motivated his dream about "my friend R." However, Freud introduced more dream material in the subsequent editions of his *Interpretation of Dreams*. By the 1919 edition he had included a fair number of dreams which were related to early childhood wishes. He reasoned that the sexualized memories and fantasies that seemed to derive from childhood suggested that children were not without sexual feelings and wishes. This might mean that the wishes and fantasies of the past were dealt with in much the same way as normal dreamers deal with current wishes that they do not wish to acknowledge. Freud was thus led to the concept of infantile fantasy.

Freud's original position had been that his patients were recalling the repressed memory of some unwanted sexual experiences which they had experienced as children as the result of an actual seduction. His realization that the memories were not of realities but of fantasies brought him to a view that was almost exactly the opposite. The patients were not recalling an unwished for experience that had actually occurred. Rather they were recalling the wish for a forbidden or dangerous experience which had never in fact occurred. Just as the dream represents in its manifest content the disguised fulfillment of a wish, so too, the neurotic symptom, as well as the transference neurosis, also expresses the disguised fulfillment of a repressed wish.

The repressed wish had originally been experienced in the form of early infantile fantasies. Freud thus gradually came to appreciate the extreme significance of fantasy in the mental life and development of human beings. The fantasies which his hysterical patients were able to recover and the wishes behind them proved to be both sexual and incestuous. This brought Freud to the next inevitable conclusion—that the child has sexual fantasies which include wishes of an incestuous and forbidden nature. Such wishes are subject to repression and disguise in much the same way as current wishes may be presented in a disguised and distorted form in dream material. Freud had to conclude, therefore, that sexuality plays a role during infancy and childhood. The common opinion up until that time—an opinion that was widely accepted in scientific circles and which Freud himself shared—was that sexuality only arose with the sexual maturation of puberty. Freud saw, however, that sexuality had a long and significant prehistory, with fantasies and wishes that extend back to the early years of life. He was thus led to develop a theory of infantile sexuality, and thus to adopt a developmental approach to the understanding of mental life which was to prove one of the most important aspects of psychoanalytic thinking.

The apparent setback that was involved in the loss of the seduction hypothesis thus proved to be one of the most important factors leading to a whole new approach to mental phenomena. The new approach laid emphasis on infantile sexuality, on the centrality of the instincts as the agency of fantasy formation and as the source of the dynamic properties of the mental apparatus, and on the development of instincts and their vicissitudes. It was only a few years after this setback that Freud wrote the *Three Essays on Sexuality* (1905), in which he described the basic elements of his libido theory. He put forth a developed theory of infantile sexuality. He described the emergence and development of the oedipal situation. He also described the precursors of genital sexuality in the instinctual life, namely, the different phases of psychosexual development—the oral, anal, and genital phases of libidinal development. The phallic phase was only recognized later on. The point to be emphasized here is that the emergence of the concept of infantile sexuality—which came about as a direct result of the abandonment of the seduction hypothesis—was the important foundation upon which Freud was able to erect a developmental psychology. The developmental perspective has become a central dimension of psychoanalytic thinking and theory. One could, in fact, say quite accurately that contemporary psychoanalysis is fundamentally a developmental method. Whether or not we accept Freud's developmental approach as definitive, his attempt was historically the first to try to relate the wishes and fantasies and instinctive acts which dominate adult life and experience to their childhood precursors in the instinctual life.

As we have already suggested, psychoanalytic instinct theory and the organization of mental life around different levels of instinctual development remained for many years in the center of analytic interest. Instinct theory not only dominated psychoanalytic attempts to explain symptoms, but also served as the basis for a classification of mental illness until relatively recent years. Levels of instinctual fixation and/or regression remain its central focus of attention. Types of neuroses or character types were described in terms of the fixation of development at one or other psychosexual level, or in terms of a pathological and regressive retreat to such levels of psychosexual organization as a result of stress. As we have already noted in our discussion of intrapsychic and interpersonal dynamics (see Chapter 2), there are many difficulties in trying to rely on an explanation or diagnosis which is based solely on the instinctual content of symptoms of behavior. Other factors besides those which concern instinctual levels of development must be taken into consideration; this is a lesson that psychoanalysis has had to learn in the development of ego psychology and it is a lesson that it is still learning.

Even so, it is important at this point in our discussion to realize what an enormous vista Freud's concept of early fantasies and early instinctual life opened up for the pioneer analysts. When we look back and read the works of the early analysts, it is hardly surprising that for many years their major interests, both as therapists and as theorists, focused on the vicissitudes and development of instinctual life. The recognition that different levels of instinctual development were reflected in both neurotic symptoms and in certain character traits was overwhelming in that era—and remains by no means a negligible feature of psychoanalysis even today. Clinical psychoanalysts still see many patients who present us with clear evidence that they have failed to master the oedipal situation and its associated conflicts. The anal implications of many obsessional symptoms and character traits are easily recognized. And we are all quite familiar with the dependence and immaturity of the oral character types.

It deserves to be emphasized, however, that the recognition of such instinctual derivatives is not a sufficient ground on which to form a sound clinical diagnosis, prognosis, or recommendations for specific treatment. We must remember that Freud's discovery of infantile sexuality and his recognition of its importance occurred at a time when he regarded repression as the major explanation for the existence of unconscious mental life. He laid great emphasis, therefore, on the need to overcome the patient's resistances. Although he acknowledged that the memories concerned were painful because they involved the continued pressure of early wishes, he nevertheless continued to regard repression as the major mechanism responsible for the existence of unconscious pathogenic material.

Development of Repression

The concept of repression, as Freud first developed it, remained for some time equivalent to the notion of defense. Defense of any kind was interpreted as a form of repression or at least involving repression in some way. Repression, therefore, accounted for all that was unconscious, regardless of the level of instinctual development that was concerned. Within the confines of this early Freudian perspective on defense and repression, the difficulties in analyzing certain patients— particularly the borderline personalities and psychotics—were ascribed to the operation of repression at such early levels of development that instincts were not able to progress to the point where they could become attached to real persons outside of the subject. In terms of object-relations theory, it was held that instincts in such individuals never reached the level of real object-directedness. Early efforts to study psychotics also led to a similar conclusion, that the same mechanism of repression could also be held accountable for the later development of psychosis. It was felt that repression had occurred at a level of development in which the differentiation of self and external objects had not been achieved. Consequently, the individual's instinctual drives were still directed only at himself—a phase of instinctual development that Freud called "autoerotic." Such patients were thought to be unable to form a transference. Hence, the formation of a transference neurosis was thought to be impossible and the therapeutic approach through transference analysis inapplicable.

We might agree with these early analytic conclusions about the difficulty of applying psychoanalytic methods to the therapy of borderline and psychotic patients. We would not appeal, however, to a unitary and overgeneralized concept of repression to account for the problem. The view that such patients are unable to form a transference has been radically revised in recent years. As analysts gained greater experience in the therapy of psychotic patients, it became apparent that instead of a repressive barrier to transference feelings, the problem in psychotics was quite the opposite. It was found that schizophrenics and psychotics in general tend to have extremely intense transference feelings. The problem was not the absence of such feelings, but rather the intensity and destructive ambivalence they displayed in the psychotic transference.

The concept of repression, therefore, underwent a significant development in Freud's early thinking. It involved a number of significant progressive shifts in Freud's thinking as well as in the development of his technique that led to the conceptual and therapeutic foundations of psychoanalysis. The notion of repression and its related basic assumption about the nature of mental functioning, namely, the dynamic hypothesis, became the focus of a variety of significant intellectual and theoretical influences which have provided the background and conceptual substructure of psychoanalytic theory. The concept of repression held a unique position in the emergence of early psychoanalytic thinking. And it had a subsequent history and underwent a further process of modification—some of which we shall examine in these pages. But in following the steps of Freud's early struggles and in retracing the vicissitudes surrounding the emergence of the concept of repression, we are following Freud's own intuitive conviction: that in understanding the process and the causes of repression, we come closest to the understanding of that human distress and anguish that goes by the name of neurosis.

[5]

Repression and Anxiety

We have considered at some length the conceptual and clinical origins of the notion of repression in the preceding chapters. Our discussion considered repression in its relation to resistance, both intrapsychically and in the transference situation. We have also seen its involvement in intrapsychic conflict and defense. However, this understanding of the origins of repression does not tell the whole story. We have reviewed some of the significant evidences and the meaningful shifts in thinking that brought Freud to his formulation of repression as a manifestation of underlying dynamic mental capacities. Our consideration of repression would remain incomplete if we were not able to relate it to its motivating cause. The underlying causal stimulus which brings repression and other related defenses into play is anxiety.

Anxiety

Our discussion in the case of the young man who developed an anxiety neurosis at the prospect of facing challenging new responsibilities in his life (see Chapter 2) raised the question of the relationship between anxiety and defense. The patient had to defend himself against underlying unconscious feelings of competition and aggression toward his older brother. The dynamics of the case made it clear that the meaning of the patient's anxiety was a complex and difficult matter. It could not be explained exclusively in terms of either interpersonal or intrapsychic factors. However, we did not consider in detail the relation between the anxiety and the patient's need to repress.

Consequently, we shall retrace our steps at this point and examine the relation between repression and anxiety more carefully. Many of the developments in our understanding of ego defenses and of the intrapsychic events which lead to repression have to be considered from the point of view of motivation, i.e., from a consideration of the stimulus for defense. Consequently, we must retrace another path in the emergence of Freud's thinking, this time about the nature of anxiety. What were his first theories about the nature of anxiety? How did they change? What was the importance of these theoretical changes for the development of our understanding of the meaning of defense?

In his early work on hysteria, Freud shared Breuer's view that dissociated memories that had not been sufficiently abreacted were at the root of the hysterical syndrome. They concurred that hysterics suffered from reminiscences. But Freud gradually saw these dissociated memories as a result of a dynamic process—repression. He held further that repression was in the service of defense. Defense against what? The answer came in terms of the content of the repressed memories. They were almost always sexual and had to do with seduction and trauma. Freud consequently became increasingly preoccupied with the importance and vicissitudes of sexuality in mental life. He extended his observations not only to hysterics, but to other kinds of patients who were referred to him for treatment. He began to explore the possibility that sexuality might have an even wider significance in the determination of neurotic symptoms.

The Actual Neuroses

Among Freud's patients there were a number who complained of symptoms which he described as constituting "morbid anxiety." This was similar to what we might today refer to as "free-floating anxiety," along with the variety of somatic symptoms often associated with such anxiety. In a certain number of these patients he found that there was a current situation in the patients' sexual life which seemed to be related to the development of their anxiety. The common denominator with these patients was that they were being sexually stimulated without reaching full gratification. The clinical observation that such individuals often become anxious is not without validity. But Freud went further to the conclusion that, when sexual impulses are aroused without an appropriate sexual discharge, the sexual feelings are transformed and become discharged in the form of morbid anxiety. In short, sexual impulses, if aroused and not discharged, were subject to a damming up. If this dammed-up libido exceeded the limit within which the organism could contain it, it would be discharged not as sexual excitement but in the form of morbid anxiety. The change was felt to be basically biochemical, and the patient was in effect suffering from a physical illness in a sense rather than from a psychological illness.

Freud's view of anxiety at this time derived largely from his dissatisfaction with current understanding of the clinical cases with which he was working in the early years before the turn of the century. This was particularly true of so-called neurasthenic conditions, a prominent feature of which was anxiety. By 1895, he had proposed that states in which anxiety was a central feature be separated from the main body of neurasthenic conditions and regarded as a distinct clinical entity. He named the new entity "anxiety neurosis." His view of the etiology of this condition was based on his observations of his patients, and particularly their sexual lives. Anxiety neurosis invariably involved an increase of physical sexual tension resulting from inadequate sexual discharge. The inadequate discharge was related to such practices as coitus interruptus or the use of condoms, practices which Freud regarded as inhibiting full discharge and as preventing reaching full orgasm.

Freud grouped together anxiety neurosis with neurasthenia, and somewhat more tentatively with hypochondriasis, and called them the "actual neuroses." The actual neuroses were distinguished from hysteria and obsessional states, which were psychological in origin. The etiology of the actual neuroses was regarded as nonpsychical. Anxiety neurosis was thought to be produced by incomplete coition and similar conditions. Neurasthenia was thought to be the result of excessive masturbation in which libido was depleted. In adopting this view of the actual neuroses, Freud was very much in tune with the prevailing medical and physiological mentality of his day. The basic model was a reflex one which involved physical and physiological processes—excessive sexual stimulation producing a quantitative energy accumulation as a result of inadequate discharge, a subsequent transformation of energy, and finally discharge of a toxic agent which was responsible for anxiety.

The emphasis in the actual neuroses was on the aspect of actuality, i.e., on the fact that the etiology pertained to a present, real situation in the patient's life. They were thus distinguished from the psychoneuroses in which the etiology was a matter of repressed experiences from the remote past (or repressed fantasies, as Freud was later to appreciate). Freud maintained his view of the actual neuroses without any significant alteration for a long time. He continued to stress the relationship between the actual neuroses and toxic physiological changes, even though there was little evidence to support his speculation.

By the time of his *Introductory Lectures* (1916–1917), the toxic element of the actual neuroses was represented as an actual toxic substance which was a product of disordered sexual metabolism brought about by inadequate sexual discharge. Freud was so convinced of the physiological basis of these conditions that he recommended that they be made the object of physiological research. Even in his monumental work *Inhibitions, Symptoms and Anxiety* (1926), which marks a significant shift in his views about anxiety, there was still little change in the conception of actual neurotic anxiety as rooted in the transformation of libido. But the notion of libido had undergone some subtle changes. Libido had originally been conceived in essentially physiological terms; gradually Freud began to think of it in more psychological terms as a sort of bridging concept between physiology and psychology. The shifts in the concept of libido had parallel effects on the development of the notion of anxiety as transformed libido.

Anxiety and Danger

Freud had more or less banished the actual neuroses from psychoanalysis, feeling that because of their physiological basis they were not susceptible to analytic treatment. In *Inhibitions, Symptoms and Anxiety* he tried to bring them back within the reach of psychoanalysis by developing a more unified theory of anxiety. He introduced a broader concept of trauma, specifically in terms of the relative intensity of the trauma in relation to the strength of the ego. Trauma could then be more broadly conceived as related to the relative helplessness of the ego in any situation. Any danger, therefore, could become traumatic— whether its source was internal or external, instinctual or real—insofar as the ego experienced a sense of helplessness in the face of it. Freud's advancing views of the nature of anxiety and defense left him with two views of anxiety: as either transformed libido or as a threatened breakthrough of the repression barrier by a dangerous impulse. These no longer seemed compatible and Freud was forced to distinguish between anxiety proper and anxiety generated by way of the discharge of surplus libido.

It was not until his famous chapter on anxiety in the *New Introductory Lectures* (1933) that Freud finally surrendered his idea that anxiety could originate in transformed libido. He clung tenaciously to his conviction that instincts and affects could be understood in biological terms. When he surrendered the attempt to formulate his understanding of mental phenomena in physiological terms (in the *Project*) and reluctantly accepted the "as-if," he did not in fact surrender his underlying biological convictions. The area of anxiety and the thinking about actual neuroses remained for some time the last bastion of his physiological conviction. Anxiety was viewed as due to a toxic substance produced by transformation of libido. In his reorganization of his thinking about anxiety in *Inhibitions,* he made the ego the seat of anxiety and saw the latter specifically as a response of the ego to danger.

This shift in view immediately posed the problem of how to reconcile his new understanding of anxiety in psychological terms with his older biological views. He tried to retain the older conviction by proposing a two-source theory. The actual theory was retained in the form of anxiety that was withdrawn from the ego and was produced more or less automatically and on the basis of economic principles. This type is newly produced by reason of the economic conditions obtaining in the present reality situation. Freud related this form of anxiety to the prototype of the birth trauma. Some immediate frustration—hunger, sexual, or external trauma—produces a response in the id similar to the birth situation. The lack of gratification of innate needs produces an increase of instinctual tension, which provides the economic conditions in which this type of anxiety occurs. The anxiety occurs automatically—without the ego's participation and as a result of economic factors in the accumulation and discharge of instinctual energies.

The other form of anxiety assumes a completely different source and involves the active participation of the ego. The ego is regarded as the sole seat of this anxiety. It can produce and experience anxiety specifically as a signal of danger. Freud states this in the following terms:

We thus gave the biological aspect of the anxiety affect its due importance by recognizing anxiety as the general reaction to situations of danger; while we endorsed the part played by the ego as the seat of anxiety by allocating to it the function of producing the anxiety affect according to its needs. Thus we attributed two modes of origin to anxiety in later life. One was involuntary, automatic and always justified on economic grounds, and arose whenever a danger situation analogous to birth had established itself. The other was produced by the ego as soon as a situation of this kind merely threatened to occur, in order to call for its avoidance. In the second case the ego subjects itself to anxiety as a sort of inoculation, submitting to a slight attack of the illness in order to escape its full strength.[18]

The dichotomy of points of view was clear. The older view had worked on a physicalistic model of libidinal repression producing anxiety. The newer signal theory saw the function of anxiety as signaling danger and inducing repression and other defenses.

The contradiction was apparent and Freud himself was dissatisfied with his dichotomy as to the sources of anxiety. His dilemma is no better expressed than in his own words.

Since sexual excitation was an expression of libidinal instinctual impulses it did not seem too rash to assume that the libido was turned into anxiety through the agency of these disturbances. The observations which I made at the time still hold good. Moreover, it can not be denied that the libido belonging to the id-processes is subject to disturbance at the instigation of repression. It might still be true, therefore, that in repression anxiety is produced from the libidinal cathexis of the instinctual impulses. But how can we reconcile this conclusion with our other conclusion that the anxiety felt in phobias is an ego anxiety and arises in the ego, and that it does not proceed out of repression but, on the contrary, sets repression in motion? There seems to be a contradiction here which is not at all a simple matter to solve. It will not be easy to reduce the two sources of anxiety to a single one. We might attempt to do so by supposing that, when coitus is disturbed or sexual excitation interrupted or abstinence enforced, the ego scents certain dangers to which it reacts with anxiety. But this takes us nowhere. On the other hand, our analysis of the phobias seems to admit of no correction. *Non liquet.*[19]

One can imagine with his famous *non liquet* Freud throwing up his hands in figurative despair.

Freud's thinking about the actual neuroses, therefore, underwent a slow and gradual transformation. They were at first conceived, along with their attendant anxiety, in explicitly physical and physiological terms—transformed libido as a form of toxic biochemical substance or physical excitation. The thinking behind this formulation was similar to the concept of energy transformation involved in hypnoid states and the hypnoid hypothesis of hysteria. This view led Freud to banish the actual neuroses from psychoanalysis and to treat them as entirely distinct from the psychoneuroses, which were analytically treatable. Under the influence of the abandonment of this last vestige of physicalism in his thinking and with the gradual shift of libido from a purely physiological meaning to a more psychological one, Freud attempted to salvage the actual neuroses for psychoanalysis. He tried to bring them under the analytic umbrella by reason of a newer and broader concept of anxiety as a signal of danger. The newer theory was considerably more psychological, but it raised difficult questions of the relationship between repression and anxiety. Was anxiety, then, the result of repression or was it rather the motive of repression?

Physiological Residues

In his biography of Freud, Ernest Jones reminds us of Freud's strong commitment to the scientific ideal of finding a physical explanation for all of his psychological findings. He had accepted the famous "as-if" in respect to the content of wishes and the nature of repression only reluctantly and somewhat apologetically. Jones suggests, however, that Freud might have hoped to be able to salvage at least one significant area in which he could find a physiological explanation for his findings. The area of morbid anxiety and the actual neuroses seems to have been this area. For nearly thirty years of his scientific life Freud continued to regard the expression of anxiety as due to the transformation of sexual impulses, when they are aroused under circumstances in which direct discharge is prevented. The hypothesis served an important heuristic function in its origins. It allowed Freud to separate the group of actual neuroses and to consider them in terms of their common relation to anxiety.

This concept of infantile sexuality was an important unifying point in Freud's thinking. According to this point of view, the repression of sexual wishes which he had discovered in the childhood of his neurotic patients was held responsible for both symptom formation in his hysterical patients and for anxiety in patients suffering from anxiety hysteria. The implication was that anxiety was the result of repression. The patient who has repressed sexuality, when he is sexually stimulated, will not respond with sexual feelings, but will respond rather with morbid anxiety. The anxiety was due in this view to a biochemical transformation of sexual instinctual energy into morbid anxiety.

This point of view was of particular importance since it has remained an area of controversy in analytic thinking and has been an area in which some significant theoretical changes have taken place. Freud's original theory was never fully accepted. Some analysts were unwilling to accept Freud's more or less physical and biochemical presumption. Ernest Jones, for example, even as early as 1911, could not agree with Freud that an emotion like anxiety which is so closely related to fear could be explained on the basis of such physical changes. Jones did not elaborate a theory of anxiety, but he suggested that anxiety represented the individual's fear of his own instinctual drives. The suggestion was in fact much closer to Freud's own later theory of signal anxiety than it was to Freud's initial theory of anxiety as transformed libido.

There was more to it, however. There were some important shifts taking place in Freud's thinking generally. From about 1914 on, with the publication of his paper on narcissism, the structural viewpoint began to play an increasing role in his thought. With the development of a structural analysis, his conceptualization of the ego and its functions and its relationship to the drives became clearer. In addition, the role of aggression and its place in the economy of the drives was taking a more prominent and significant place. There were many personal influences that brought home this latter aspect of human instinctual life to Freud. There was the war and its horrors. Freud's sons were in the fighting. He began to suffer some significant losses as well: the death of his daughter Sophie, the death of his favorite niece, the death of his dear friend Anton von Freund, and finally the conjunction in 1923 of two events that left a permanent and indelible mark on Freud's spirit —the death of his grandson and the onset of his own ultimately fatal cancer. The themes of castration, death, and aggression play a much more significant role in Freud's later views on anxiety. The realization that the danger of which anxiety became the signal was derived not only from libidinal impulses but from aggressive impulses as well was a significant development in psychoanalytic understanding of man's emotional life. The understanding of aggression is still a problem for contemporary psychoanalysis.

The Role of Repression

Repression remained the major dynamic process by which mental content became unconscious. It continued to be held responsible for amnesia and for neurotic symptoms which, like dreams, gratified repressed wishes in a disguised form. Finally in his first approach to the complex problem of anxiety, Freud attributed it to the damming up and biochemical modification of sexual excitation and its products. When this was current and discernible he regarded it as an actual neurosis. But when the repression of sexuality derived from infantile levels of experience, the individual in adult life would become anxious in situations of sexual stimulation when one would normally expect sexual excitement. Repression was thus viewed as the cause of anxiety, and according to this view the undoing of repression should diminish anxiety. But relatively common psychiatric experience shows that this often does not happen. The lessening of repression is often accompanied by an increase of subjective anxiety. This was one of the basic clinical findings that led Freud to alter his thinking and to develop his theory of signal anxiety.

The explanation of anxiety that Freud had developed in his understanding of the so-called actual neuroses, i.e., in terms of the transformation of libido, was gradually extended in his thinking to apply to cases of phobic anxiety and other anxieties which were clearly psychoneurotic. The anxiety in these states could not be explained by such a simple and straightforward mechanism. The appeal to repressed instinctual drives, particularly to repressed sexuality, has a certain validity and explanatory power, but it does not satisfy many of the basic questions about the relation between anxiety and repression. According to the original theory, the child who will become an adult neurotic deals with the infantile oedipal situation by extensive repression. For example, the young girl not only represses her incestuous feelings for her father, but in addition at the time of the passing of the oedipal situation represses her sexual impulses generally.

From a more contemporary perspective, we would still agree that the future neurotic employs repression as a general defense, more extensively than would be compatible with the achievement of satisfying adult heterosexual object relations. The future neurotic may demonstrate considerable success in his capacity for learning and attainment through the years of latency and early adolescence. He may also be relatively successful in establishing and maintaining significant friendships during his growing years. In some cases, their level of achievement and adjustment may remain adequate even into the years of young adulthood. It is only when they are faced with the problem of achieving adult heterosexual object relations that they begin to run into difficulty. According to Freud's original hypothesis, the attempt to achieve an adult heterosexual object relationship would inevitably result in the emergence of anxiety. The basis of the anxiety would be the transformation of repressed and undischarged libido.

A Clinical Case

A clinical case may help to focus some of the difficulties. The following incident was described by a young woman who had been an extremely inhibited and repressed young girl. She was the oldest child and only daughter in her family. She had a brother who was two years her junior. Her father had died when she was six years old. Despite this loss she had been relatively successful and well adjusted in her childhood and adolescence. She had been popular with both girls and boys and was frequently invited to parties. She had been quite successful academically in high school and at college. Her heterosexual experience was generally limited to double dates and being escorted to formal dances. During one of her spring vacations at college she went to New York City with a group of friends. One night, after the group had spent a pleasant and entertaining evening together, one of the most attractive boys in the group wanted to escort her back to her hotel in a hansom cab. At this point she became panic-stricken. She ran away from him and ran in a panic through the streets of the city, stumbling and falling in the mud and ruining her good dress. She finally returned to the hotel alone, extremely anxious, upset, and disheveled. The whole incident was described in her analysis with a sense of wry humor. She described this anxiety she had experienced as a young girl with a sense of regret.

According to Freud's original view he would say that this girl had repressed her sexual feelings at the time of her infantile neurosis. Consequently, when she began to feel sexual attraction toward the young man who wanted to take her for a cab ride, sexual feelings were aroused. Instead of feeling sexual arousal and excitation, the feelings were expressed as morbid anxiety. From our contemporary standpoint we would offer a somewhat different explanation. We would take the position that her sexual feelings were repressed in childhood because she experienced them as threatening and dangerous. Thus when she was confronted in adult life with a situation in which sexual feelings were stirred and her repression threatened, the anxiety which had previously motivated her defenses re-emerged once again as a signal of danger. She responded to this signal with the classic response to danger—fright and flight.

Both explanations concur that sexual instincts were repressed. But in Freud's original definition, no reason is given for the repression. The theory states simply that if repression takes place earlier anxiety will replace sexual feelings in later adult experience. Today we would propose that there is indeed a reason which lies in the internal psychic life of the individual who has responded to sexuality as the source of a danger to the ego. On the infantile level sexual impulses are a source of danger. In the context of the oedipal situation, sexual impulses of a son toward his mother call forth the threat of retribution from the father and the resulting castration anxiety. The sexual impulses and wishes of the girl to be loved by her father and to have a baby by him and so replace her mother call forth the threat of retribution from the mother and loss of love. Thus sexual impulses at the level of the infantile and oedipal involvement carry with them a threat and a danger. Individuals who have been sufficiently threatened by these dangers and have to repress their sexual feelings are prevented from effectively resolving their incestuous feelings and infantile fears. They cannot, therefore, pass on to further emotional development and to the establishing of meaningful love relations with nonincestuous and adult heterosexual objects. Such individuals will re-experience the threat of danger and anxiety which originally motivated the repressive defense, when the defense itself is threatened by a new sexual stimulus.

This latter explanation is quite different from Freud's original approach to the meaning of morbid anxiety. According to the original theory, anxiety occurs as a result of repression. According to a more contemporary view, however, repression occurs because anxiety presents the ego with an internal danger situation against which it must defend itself. Although the two views are substantially different, we must admit some area of overlap. It is obvious, for example, that the more the girl felt attracted to the young man the greater would be the conflict between her present, actual wish to respond sexually and the internal reality which still led her to regard sexuality as dangerous. The more, therefore, she felt attracted to the boy the more anxious she would become. There is, consequently, a certain economic factor involved. Her anxiety is related to the circumstances in which sexual excitation is not permitted direct and adequate expression and discharge. Anxiety is the result. Nonetheless, we would have to consider that if the original theory had been correct, i.e., if the anxiety occurred as the result of repression, we would expect the anxiety to diminish as repression gives way. This, however, was exactly the opposite of what actually took place. The patient had been quite well adjusted and functioning relatively normally until the situation arose in which her repression was seriously threatened. In the circumstances, far from becoming less anxious, she became increasingly anxious and developed a state of panic. This girl's experience is supported by the common therapeutic experience that patients who have used repressive defenses tend to become more anxious rather than less anxious as their defenses begin to break down.

The Motive for Repression

As long as Freud held on to his view of anxiety as transformed libido, he was really without any explanation of the initiation of repression. Given the fact of repression his theory offered an explanation for the subsequent vicissitudes of instinctual forces in the generation of anxiety. But he was not able to explain the fact of repression. His explorations into the sexual lives of his patients and his own instinctual life through his self-analysis led him to see that sexuality was much more important and asserted itself much earlier in life than he or anyone else had previously suspected. His ideas about infantile sexuality were at first uneasy and not altogether comfortable. Freud's early treatment of repression gave the impression that it was almost self-explanatory. It took time for the connection between infantile sexuality and repression to come into focus. We can readily understand the tendency to want to repress or deny the unpleasant possibility that little children—the paragons of human innocence—might want to sexually possess the parent of the opposite sex and enter into sexual rivalry with the parent of the same sex. Expressed in such blatant and direct terms, the idea is rather unacceptable.

Nonetheless, the contemporary psychoanalytic psychiatrist would regard it as an essential feature of early psychic maturation that the child reach a level of development in which a genuine triangular conflict with parents or parent substitutes is established. In Freud's time, however, the discovery of the oedipal situation was new, alien, strange, even a repulsive idea. But today we have come to accept the fact that the oedipal situation represents a normal developmental stage. In addition, we still regard repression as an important defense which every human being uses to a greater or lesser extent. Excessive repression, however, lies at the foot of many psychic disturbances, particularly in the psychoneuroses. We can say that excessive repression of childhood sexual feelings is not the preferred or normal way to resolve the infantile neurosis which is rooted in the oedipal situation.

Patients, like the young girl described above, who use excessive repression as a means of dealing with threatening sexual impulses find themselves unable to reach a genuine resolution of the oedipal situation. Consequently, they are unable to attain a full capacity for adult sexual maturity and heterosexual adjustment. They remain fixated at an earlier level of psychosexual development. The early view of repression and the related theory of anxiety as transformed libido provided the basis on which early forms of psychoanalytic treatment developed. Repression was generally regarded as the major cause of anxiety and mental distress. The goal of analysis, therefore, was to undo repression. According to the hypothesis, the lifting of repression would release the individual from his anxiety and related neurotic symptoms. In terms of our preceding discussion, it can be seen that analytic treatment was on precarious footing.

Freud also had applied his anxiety theory to the understanding of anxiety dreams. In the *Interpretation of Dreams* (1900), he related the hypothesis of anxiety as transformed libido to his theory that dreams were a form of wish fulfillment. He suggested that, if a patient had an anxiety dream, the anxiety was the expression of a repressed sexual wish. In the relaxation of censorship which is associated with the dream state, the sexual wish escapes from the usual state of repression exercised in the waking state. But even the partial gratification of the wish in the dream leads to its being experienced as anxiety. At the same time —in a fashion so characteristic of him—Freud provides hints which foreshadow the later theory of anxiety which had to wait a quarter of a century for such seminal hints to come to fruition. In describing the activity of the dream censor and its function in bringing about the dreamwork, Freud states quite explicitly that the censor must receive some sort of signal which would stimulate it and thus elicit dreaming activity. The activity of the dream censor thus prevents the individual from experiencing a more severe anxiety or other painful affect which might disturb him and interrupt sleep. The censor and its capacity for producing dreams served as the guardian of sleep.

It is interesting from the point of view of the development of Freud's ideas that as early as 1900 in a theoretical discussion of the function of dreaming he should introduce the idea that a repressing agency, the censor, should have to receive a signal of some sort in order to undertake the dreamwork. The dreamwork, therefore, was set alongside repression and symptom formation as analogues of the defensive activity by which the mind dealt with instinctual impulses that it could not tolerate. This formulation went hand in hand with Freud's explicit theory of anxiety as a biochemical equivalent of repressed sexual impulses until the publication of *Inhibitions, Symptoms and Anxiety* in 1926. It was only then that these more scattered and fragmentary views were pulled together into a coherent theory of anxiety which was to supersede the earlier formulation.

Even as Freud reached a new and more meaningful formulation of the nature of anxiety, he did not, as we have seen, entirely abandon the earlier view or the relation between overwhelming stimulation and anxiety. Instead he made a distinction between two forms of anxiety—a more situational and economically determined one which more or less bypassed the ego and the form of anxiety which involved repression and which actively involved the ego. Writing of repression-related anxiety, he made it clear that it was not repression which caused anxiety—as he previously had thought—but anxiety which caused repression and other defenses. We can refer back to the case of anxiety neurosis and phobic anxiety in the young man who was afraid that he was going to suffer a psychotic breakdown (see Chapter 2). This case provides several interesting points of discussion. Our discussion of the case indicated that the patient was deeply troubled by his aggressive impulses. Aggression, particularly in the form of competition and rivalry with his older brother, had become a source of internal danger for him. This brings into focus the realization that not merely sexual impulses can become a source of internal danger, but also—and perhaps even more frequently —aggressive impulses. Anxiety is related to the repression of instinctual impulses—both sexual and aggressive—insofar as they become sources of internal danger.

The young man had developed a number of defensive functions to deal with these aggressive impulses. They included not only repression, but also reaction formation. That is, instead of allowing the hostile and rivalrous feelings to reach consciousness he turned them into opposite feelings of affection and regard—for his father and brother. This is a similar process to that Freud described in discussing his dream, his friend R. being his uncle. In that dream hostile and competitive feelings were transformed into masking positive affects. Our young man also demonstrated some regression in his adapting to demands and responsibilities, retreating into a rather passive and compliant position in relation to his father and his brother. All of these defenses were stimulated by and were responses to signal anxiety. The patient's aggression had become a source of internal danger to him during the emergence and resolution of his infantile neurosis. He had been unable, therefore, to resolve his basic conflicts over aggressive impulses. In his adult life, it turned out that he found himself drawn into a situation in which he had to mobilize aggression and competitive effort in the service of adaptation. He responded to these internal stirrings of aggression as if they still presented him with a threat of internal danger, a carry-over from the infantile situation. In these circumstances, his defenses were threatened and he was plunged into a state of anxious agitation and partial decompensation.

The Signal Theory of Anxiety

If we approach this case from the point of view of Freud's original theory, shifting the focus from the vicissitudes of sexual instincts to the aggressive instincts, we might view the young man's anxiety as due to a transformation of his aggression. If we look at it from the point of view of contemporary theory, however, we would have to say that the anxiety was not merely related to the aggression as such, but to the fact that the patient still continued to regard his aggression as a source of internal danger. We are forced, therefore, to focus on the signal aspect of this dynamism rather than on the merely instinctual aspect. The question, therefore, arises as to how the signal arises and what its relation to the functioning of the ego is. To what extent and in what manner does the signal derive from the instinct? To what extent and in what manner does it arise from the ego? In the light of this case, we might still believe that there is a relationship between the arousal of instinctual forces and the ego's experience of anxiety as a signal of danger.

We have to recognize that there is a crucial and continuing problem in understanding how the ego comes to regard its own impulses as a signal of danger. There is an important difference between recognizing one's own impulses as dangerous and anxiety as a signal of that danger, and regarding instinctual impulses as changed into the affect of anxiety. The problem brings us to the threshold of the problematic area of the nature of affect and the capacity of the ego to tolerate affect under conditions in which impulses are aroused and cannot be directly gratified or discharged. The whole question of tolerance for psychic distress, tolerance of danger, and tolerance of loss becomes extremely important.

There is a crucial difference, however, between regarding anxiety in terms of biochemical discharge without psychological meaning and regarding it in terms of awareness of a threat arising from impending danger or challenge. It is easier to think about this in terms of external threats or challenges—for example, examination anxiety. The threat posed by an impending examination and the anxious fears associated with it are easy to understand. What is much more difficult to understand is the fact that one can respond to an internal and subjective danger in much the same way as one responds to an external and objective danger. There is much lacking to our understanding of what it is that constitutes the internal danger. How does the ego produce the signal that makes it possible for the ego to mobilize its resources in the service of defense?

Signal Anxiety in Development

But there is a further dimension of the problem of anxiety, which Freud's theory of signal anxiety leads to, but which he did not explicitly develop. We have learned that the ego does not develop its resources fully without the stimulus of challenge and the provocation of danger. As Hartmann has impressed on us in his *Ego Psychology and the Problem of Adaptation* (1939) and his subsequent works, the development of the ego is a complicated matter. Not all of the functions and capacities of the ego develop out of the instinctual level of conflict and defense. The ego is developed out of certain autonomous capacities and functions which do not derive from defense organizations. They are structures of primary autonomy, the given capacities of the mind for perception, memory, and the organization of cognitive functions which do not pertain to or derive from instinctual conflicts. Part of the development of the ego lies in the maturation and integral functioning of these primary autonomous functions.

However, perhaps more important to the overall adjustment and capacity for mature and adaptive functioning, the ego also develops some of its significant capacities through the working through of instinctual developmental vicissitudes. Functions that may arise in the process of responding to and dealing with instinctual impulses, i.e., functions that arise out of a matrix of conflict and defense, may undergo what Hartmann calls a "change of function." Such structural capacities then become relatively autonomous and constitute structures of secondary autonomy—secondary because they derive from drive-dependent processes and only secondarily become relatively autonomous. The structures and functions of both primary and secondary autonomy combine to form the conflict-free sphere of the ego. One of the most important aspects of psychic development, therefore, depends on the ego's capacity to experience internal conflicts and developmental challenges and to be able to mobilize defensive resources in response to the internal signal of danger. Within a certain optimal range of functioning, such defenses serve to moderate anxiety and allow the ego to maintain a certain adaptive balance in its internal economy. Such defenses can be used excessively to the detriment of adaptation as well: the ego may resort to primitive defenses of denial, avoidance, or projection, or even severe degrees of repression which interfere with its capacity to test reality and master basic conflicts. Such excessive defenses may banish anxiety, but they do so at the expense of genuine mastery; nor do they provide the necessary stimulus for eliciting the growth potential of the ego. Such defenses inhibit growth insofar as they banish anxiety. Unless some anxiety is not only experienced as a signal, but also tolerated in the service of adaptation, the development of adaptive defense structures and the formation of certain types of character structure in later childhood and adolescence may be severely impaired.

The perspective that we are proposing here provides a distinctly different orientation to anxiety than that contained in Freud's view of anxiety as the morbid product of repression. We are suggesting that anxiety, taken as the signal of internal danger, is not only a stimulus to the mobilization of defenses, but it is also a crucial developmental stimulus to the mastery and adaptive channeling of instinctual energies. Although anxiety may undeniably at times be a relatively, even severely, disabling symptom, it is nevertheless to be regarded as an affect which is absolutely inseparable from successful growth and maturation in almost every developmental phase of the life cycle. In summary, not all anxiety is to be regarded as pathological.

The experience with war neuroses is illuminating in this regard. The patients who tended to develop the most severe forms of war neurosis were not soldiers who had a previous history of pathological anxiety or neurotic symptoms. Frequently enough, rather anxious and relatively neurotic individuals went through the entire war, had a great deal of active battle experience, and yet suffered only minor decompensations—if any—after severely stressful experiences. They were often able to recuperate quickly and return to duty. In contrast, the cases which developed the most severe, and often relatively irreversible, traumatic neuroses were individuals who had no history or no recollection of previous neurotic difficulties or incapacitating anxiety. They often showed a rather counterphobic attitude, convinced that they would never experience fear and not even developing any anticipatory anxiety before going into action. We would view such cases as representing a pattern of development in which the internal conflicts of early childhood had been subjected to massive repression and denial of anxiety. This massive avoidance of anxiety prevented the necessary developmental resolution of internal conflicts from taking place. Confrontation with real dangers of the battlefield broke through their fragile defenses and they were overwhelmed. They would sometimes collapse at the first sound of gunfire. And they were frequently unable to recover their previous self-assurance and confidence. These patients demonstrate very well the crucial importance of anxiety as a developmental prophylactic against psychic disaster. We should note once again that what proved the undoing of these men was not the external danger to which the proportional response is fear, but it was the internal danger from inner instinctual impulses to which the proportional response is anxiety.

This is what Freud meant when he described anxiety as signaling a threat from a traumatic situation—whether real or fantasied. He appealed to the birth trauma as the primary analogue of anxiety. The primary anxiety of birth was due to the primitive and relatively weak ego being overwhelmed by stimuli, before the primitive ego had erected or formed any protective barriers. The situation of some traumatic neuroses was similar; their incapacity to tolerate and use adaptively an adequate amount of anticipatory anxiety left them with an almost total and regressive loss of defensive capacity in the face of an overwhelming stimulus. In other words, without a signal of impending danger and trauma which would allow the mobilization of some of the ego's defensive resources, the ego was left defenseless and the response resembled very closely Freud's description of primary anxiety.

This discussion brings into focus the difference between Freud's original theory of anxiety, which described all anxiety as pathological, and more contemporary efforts to differentiate between anxiety as a stimulus for mastery and growth and pathological forms which represent the failure of mastery and development. Most contemporary psychoanalysts have come to appreciate that anxiety is an integral part of the affective life, which also undergoes development. Anxiety is, therefore, a heterogeneous phenomenon—or rather group of phenomena. The anxiety experienced by the infant is different from the separation anxiety of the young child. Both of these are again different from the anxiety which represents the signal of an internal danger. All of these anxieties have their role and function in the economy of psychic defense and development. But they are never completely dispelled. We can recognize the kind of signal anxiety which afflicted the young girl in New York when confronted with a sexual stimulus as an anxiety which ultimately derived from an infantile sexual and oedipal conflict. Similarly we can recognize behind the anxiety of many of our more disturbed patients the more primitive separation anxiety which is a common feature among young children. And finally, in the traumatic neuroses and in certain acute psychotic states, we can recognize the decompensation and loss of defensive capacity which Freud described in traumatic situations and which mirror the weakness and vulnerability of the ego in primitive states of defenselessness.

Thus we can begin to appreciate that the contemporary view of anxiety has by no means reached theoretical closure. Our view of anxiety has become considerably more complex than even Freud had envisioned. Its consideration has broadened to touch on more inclusive aspects of problems of development and adaptation. It can no longer be considered merely in terms of pathological functioning. The role of the ego in relation to anxiety has also become considerably more complex, no longer merely a matter of signaling instinctual danger. The relation between anxiety and repression can no longer be cast simplistically in terms of which came first or which produces what. As with the rest of psychoanalytic theory, the considerations of anxiety and repression and their relationship must now be cast in terms of developmental and adaptive perspectives which involve the full range of processes and interactions which constitute the complexity of human psychic functioning.

[6]

The Developmental Hypothesis

At a number of points in our discussion, it has become apparent that Freud's gradually emerging ideas about the human mind and human behavior not only embraced a hypothesis about the dynamic properties of the mental apparatus, but also extended to a view of how the mind came to possess the characteristics it did. We have seen the crucial importance for the development of psychoanalytic thinking of Freud's realization that the reports of his hysterical patients of infantile traumatic seductions were based on fantasies and not on realities. The conjunction of this realization with the results of his own self-analysis brought Freud not only to a realization of the role of fantasy in the economy of mental life, but to a realization of the importance of instinctual energies and of their course of development. The abandonment of the seduction hypothesis, therefore, opened the way to an understanding of the development of instinctual drives. The developmental hypothesis followed hard on the heels of the dynamic hypothesis. It was the first theory of psychological development in any real sense.

Psychoanalysis As a Developmental Theory

The two points of view remain central to psychoanalytic understanding. It can be said, in this sense, that psychoanalysis is in a primary way a developmental psychology. The developmental approach is obviously linked closely to Freud's methods of investigation. From the beginning, even in the days when he was using a fairly straightforward hypnotic technique, his investigations took the form of uncovering the past and trying to relate current symptoms to past experience. The dynamic and developmental approaches in psychoanalysis have remained closely linked. In describing psychoanalysis as a body of hypotheses, Hartmann and Kris outline the two views in these terms:

> Two groups of hypotheses will be discussed: some dealing with genetic propositions. The former are concerned with the interaction and the conflicts of forces within the individual and with their reaction to the external world, at any given time or during brief time spans. The genetic propositions describe how any condition under observation has grown out of an individual's past, and extended throughout his total life span. Representative examples of dynamic propositions are those concerned with defense against danger and reaction to frustration. Genetic propositions state how these reactions come into being and are used in the course of an individual's life.[20]

A developmental psychology implies not only progress in mental development and maturation, but also the various manifestations of regression. We have discussed the problem of regression briefly in relation to anxiety. We will have further opportunity to consider the progressive and regressive aspects not only of the instinctual life, but of the ego, object relations, and also thought processes. As with the other metapsychological assumptions, the developmental hypothesis embraces all aspects of psychological functioning. Psychoanalytic understanding of any capability or function or organization of the human psyche requires that it be understood in terms of its origins and the course of its development. We would like to emphasize that the developmental approach is intrinsic to psychoanalytic understanding—it is not merely accidental or additional. The developmental understanding is a necessary consequence of the methods and investigative approach of psychoanalysis. The relationship between past experience and present functioning, between previous trauma and present symptoms, or in broader perspective, between historical actualities and psychological realities, is at the very core of psychoanalysis as a theory of human functioning and as a therapeutic process.

Freud's early investigations focused primarily on instinctual development. The conjunction of his realization that his patient's reports of seduction were based on fantasy with his own self-analysis led him to formulate the rudiments of a theory of infantile sexuality. He postulated the oedipal situation as a crucial developmental conflict in the emergence of the human psyche. But, as he extended his investigations, he found that the emergence of genital sexuality and the oedipal configuration had an instinctual prehistory. He focused on drives and tendencies that related to oral activity early in infantile development and later on terms of anal preoccupations and activity. Early instinctual drives were channeled through oral and anal paths. These early instinctual develop-ments and their relationship to the emergence later in development of genital instinctual expression enabled Freud to formulate his theory of infantile sexuality. He conceptualized these early instinctual manifesta-tions in terms of pregenital sexual development and brought the whole together under a single theory of libidinal development.

Instinctual Fixation

Freud suggested that the predisposition to later illness was related to developmental difficulties in progressing from one level of instinctual organization to another. In this context he proposed the concept of in-stinctual fixation. He proposed that sexual aberrations and perversions could be understood as developmental arrests in which earlier phases of sexual growth persisted and, instead of becoming integrated into an overall pattern of adult heterosexual and genital functioning, they per-sisted as the dominant mode of sexual expression. Thus he suggested that a preference for anal intercourse reflected a fixation at a level of anal instinctual development which brought it about that anal erotic wishes and tendencies predominated over more normal genital desires. Thus he was able to bring the development of sexual aberrations into relation with his theory of instinctual and sexual development.

He then extended this theory of instinctual and libidinal fixation to other developmental failures that gave rise to mental disturbance. For example, certain individuals might have retained a considerable amount of sexual libido at an oral level of development. This would imply that a smaller amount of libido or instinctual energy would be available for employment at later developmental stages. He drew the analogy of an army which would set up a base and then try to send out troops to more advanced stations. In the face of attack, the advanced troops would fall back to the more firmly established base. He wrote:

The second danger in a development by stages of this sort lies in the fact that the portions which have proceeded further may also easily return retro-gressively to one of these earlier stages—what we describe as a *regression*. The trend will find itself led into a regression of this kind if the exercise of its function—that is, the attainment of its aim of satisfaction—is met, in its later or highly developed form, by powerful external obstacles. It is plausible to suppose that fixation and regression are not independent of each other. The stronger the fixations on its path of development, the more readily will the function evade external difficulties by regressing to the fixations—the more incapable, therefore, does the developed function turn out to be of resisting external obstacles in its course. Consider that, if a people which is in movement has left strong detachments behind at the stopping-places on its migration, it is likely that the more advanced parties will be inclined to retreat to these stopping-places if they have been defeated or have come up against a superior enemy. But they will also be in the greater danger of being defeated the more of their number they have left behind on their migration.[21]

Thus Freud linked the concept of regression to the developmental notion of fixation. The level of regression would be a function of the level and degree of fixation. This notion assumed a central position in Freud's ideas about the etiology of the neuroses.

Instinct Theory

In this fashion Freud first explained the concept of instinctual fixation. He applied it to the understanding of instinctual regression in the process of symptom formation and also to the development of character traits. This schematic view of development remained for some time the major basis for a psychoanalytic classification of mental disorders. Freud's focus during this period was on the instinctual and libidinal aspects of development. His thinking was cast in terms of a dualistic theory of instincts, an approach which he maintained with some significant variations throughout the better part of his career. During this period of the development of his thinking his instinct theory postulated a dichotomy between the sexual instincts on the one hand and the self-preservative or ego instincts on the other. The sexual instincts were considered to constitute the major content of the repressed unconscious. The self-preservative instincts were, on the whole, associated with the preconscious-conscious part of the mind.

The further emergence of Freud's developmental hypothesis was a consequence of two major theoretical shifts. The first was the shift in his theory of instincts. The second was the development of his thinking about the ego. Both these aspects were related to each other and each had considerable effect on his views regarding mental development. The dichotomy of sexual and ego instincts did not prove adequate. Freud's use of this dichotomy was complicated by two factors which proved to be of the utmost importance in the development of his later thinking—narcissism and aggression. When Freud came to the consideration and initial understanding of narcissism, it became apparent that it represented a libidinal component that seemed to fall within the area of ego instincts. Thus Freud was forced to abandon his concept of ego instincts and reformulate his views about instincts in general. Concomitantly, the nonlibidinal aspects of ego functioning came more clearly into view. We shall have more to say about narcissism later (see Chapter 8).

Aggression was the other factor that assumed increasing importance in Freud's thinking. From the earliest investigations he was aware of aggression but seemed to pay little attention to it, especially after his views of the role of libidinal instincts and their investigation assumed their predominant place. Aggression was considered in terms of sadism and its correlative masochism; he treated them as "component instincts" whose status in the theory was never quite secure. Aggression gradually came to be included under the ego instincts and was thus regarded as a nonlibidinal response of the ego. Finally, with the emergence of the structural theory and its revised view of the ego and its functions, aggression was separated from the ego and assigned to the id along with the libidinal instincts. Thus the distinction between ego instincts and libidinal ones was broken down and the status of aggression and the sexual instincts as independent and comparable sources of instinctual force established. The evolution of instinctual theory had to be paralleled by a development in Freud's notion of what the ego was and what it did.

The Theory of the Ego

Freud's understanding of the ego and its functioning underwent a significant development during the course of his career. The impetus he gave to the development of an ego psychology has continued after his death and today provides perhaps the most active area of psychoanalytic investigation and concern. The development of the psychoanalytic thinking about the ego has been traced by Rapaport.[22] In the earliest phase of Freud's work, the concept of the ego was relatively primitive and nonsystematic. The term "ego" was used variably for the person, the self, or for consciousness. The ego was identified with the mass of ideas or memories which are either conscious or available to consciousness. Defensive activity, which was loosely associated with the ego, split off certain ideas from the associative network and thus provided the basis for damming up of affect and the dissociation of unconscious ideas.

The discovery that infantile seductions were not facts but fantasies brought the understanding of the ego to a new phase. Freud's interest shifted to the agent that created the fantasies. His interest in defense declined and the notion of defense took the form of a rather global concept of repression. Repression was conceived as a function of ego instincts, so that even crucial ego functions at this stage of Freud's thinking were conceived in terms of instinctual forces. The gradual formulation of his ideas about secondary process and the reality principle, however, provided a set of regulatory processes which were somehow set over against instinctual processes—even if they were still conceived of as instinctual derivatives. Repression, moreover, came to be seen not merely as a matter of topographic defense by ego instincts, but rather as a matter of the establishment of more or less permanent countercathexes. The discovery of permanent countercathexes and their correlative resistances—and that these resistances were also unconscious—led to the revamping of Freud's earlier topographic ideas and provided the basis for his development of the structural theory. What was unconscious could no longer be simply ascribed to instinctual forces and their repression. The ego was found to include countercathectic structures which were also unconscious.

Freud's struggles with the concept of narcissism provided a turning point. Through them the concept of the superego gradually emerged as a split-off structure within the ego. Freud moved inexorably toward greater clarification and separation of the instincts, both libidinal and aggressive, and a more coherent view of the ego. Finally in the *Ego and the Id* (1923) the ego emerged as a coherent organization of mental processes and functions. It was organized primarily around the system of consciousness, but it included structures which caused unconscious resistances; it had neutral energies at its disposal and could transform the energy of instinctual drives for its own independent uses. At this stage, the ego was still seen as relatively weak and acting as mediator between more powerful contending forces—id, superego, and reality. It was only with his development of his theory of anxiety and particularly the notion of signal anxiety that the ego achieved a position of autonomy and strength. In *Inhibitions, Symptoms and Anxiety* (1926), the ego emerges as relatively autonomous, capable of mastery, initiating defense by the anxiety signal, having a variety of relatively effective defenses at its disposal, restraining instinctual impulses in terms of the reality principle, and purposefully directing itself to specific goals in the interests of adaptation.

Ego Development

All of this had definite implications for Freud's views of development. The structural approach was implicit in his earlier work, but it had to pass through an evolution to become more explicit. Nevertheless, a careful reading of some of his early papers will reveal hints of his approaching the possibility that the noninstinctual and structural parts of the mind are also subject to a developmental process. The original developmental hypothesis had been formulated in reference to instinctual development. But as the concept of the ego slowly emerged and was clarified, it became apparent that it too had a developmental history and course.

As early as 1911, Freud clearly indicated that instinctual development alone might not be sufficient to provide an understanding of either the cause or the type of neurosis. In 1911 he published his important paper "Formulations on the Two Principles of Mental Functioning." This paper was of particular interest since it contained a number of statements which carry important implications for the understanding of the functioning of the ego. Freud describes the developmental transformation which takes place in the child's mind as he becomes capable of distinguishing wish from reality. At birth and in early infancy the child's mind is dominated by the pleasure principle, the need for immediate gratification, by action or by fantasy, of a wish whose fulfillment is associated with the elimination of excessive tension. The child learns that certain experiences bring reduction of tension, which is associated with discomfort and unpleasure, and pleasurable gratification. He wishes to re-create these experiences of pleasure and gratification.

It is only gradually with increasing experience and with a repeated confrontation of the interference of reality with such gratification that he comes to recognize that reality does not always respond with immediate gratification of his impulses and wishes. The dictates of the pleasure principle with its demand for immediate satisfaction and gratification run counter to the dictates of the reality principle with its requirements of delay of gratification and congruence with the structure of reality and the recognition of the laws of cause and effect. In the course of development the pleasure principle must gradually give way to and adapt itself to the reality principle. The differentiation of these two principles of mental functioning is parallel in many ways, as we shall see, to Freud's earlier distinction between primary and secondary process thinking.

In discussing the emergence of the reality principle Freud focuses on the developmental aspects. He writes:

> While the ego goes through its transformation from a *pleasure-ego* into a *reality-ego,* the sexual instincts undergo the changes that lead them from their original autoerotism through various intermediate phases to object-love in the service of procreation. If we are right in thinking that each step in these two courses of development may become the site of a disposition to later neurotic illness, it is plausible to suppose that the form taken by the subsequent illness (the *choice* of neurosis) will depend on the particular phase of the development of the ego and of the libido in which the dispositional inhibition of development has occurred. Thus unexpected significance attaches to the chronological features of the two developments (which have not yet been studied), and to possible variations in their synchronization.[23]

Object love meant mature sexual love for a heterosexual object. Freud seems to be indicating that the earlier stages of object love and object relationship were major areas which were at that time "not yet studied." From our contemporary viewpoint, we would view the early development of object relations, long before the development of the triangular conflict of the definitive infantile oedipal situation, as crucial determinants of certain basic ego capacities which serve as fundamental predispositions either for mental health or for various forms of mental disturbance.

As we have previously suggested, Freud's use of the term "ego" does not have the same connotations that it had in his later writings, in which it was used as a more specifically structural referent—or for that matter that it has in our own contemporary usage, after considerable post-Freudian development. But Freud nonetheless was drawing our attention to a most important distinction. In addition to the instinctual development which he had treated extensively elsewhere, he was pointing out the differential development and integration of certain ego capacities which in the broadest sense relate to the acceptance of the limitations of reality and to a tolerance for separation and loss. These capacities are differentiated from the fantasy content which is characteristic of various levels of instinctual development and are specifically related to the development of the ego as an independent aspect of psychic development.

Freud makes a clear distinction between problems which relate to the reality principle and problems which relate to the development of instinct in terms of instinctual zones of excitation and specific fantasies of gratification. He is saying in effect that an individual may have an inhibition of development which affects these basic ego capacities and at the same time manifest fantasies and wishes which reflect all of the levels of instinctual development. An individual may traverse all of the levels of instinctual development, and yet fail in one or another aspect of ego development. Conversely, an individual may have progressed in the early stages of ego development fairly successfully in regard to the emergence of the capacity for reality testing and object relations. Both of these are important aspects of ego functioning and form important attributes of adult character structure. Even so, such early mastery does not preclude the emergence at some later date of basic instinctual conflicts. Despite the development in ego capacities, the emergence of such instinctual conflicts can result in neurotic patterns of defense and/or in compromise of the capacity for adult heterosexual object love.

The Developmental Process

Freud's statement indicates his awareness, as early as 1911, of problems that we are only now beginning to understand in greater detail. These problems concern the complex relationship between instinctual development, ego development, and the development of object relations. When Freud was writing the paper on mental functions, it was generally believed that the child was not capable of much in the way of object investment until it had reached a genital level of development and had entered on the infantile neurosis. Study of the developmental process has helped us to understand that object relations have a course of development that originates in the first months of life. Particularly important is the growth and development of the child's relationship to the mother in the beginning of his experience of objects. From our more advanced perspective we would make a much greater differentiation than Freud implies between the capacity to form an object relationship with another person and the ability to combine love with appropriate genital sexual feelings and activities. The prehistory of adult heterosexual object love is far more complex than was envisioned in Freud's time.

It is worth pausing for a moment to comment on the seminal aspects of Freud's remarks which we have quoted. The paper on the two principles of mental functioning gives us an excellent example of the innumerable hints and observations which Freud scatters throughout his work indicating his awareness of problems which he could outline but which his theory was as yet unable to encompass. In the passage quoted he underlined the significance of the chronological relations between instinctual and ego development. Our knowledge of this area is still only partial and incomplete. It was for a long time bypassed and ignored, but it has more currently become an extremely focal point in our attempts to understand some of the important causes of the most serious mental disturbances. Freud was only able to point to and to a certain extent formulate the problems. He recognized that they would eventually be approached on the basis of the slow acquisition of greater knowledge. He carefully avoided the trap of making generalizations or providing easy solutions which he could not verify or which could not be further explored by means of the techniques he had available to him. His interest, particularly in the early years of his career, was focused primarily on areas where current theory and technique held promise of leading to a more rapid extension of knowledge. This accounts to a large extent for the great emphasis given by Freud and his early followers in the analytic movement to the elucidation of unconscious content, both in terms of a theory of mental functioning and as a technique of therapeutic intervention.

One of the major aspects of Freud's introduction of a developmental perspective to his thinking, as Rapaport has pointed out,[24] was his elucidation of instinctual drives as an intrinsic maturational factor. As we have suggested, his early work on hysteria and his initial theories were not developmental in a strict sense. The relationship between past experience and present symptoms was treated only in terms of anamnestic connections. There was no consideration of maturational factors. The abandonment of the seduction hypothesis and the realization of the role of fantasy in mental life turned Freud's attention to the instinctual drives which gave rise to the fantasies. He gradually evolved the view of these drives as innate and unconscious factors which underwent a progressive course of maturation. The maturation of such instinctual drives was intrinsic, not determined by any outside influences, and was therefore independent of and prior to experience. The treatment of instinctual drives as intrinsic maturational factors sets psychoanalysis apart from other behavioristically oriented psychologies which explain behavior solely in terms of learning, e.g., as a result of and subsequent to experience.

The genetic approach is limited by the fact that the psychoanalytic situation involves interpretations which may complicate the validation of the reconstructions. Freud himself was aware of the difficulty. In a letter to Fliess in 1897, he wondered out loud whether he wouldn't be better off going to the nursery and directly observing children. The direct observation of children was a labor that was to be taken up by others, and it has proven to be a richly rewarding and fundamental area of research. But it too has its disadvantages. Study of preverbal infants is limited to direct observation and external measurement. The internal mental processes are not available for study. They can only become available when the child has reached a level of verbal capacity and introspective facility to allow expression of his inner experience. The genetic method in psychoanalysis, however, must approach genetic influences indirectly from the perspective of adult retrospection. This opens the possibility of suggestion and distortion, even as it offers the possibility of insight into genetic processes by way of the developmental hypothesis.

These approaches to the genetic process are different, and each offers a different perspective on the developmental process. They are complementary as well. Freud saw this clearly when he wrote:

Psychoanalytic investigation, reaching back into childhood from a later time, and contemporary observation of children combine to indicate to us still other regularly active sources of sexual excitation. The direct observation of children has the disadvantage of working upon data which are easily misunderstandable; psychoanalysis is made difficult by the fact that it can only reach its data, as well as its conclusions, after long detours. But by cooperation the two methods can attain a satisfactory degree of certainty in their findings.[25]

The genetic approach allows the tracing not only of intrinsic maturational factors but also of complex behavioral patterns. It made it possible for the development of personality as such, independently of the extrinsic development of organs, functions, abilities, or simple behaviors, to be brought within the compass of a developmental psychology.

Parallel to the development of the instinctual drives, there is a development of intrinsic factors which operate to restrain and direct drives. A discussion of intrinsic developmental factors must include these factors as well. These are the factors that permit delay of discharge and which account for intrapsychic conflict. Freud saw the functioning of such restraining factors as derived from experience. Only gradually and hesitatingly did he come to acknowledge them as manifesting another and separate intrinsic maturational factor—as we have seen in our discussion of the development of the ego.

Drives and Experience

The relationship between instinctual drives and experience remained central to Freud's developmental views. In applying the genetic method, he was presented with a certain set of neurotic symptoms and behaviors together with a situational context in which these phenomena took place. The analytic search into the background of this presenting pathology through the patient's memories and associations tended to reveal other situations and behaviors at various stages of his life history which seemed to have a similar quality to the present difficulties. Freud was able to link these various episodes in the patient's life history into a pattern by seeing them as separate but similar efforts to deal with the intensity of instinctual drives. He was also able to relate this pattern of observable regularities to the maturational course of the instinctual component.

In tracing these series of behaviors, Freud noted that the intrinsic maturational forces and the external environmental conditions derived from the patient's experience enjoyed considerable variability in the degree to which they seemed to influence the behaviors under investigation. The further back into the patient's life history he carried his investigation of the series of antecedent behaviors, the more the relative significance of the experiential factor seemed to diminish. Also, the further back his investigation carried him, the more did the pattern of behavior seem to reflect the operation of intrinsic instinctual maturational factors and the specific developmental vicissitudes of the phase of development in which the original pattern of solution arose and became dominant.

To explain the patterns of interplay between intrinsic maturational factors and extrinsic experiential factors, Freud postulated what he called a "complemental series." In the *Three Essays on Sexuality* (1905) in which his developmental views were given their earliest coherent expression, he wrote:

No other influences on the course of sexual development can compare in importance with releases of sexuality, waves of repression and sublimations —the two latter being processes of which the inner causes are quite unknown to us. It might be possible to include repressions and sublimations as a part of the constitutional disposition, by regarding them as manifestations of it in life; and anyone who does so is justified in asserting that the final shape taken by sexual life is principally the outcome of the innate constitution. No one with perception will, however, dispute that an interplay of factors such as this also leaves room for the modifying effects of accidental events experienced in childhood and later. It is not easy to estimate the relative efficacy of the constitutional and accidental factors. In theory one is always inclined to overestimate the former; therapeutic practice emphasizes the importance of the latter. It should, however, on no account be forgotten that the relation between the two is a co-operative and not a mutually exclusive one. The constitutional factor must await experiences before it can make itself felt; the accidental factor must have a constitutional basis in order to come into operation. To cover the majority of cases we can picture what has been described as a "complemental series," in which the diminishing intensity of one factor is balanced by the increasing intensity of the other; there is, however, no reason to deny the existence of extreme cases at the two ends of the series.[26]

The relationship between these factors was governed by the developmental principle. At the beginning end of the developmental series the instinctual drive dominates in influencing the behavioral solution which is employed to allow discharge of the instinctual energies. As development proceeds, environmental influences and experience (accidental factors) play an increasingly greater role in the shaping of behavior.

Speaking a dozen years later, in his *Introductory Lectures* (1917), Freud applied the same developmental logic to the etiology of the neuroses. He observed:

As regards their causation, instances of neurotic illness fall into a series within which the two factors—sexual constitution and experience, or, if you prefer it, fixation of the libido and frustration—are represented in such a manner that if there is more of the one there is less of the other. At one end of the series are the extreme cases of which you could say with conviction: these people, in consequence of the singular development of their libido, would have fallen ill in any case, whatever they had experienced and however carefully their lives had been sheltered. At the other end there are the cases, as to which, on the contrary, you would have had to judge that they would certainly have escaped falling ill if their lives had not brought them into this or that situation. In the cases lying within the series a greater or lesser amount of predisposition in the sexual constitution is combined with a lesser or greater amount of detrimental experience in their lives. Their sexual constitution would not have led them into a neurosis if they had not had these experiences, and these experiences would not have had a traumatic effect on them if their libido had been otherwise disposed.[27]

The implications of these developmental views are far-reaching and carry considerable influence on psychoanalytic thinking. The intrinsically maturing core of the personality includes not only sources of force and drive as important energic determinants of behavior, but it also includes other forces which regulate and control instinctual drives. Both these aspects undergo a pattern of intrinsic development. Freud vacillated between viewing these regulative and socializing forces as determined by experience on one hand and as constitutional givens on the other. Gradually he came to the view that these regulative aspects of the personality underwent an intrinsic development independently of experience. Consequently, unlearned instinctual forces and restraining regulative mechanisms interact in such a way during the course of development as to give rise to various developmental (psychosexual) stages. The patterning of this developmental interaction determines in part how the child experiences and interprets the influences impinging on him from his environment. Thus the developmental pattern emerges prior to and independently of experience—in the biological sense of intrinsically determined vectors of growth; but it does not take place without constant interaction with and subjection to the shaping influence of environmental influences and subjective experience. John Benjamin concluded an extensive review of the influence of innate and experiential factors on development in the following terms:

We have every reason, empirically, to state the following: not only can innate differences in drive organization, in ego functions, and in maturational rates determine different responses to objectively identical experiences; *but they can also help determine what experiences will be experienced, and how they will be perceived.* [Italics in original.] [28]

Thus the developmental approach brings the innate factors in personality organization into much sharper focus. It is this innate and intrinsic maturational aspect of psychoanalytic thinking that sets it apart from other contemporary theories of personality development in which such development is conceived in terms of learning and experience. Thus the developmental perspective has the effect of balancing the view of personality organization and functioning that is emphasized in the other basic perspectives and assumptions about mental processes—specifically in the dynamic and adaptational considerations in which the role of experience looms large.

Keeping the innate dispositional factors in mind, we can return to a consideration of the developmental role of experience. Freud's analysis of instinctual drives was cast in terms of the concepts of zone, aim, object, and cathexis. He conceived of the drives as psychic forces which expended energy in accomplishing work. The energy had a source (the organically based "zone" from which it derived), an aim (the tendency to discharge accumulated energy and thus reduce tension), and an object toward which the energy was directed outside the subject. If drive discharge is limited or excessively restrained—either by intrinsic restraining factors or extrinsic prohibitions—drive energy will be diverted to other forms of expression within the same modality, or by regressively shifting to another modality which had been employed earlier in the course of development. Such displacements of energy could undergo fixation in the course of development with severe implications for the functioning of the personality, as we have already seen.

Instinctual Drives and Objects

The concept of cathexis is crucial to this whole consideration. It is the concept that links instinctual drives with objects; consequently, it is the concept that bears the burden of integrating the intrinsic maturational aspects of instinct with the experience of objects. The universal tendency of drive was toward discharge, but not discharge without direction toward an object. Drive discharge involves the interaction of instinctual energies and regulating structures. Regulating structures control and inhibit the processes of discharge and displacement. The discharge of drive energy can take place along a continuum, extending from drive-dominated forms of behavior, in which controlling structures exercise a minimal curtailment of the tendency for discharge and displacement, to more regulated forms of behavior in which these tendencies are restricted. Thus there is a developmental transition from less mature instinctual discharge which is immediate, direct, and generally socially inappropriate, to more developmentally advanced forms of discharge which are much more differentiated, usually delayed or detoured in some fashion, and generally socially appropriate and adaptive.

The accomplishment of the complex course of development is dependent not merely on innate factors, however significant and determining they may be in any given case. The emerging cathexis of appropriate objects in the respective phases of psychosexual development is a critical aspect of human development. The success with which the infant and growing child move from one stage of libidinal development to another is a function of the degree to which cathexis of age- and phase-appropriate objects has been achieved. Such cathexes take place in the context of object relatedness. The interplay between subject and cathected object and the mutual regulation that works itself out between them becomes central to the whole process. This becomes important not merely in terms of libidinal and instinctual organization, but even more crucially for the differentiation and integration of the ego. Freud saw this aspect of development all too clearly when he conceptualized the ego as an organization of abandoned object cathexes. The processes of introjection and identification assumed a central role in his conceptualization of the development of the structural aspect of the personality. When he finally came to the formulation of his structural theory, it was clear that the integration of the ego was correlative with and derivative from the status of object relations.

The Developmental Hypothesis

Thus there is no aspect of psychoanalytic developmental theory in which the respective contributions of innate and experiential factors do not have their place. The developmental process is cast in terms of their complex interplay and mutual interaction and determination. From the earliest stages of development, experience—particularly in the form of object relations—modulates and modifies the emerging pattern of innate developmental forces. Correspondingly, at every level of development, innate constitutional factors set the conditions for and contribute to the patterning of experience. The interplay of the factors gives rise to the stages of psychosexual and psychosocial development, in a pattern of growth that is no better described than in Erikson's term "epigenesis." The organism obeys those inner laws which dictate that one organ should be formed after another, that one item of the behavioral repertoire should be created after another. He writes:

. . . this evolutionary principle of epigenesis . . . governs the unfolding before birth of the organic basis for all behavior and continues after birth to govern the unfolding of an individual's social potentialities in the successive encounters of impulse systems and cultural realities.[29]

To recapitulate—the developmental hypothesis in psychoanalysis can be spelled out in a series of interrelated propositions. The psychoanalytic understanding of the developmental process sees it as the result of two interacting factors—intrinsic maturational organismic forces, which are antecedent to and independent of experience, and an experiential factor, which is based on learning, training, or other forms of environmental influence or stimulus input. The intrinsic forces include both instinctual drives, which are constantly seeking immediate and direct discharge, and drive regulating and controlling structures, which are ordered to delay of drive discharge and maintenance of tension states.

The role of experience in shaping and modifying the development of behavior is to enable the individual to learn to use substitute objects and alternative aims in the expression and gratification of an instinct. The availability of multiple means and goals for drive discharge allows for delay of gratification and searching out of drive-satisfying alternatives which are congruent with reality demands. The developmental process takes place in more or less discontinuous and qualitatively distinct (psychosexual) phases. In the process of development there is a transition from the dominance of primitive behavioral organization (primary process) to more mature, advanced, and better differentiated forms of organization (secondary process). The more developed secondary process organization consists of drive-regulating structures whose relatively autonomous functions are required for maximizing the adaptive balance between drive derivatives and reality factors. Earlier and more primitive forms of behavioral organization are not replaced by later developing forms, but remain potentially active by incorporation in and integration with later more developed and more differentiated patterns of organization.

The notion of instinctual zones and their related modalities of activity are most helpful in conceptualizing this developmental sequencing. All instinctual zones (and their organic correlates), as Erikson has made clear, have their respective modes of functioning. This is determined largely by the mechanics of their operation, e.g., the anus expels and retains. The distinctive quality of instinctual drives derives from the functional patterns of their respective modes. During the course of maturation the epigenetic shifts from zone to zone are accomplished by shifts in cathexis. These cathectic shifts gain increasing differentiation of the instinctual drives which is antecedent to and therefore not specifically determined by experience. Their maturation is intrinsic, but their differentiation is codetermined by experience. As the instinctual mode attains its specific phase of epigenetic ascendancy, the accumulation of experience acts to generalize the particular mode so that its characteristics extend to other zones and behaviors; thus the retentive mode of the anal phase may be extended to manipulative behavior giving it a grasping, possessive, and retentive quality. Thus the estrangement of modes from their respective zones gradually changes them from instinctual drive derivatives into modes of action which are available for adaptive and purposeful activity. Such adaptive behaviors are subject to learning and experience, so that the progressive separation of zone and modality is in part due to the modifying influence of experience.

These propositions and processes are central to contemporary psychoanalytic understanding and work. Psychoanalytic understanding of behavior and psychopathology is inherently a genetic understanding. It gains insight by an understanding of the genetic roots of behavior, not merely as historical actualities but specifically as present psychological realities. It understands not merely in terms of the causal action of innate factors and earlier experiences as part of the patient's past, but it seeks to understand the historical residues insofar as they represent aspects and elements in the patient's present psychological reality and psychic organization. That genetic understanding is the objective not only of psychoanalytic theory, but of psychoanalytic technique as well.

[7]

Primary and Secondary Process

In our preceding discussion of the developmental process, we had occasion to observe that the psychoanalytic account of the growth and maturation of the mental apparatus embraced both instinctual and noninstinctual elements. We also noted that both aspects of development derived from both intrinsic maturational factors and environmental-experiential influences and the interaction between them. Freud had described this complex interaction in terms of a "complemental series" —although the exact working out of these complemental influences may in fact turn out to be more complex than Freud's formulation of their interrelation would allow. We saw that Freud himself for most of his career thought of the development of the ego as simply a result of experiential influences. Even so, there were hints that intrinsic developmental factors might have a place in the genesis of the ego; this became more evident in his later thinking. These hints were taken up and elaborated later by Hartmann and others into a theory of structure of primary and secondary autonomy. Structures of primary autonomy which subserved functions of perception, memory, etc., were more or less given, while structures of secondary autonomy were derived from the influence of experience. The developmental interplay between these structures remains a problem for contemporary analytic theory.

Freud seemed to have grasped the complexity of these problems intuitively, but did not possess the theoretical basis to conceptualize them. Despite its historical interest as evidence of the understanding of these difficulties, Freud's 1911 paper on the two principles of mental functioning had little substantial influence on the direction of his own interests or the interests of the rest of the psychoanalytic pioneers. For a number of years, their attention was taken up almost exclusively with the exciting and fruitful discoveries that lay in the elucidation of the contents of the unconscious. Each new discovery was a revelation and opened new realms of interest and meaningful exploration. Psychoanalysis in those days, indeed, amounted to a dark continent.

From Content to Concept

As analytic technique became more skillful and as some of the more gross outlines of the dark continent of the unconscious were mapped out, some of the major areas of unconscious thinking together with new patterns of organization of the fantasy life became increasingly accessible to psychoanalytic understanding and formulation. It was some time, however, before analytic interest concerned itself with the ways in which the ego as we now understand it can defend against, distort, and disguise the material of such fantasies and wishes. The organization and operation of such processes was much more poorly understood than the content of the material that was elicited in the analytic process. It was only gradually and after a number of years that there evolved a shift in interest from the content of analytic productions to the processes involved—from content to concept.

Up to this point in our discussion we have focused primarily on the development of concepts. We have not paid any attention to content, except insofar as it helped us to understand or put into focus some of Freud's basic hypotheses. We have referred to sexual memories or fantasies only in terms of their conceptual implications, as empirical findings which led Freud to shift his emphasis from a theory which put primary emphasis on repression of traumatic experience to one which postulated the development of instinct. We have dealt with matters of content particularly in relation, first, to the dynamic nature of both the repressed content and the forces by which it becomes repressed. Second, we have suggested that an economic or quantitative factor is implicitly involved in the idea that fantasies can be displaced in dreams or in neurotic symptoms. Third, we have discussed the steps which led to the formulation of the developmental hypothesis. We have not, however, paid much attention to the specific nature of the mental processes which characterize unconscious mental life.

At this point we can turn to a consideration of one of the basic psychoanalytic distinctions dealing with the nature of mental processes. The distinction between primary and secondary thought processes remains one of Freud's most significant formulations. He gave this distinction its definitive expression in the famous Chapter 7 of his *Inter-*

pretation of Dreams. In that chapter Freud summarized and recast all that he had learned about the functioning of the mind in his years of study not only of dreams and the dreaming process, but also of hysteria and other forms of neurosis. The seventh chapter, therefore, became a major statement of Freud's formal conceptualization of the mental apparatus—and the distinction between primary and secondary process was at the heart of it.

Dream Mechanisms

Freud described the generation of dream thoughts as involving a train of thought which arises in the preconscious. But instead of receiving a cathexis from the preconscious level, it receives its cathexis from the unconscious level. The cathexis from the unconscious is derived from an unconscious wish which has infantile determinants. As a result of this unconscious cathexis, the dream thoughts undergo a series of transformations which constitute the dreamwork and which lead to psychical processes which we can no longer recognize as normal. He describes the specific mechanisms by which such transformations are accomplished. The process involves the translation of latent dream thoughts into the manifest dream content.

The first of the mechanisms by which the dreamwork is carried out is condensation. In the formation of the dream contents, a broad range of latent dream-thoughts may be compressed into a small compass of manifest material. Thus the dream content serves as nodal points upon which a great number of dream-thoughts may converge. Freud describes this mechanism in the following terms:

The intensities of the individual ideas become capable of discharge *en bloc* and pass over from one idea to another, so that certain ideas are formed which are endowed with great intensity. And since this process is repeated several times, the intensity of a whole train of thought may eventually be concentrated in a single ideational element. Here we have the fact of "compression" or "condensation," which has become familiar in the dream work. It is this that is mainly responsible for the bewildering impression made on us by dreams for nothing at all analogous to it is known to us in mental life that is normal and accessible to consciousness. . . . In the process of condensation, on the other hand, every psychical interconnection is transformed into an *intensification* of its ideational content. The case is the same as when, in preparing a book for the press, I have some word which is of special importance for understanding the text printed in spaced or heavy type; or in speech I should pronounce the same word loudly and slowly and with special emphasis.[30]

Thus the images formed are collective or composite. The figure of Irma, for example, as it appears in the famous Irma dream, is a collective figure who possesses contradictory characteristics—including differences —insofar as she represents a number of other figures. The figure of Dr. R. who appeared in Freud's uncle dream—we have discussed this dream previously (see Chapter 3)—was, on the contrary, a composite figure in which the characteristics common to two or more persons are combined while the differences are canceled out.

Freud noted that condensation in the dream process tended to give rise to intermediate ideas which were very much like compromises. This phenomenon was quite foreign to normal conscious thought processes, in which emphasis is laid on selection of correct ideas and on their segregation from incorrect ideas. Moreover, such ideas are linked to each other in the loosest fashion. The dreamwork uses and gives equal value to associations that normally would be scorned by normal thought. Such associative links are tolerated at best only in jokes in conscious thought. The thought processes of the dream may also tolerate contradictory ideas and allow them to stand side by side. Sometimes they are even combined to form condensations, as if the contradiction were nonexistent, or they are brought into compromises that conscious thought would never tolerate.

The second major characteristic of the dream-thought processes is displacement. Freud describes it in these terms:

In the dream work a psychical force is operating which on the one hand strips the elements which have a high psychical value of their intensity, and on the other hand, *by means of overdetermination,* creates from elements of low psychical value new values, which afterwards find their way into the dream-content. If that is so, a *transference and displacement of psychical intensities* occurs in the process of dream-formation, and it is as a result of these that the difference between the text of the dream-content and that of the dream-thoughts comes about. The process which we are here presuming is nothing less than the essential portion of the dream work; and it deserves to be described as "dream displacement." [31]

Freud later amplified this account somewhat by adding that displacement may be effected either by replacing a latent element of the dream content by a more remote element or by shifting the psychical cathexis from a relatively important to a relatively unimportant element.

Freud recapitulated the characteristics of the dreamwork in the following terms:

The dream-work is not simply more careless, more irrational, more forgetful and more incomplete than waking thought; it is completely different from it qualitatively and for that reason not immediately comparable with it. It does not think, calculate or judge in any way at all; it restricts itself to giving things a new form. It is exhaustively described by an enumeration of the conditions which it has to satisfy in producing its result. That product, the dream, has above all to evade the censorship, and with that end in view the dream-work makes use of a *displacement of psychical intensities* to the point of a transvaluation of all psychical values. The thoughts have to be reproduced exclusively or predominantly in the material of visual and acoustic memory-traces, and this necessity imposes upon the dream-work *considerations of representability* which it meets by carrying out fresh displacements. Greater intensities have probably to be produced than are available in the dream-thoughts at night, and this purpose is served by the *extensive condensation* which is carried out with the constituents of the dream-thoughts. Little attention is paid to the logical relations between the thoughts; those relations are ultimately given a disguised representation in certain *formal* characteristics of dreams.[32]

There is little of the characteristics of the dreamwork that is not expressed in this statement. And Freud added by way of comment:

It will be seen that the chief characteristic of the processes is that the whole stress is laid upon making the cathecting energy mobile and capable of discharge; the content and the proper meaning of the psychical elements to which the cathexes are attached are treated as of little consequence.[33]

Primary vs. Secondary Process

These considerations of the characteristics of dream-thought processes carried Freud on to the further formulation of the distinction between primary and secondary processes. He remarked:

Thus we are driven to conclude that two fundamentally different kinds of psychical process are concerned in the formation of dreams. One of these produces perfectly rational dream-thoughts, of no less validity than normal thinking; while the other treats these thoughts in a manner which is in the highest degree bewildering and irrational.[34]

He noted that the characteristics of the irrational dream process were similar in their formal aspect to neurotic symptoms he had studied in his patients. In hysteria, he argued, relatively normal thoughts are transformed into symptoms by similar mechanisms of condensation, formation of compromises, and contradictory associations. In hysteria, these formations were the result of the activity of unconscious and often in-

fantile wishes. Freud thus argued by analogy that the irrational characteristics of the dream-thoughts were due to the operation of repressed
and unconscious infantile wishes.

Such wishes, coming from the unconscious, have no other objective
than immediate discharge of impulse and immediate gratification. They
operate in terms of and are governed by the pleasure principle. Freud
argued, however, that the activity of a second system was necessary
since the first system, ordered to pleasure and satisfaction, could not
achieve anything further than hallucinatory gratification. The first primitive wishing had to be the hallucinatory cathexis of a satisfying memory. The wish could, therefore, set the apparatus in motion to re-create
and cathect such satisfying memories, but the hallucination could not
bring about cessation of the need. A second system was necessary to di-
vert the excitation aroused by the need in such a way as to allow voluntary action which could alter the environment to give real rather than
hallucinatory gratification.

The difference and the nature of the interaction between the two systems was conceived in terms of the economic problem of energy discharge. Freud wrote:

All I insist upon is the idea that the activity of the first ψ-system is directed
towards securing the *free discharge* of the quantities of excitation, while the
second system, by means of the cathexes emanating from it, succeeds in *inhibiting* this discharge and in transforming the cathexis into a quiescent one,
no doubt with a simultaneous raising of its level. I presume, therefore, that
under the dominion of the second system the discharge of excitation is governed by quite different mechanical conditions from those in force under the
dominion of the first system. When once the second system has concluded
its exploratory thought-activity, it releases the inhibition and damming-up of
the excitations and allows them to discharge themselves in movement.[35]

The tenor of these remarks must have seemed rather obscure to Freud's
contemporaries, and it was not until the discovery and publication of
his *Project* (1895) that the conceptual context for them became clear.
Nonetheless, it becomes apparent that in Freud's thinking the first system was ordered to direct discharge and immediate satisfaction. Its activity was, therefore, governed by the pleasure principle. Similarly, the
second system was under the governance of the reality principle. The
above statement expresses in terms of energy discharge the role of the
reality principle in serving the needs of the pleasure principle. The
psychical process which characterizes the first system he called "pri-

mary process," and that which results from the inhibition imposed by the second system he called "secondary process."

Freud concluded his analysis of these two psychical systems with a generalized statement which underlines their relative importance in the understanding of the functioning of the mental apparatus. He commented:

> The two psychical systems, the censorship upon the passage from one of them to the other, the inhibition and overlaying of one activity by the other, the relations of both of them to consciousness—or whatever more correct interpretations of the observed facts may take their place—all of these form part of the normal structure of our mental instrument, and dreams show us one of the paths leading to an understanding of its structure. If we restrict ourselves to the minimum of new knowledge which has been established with certainty, we can still say this of dreams: they have proved that *what is suppressed continues to exist in normal people as well as abnormal, and remains capable of psychical functioning.*[36]

Freud's formulation makes it clear that he felt he had come upon a basic characteristic of human mental functioning. His formulation and the basic differentiation of primary and secondary thought processes still stands as an important and fundamental insight into the organization of mental processes.

Freud used the distinction between primary and secondary process to characterize the difference which he observed between the functioning of the mind during dreaming activity and in the formation of symptoms and its functioning in the normal, conscious, waking state. He suggested that the organization of thought exhibited in dreams reflected the pattern of thought that took place in the unconscious levels of the mind, while the less primitive and more rational and logical organization of the secondary process was characteristic of the conscious and preconscious levels of mental functioning. The primary process, then, was much more closely related to unconscious processes and reflected more immediately a derivation from and dependence on instinctual drives. The organization of the primary process was, therefore, drive dependent. Rapaport has synthesized the elements of this drive dependence in these terms:

> Thus the primary organization of memories occurs around drives. All the memories organized around a drive, and dependent for their emergence in consciousness on drive-cathexis, are conceptualized as *drive-representations.* In this drive-organization of memories the following hold: (a) Any representation may stand for the drive; that is, the memory of any segment or aspect

of experience accrued in the periods of delay, and around the gratification, may emerge as an indicator of mounting drive-tension. (b) The characteristic of energies which makes for this extreme freedom of representation, and allows representations to be raised to hallucinatory vividness, is conceptualized as *"mobility" of cathexis.* The cathectic energy in a drive-organization of memory can freely move and center on any representation. (c) This free mobility is inferred from the observations which are conceptualized as the mechanisms of *displacement, condensation, substitution,* and so on. . . . (d) The thought processes based on drive-organizations of memory, and using cathexes which are freely displaceable and strive towards discharge in terms of "wishfulfillment," are conceptualized as the *"primary process."* The free displaceability is a corollary of the unrestrained tendency toward full discharge by the shortest path (wishfulfillment), which is the characteristic of the "mobile" drive-energies.[37]

Thus the quality of primary process thought derives from and represents the influence of instinctual drives and it is calculated to achieve immediate drive discharge and fulfillment of wishes.

Dream Research

It can be noted in passing that Freud's insight into the primary process was based essentially on his study of dreams. Dream research has undergone a revitalization in the last score of years. This resurgence of interest in dream processes has been occasioned particularly by the discovery of rapid eye movements and their measurable correlates. Aserinsky and Kleitman discovered in the early 1950's that there were regular bursts of active and rapid movements of the eyes during sleep. Further investigation has showed that these periods of so-called REM activity were associated with a higher percentage of dream recall and also that there were identifiable differences in the organization of mental activity during REM and non-REM (NREM) periods of sleep. This has suggested that the pattern of physiological activation associated with the REM periods—cortical desynchronization and hippocampal slow waves on the EEG, active extraocular muscle movements, respiratory and cardiovascular activation—represents a state of physiological arousal. The major difference from normal waking arousal is that the activation of voluntary muscle is inhibited at the same time.

These discoveries have given rise to active and elaborate research into the future of these varied sleep and dream states. They have also given rise to the realization that dreaming is a much more varied and complex activity than even Freud appreciated, suggesting that different states of physiological organization are related to different patterns of thought organization. It is possible that dreaming activity embraces a variety of patterns of cognitive organization which can be differentiated with the help of physical and physiological indicators that Freud did not have available. The possibilities are stimulating, and the findings will deepen and possibly alter much of our understanding about dreams, their nature and function. Even so, it is remarkable that Freud's descriptions of dream cognition and his basic insight into the primary and secondary organization of thought processes is not only still valid but forms one of the major bases for the ongoing research into dream processes and dream thought. What Freud described as dreaming may represent a variety of patterns of dream organization of which primary and secondary organizations represent polar types.

Pleasure vs. Reality

The account of mental processes which Freud gave in his 1911 paper on the two principles of mental functioning presents a somewhat simplified picture. In it, however, he explicitly connects the primary process with the operation of the pleasure principle and the secondary process with the operation of the reality principle. The primary process is envisioned as thinking which is governed only by the need for gratification without any consideration of reality, whereas the secondary process functions in relation to and in terms of the structure of reality. Freud also makes it clear that he is not merely giving an account of the organization of unconscious mental activity, but he also specifically relates such unconscious activity to infantile stages of psychic development. He contrasts such mental activity with the conscious mental life of the individual who has matured to the point where he can adapt to the demands of reality.

The pleasure principle is the first principle of mental functioning. It governs the operation of the primary process to bring about immediate and direct gratification of any impulse or wish as it arises. The gratification takes place without any regard for what might be happening in reality at the moment. Freud makes the implicit assumption that in the absence of a real satisfying object, the mind automatically provides a substitute satisfaction in the form of an hallucinated object. This represents the paradigm of primary process thinking. Whether the real object is present or not is not significant since, under the dominance of the pleasure principle, the impulse will find gratification by making use of any available mode of discharge. Thus, according to the paradigm, the hungry infant seeks for the breast which he associates with satisfaction and relief of his hunger. When the breast is not immediately available in reality, however, he gains an immediate, if substitute, satisfaction by hallucinating the breast. The peremptory demands of the infant's internal needs disturb his equilibrium and seek immediate satisfaction. Freud comments:

When this happened, whatever was thought of (wished for) was simply presented in a hallucinatory manner, just as still happens today with our dream-thoughts every night. It was only the non-occurrence of the expected satisfaction, the disappointment experienced, that led to the abandonment of this attempt at satisfaction by means of hallucination. Instead of it, the psychical apparatus had to decide to form a conception of the real circumstances in the external world and to endeavour to make a real alteration in them. A new principle of mental functioning was thus introduced; what was presented in the mind was no longer what was agreeable but what was real, even if it happened to be disagreeable. This setting-up of the *reality principle* proved to be a momentous step.[38]

The initiation of the reality principle, then, implies that the infant has begun to recognize that mere hallucination of the breast, whatever satisfaction may accompany that, will not appease his hunger pangs. Little by little, however, he begins to realize that there are available to him means by which he can modify reality and thus achieve real satisfaction —i.e., he can control his mother's availability by crying.

At the beginning of life such adaptive maneuvers are largely automatic. They are originally more reflex than conscious or reflective. The origins of the reality principle as Freud initially formulated it had to do with the time in the infant's developing experience when he begins to realize that certain maneuvers on his part can have an effect on his environment. When the gratifying object or condition is not present, he learns that certain forms of his own activity are followed by modifications of reality and real gratification of his inner needs and wishes. Thus, according to this formulation, the reality principle comes into play in the service of the pleasure principle. The infant realizes that hallucinatory gratification will not satisfy his needs and begins to make purposive efforts toward the goal of modifying reality. In the beginning his crying is more or less automatic and reflexive. But there comes a time when it becomes quite clear that the infant is crying in a purposive way in order to bring about a change in his environment—e.g., his mother's presence.

Primary Process and the Unconscious

Freud's discussion of the characteristics of these thought processes, both in the *Interpretation of Dreams* and in his 1911 paper, focuses on the differentiation between primary and secondary process. In describing primary process thinking he characterized it as involving vivid and concrete imagery. It recognizes no negatives. It knows no time. It readily finds substitute gratification by the use of displacement or symbol formation. It accepts the most immediate and direct path of gratification for any wish that may arise—even hallucinatory gratification where real gratification is unavailable. This extremely unrealistic and primitive form of thinking was contrasted with the more realistic thinking of the secondary process. Freud saw the primary process as finding expression in dreams and neurotic symptoms which tend to make use of mental processes which are far more primitive and archaic than more mature thought which takes consideration of reality into account. Thus it is the tendency of our conscious waking minds to introduce logical constructions, to explain and make sense out of dreams or symptomatic actions by imposing on them a logical and consistent ordering through the processes of secondary elaboration or rationalization.

Freud proposed, therefore, that the repressed unconscious was governed not by reality-oriented modes of thinking, but by primitive, primary process modes of organization and functioning. The combination of this premise with his discoveries relating to the content of the repressed unconscious material led to the conclusion that the content of the unconscious consisted of infantile wishes and fantasies. In addition, however, the quality of the thought processes governing these unconscious wishes is primitive and infantile when compared with secondary process thinking. The synthesis of these ideas really implied a developmental concept which reached beyond and included more than simply instinctual development. Freud wrote:

Among these wishful impulses derived from infancy, which can neither be destroyed nor inhibited, there are some whose fulfillment would be a contradiction of the purposive ideas of secondary thinking. The fulfillment of these wishes would no longer generate an affect of pleasure but of unpleasure; and *it is precisely this transformation of affect which constitutes the essence of what we term "repression."* The problem of repression lies in the question of how it is and owing to what motive forces that this transformation occurs. . . . It is enough for us to be clear that a transformation of this kind does occur in the course of development—we have only to recall the way in

which disgust emerges in childhood after having been absent to begin with
—and that it is related to the activity of the secondary system.[39]

Thus the development of repression was linked with the elaboration of
those noninstinctual aspects of psychic structure which allow for inhibition of instinctual discharge and transformation of the pleasur-
able/unpleasurable effects of such discharge under the influence of the
reality principle. The content of the unconscious, therefore, relates
to the undischarged infantile past, and the thought processes related
to them remain primitive and archaic in their organization.

Regression

In developing his ideas about the functioning of the mental apparatus,
Freud formulated a model which he used to explain his finding about
the dreaming process. He envisioned the mental apparatus as having a
sensory and a motor end. He reasoned that the psychic apparatus must
be built along the basic lines of a reflex model. Sensory input was introduced at the perceptual end of the apparatus and was then transcribed
into memory traces which were stored in mnemonic systems. The memory traces were linked with each other in patterns of association within
the memory or mnemonic systems. The perceptual system was entirely
without memory or associative capacity. It functioned merely in the
conscious reception of sensory input. The association and integration of
memory traces was carried out in the memory systems. Freud envisioned a series of such systems in which the memory traces were related
and integrated according to increasing complexity and in accordance
with increasingly logical patterns of organization. Thus the first mnemonic system would involve the association of traces only on the basis
of temporal simultaneity. Other memory systems would associate the
same perceptual content in terms of other patterns of coincidence; another system might record these traces in terms of relations of similarity; and so with other systems. As the memory systems became more
and more removed from the perceptual end of the apparatus, the organization of traces was more elaborate, more in accord with logical principles, and consequently more integrated in terms of secondary process
forms of organization.

The pattern of excitation within this organization of systems was normally from the sensory end toward the motor end where appropriate
discharge could be achieved. But in sleep, discharge from the motoric

elements of the apparatus was blocked. The discharge, therefore, moved in a retrograde direction toward the sensory end of the apparatus instead. Freud commented:

The only way in which we can describe what happens in hallucinatory dreams is by saying that the excitation moves in a *backward* direction. Instead of being transmitted towards the *motor* end of the apparatus it moves towards the *sensory* end and finally reaches the perceptual system. If we describe as "progressive" the direction taken by psychical processes arising from the unconscious during waking life, then we may speak of dreams as having a "regressive" character.[40]

Thus the movement, content, and organization of dream processes were regressive in character—and the regression was associated with the emergence of primary process forms of thinking which were linked with the pattern of organization of memory traces in the primary mnemonic systems. Freud goes on to say:

If we regard the process of dreaming as a regression occurring in our hypothetical mental apparatus, we at once arrive at the explanation of the empirically established fact that all the logical relations belonging to the dream-thoughts disappear during the dream activity or can only find expression with difficulty. According to our schematic picture, these relations are contained not in the *first Mnem.* systems but in *later* ones; and in case of regression they would necessarily lose any means of expression except in perceptual images. *In regression the fabric of the dream-thoughts is resolved into its raw material.*[41]

By the time the 1914 edition of the *Interpretation of Dreams* was published, Freud had elaborated his notion of regression and had delineated three types. He added the following paragraph in 1914:

It is further to be remarked that regression plays a no less important part in the theory of the formation of neurotic symptoms than it does in that of dreams. Three kinds of regression are thus to be distinguished: (a) *topographical* regression, in the sense of the schematic picture of the ψ-systems which we have explained above; (b) *temporal* regression, in so far as what is in question is harking back to older psychical structures; and (c) *formal* regression, where primitive methods of expression and representation take the place of the usual ones. All these three kinds of regression are, however, one at bottom and occur together as a rule; for what is older in time is more primitive in form and in psychical topography lies nearer to the perceptual end.[42]

All three forms were characteristic of dream formation. Topological regression referred to the fact that an impulse which in waking life might be expressed in thought or action is prevented from such expression during sleep. Consequently, the impulse undergoes a regressive change and appears in the disguised form of an hallucinatory gratification of the wish that has been aroused. The dream itself, therefore, is a form of sensory hallucination which serves the immediate gratification of wishes, and is therefore governed by the principles of primary process organization and the operation of the pleasure principle. The retrogressive movement toward the sensory end of the psychic apparatus also involves a shift from logical, reality-oriented thinking to a more primitive form of expression in terms of concrete imagery. The regression is, therefore, also formal.

Freud also saw the dream process as related to specifically developmental issues. The temporal aspect of regression—the fact that dream processes involved a regression to the use of psychic structures derived from an earlier level of development—underlined this aspect. Freud became more aware of this aspect as his concept of the developmental hypothesis became more differentiated. In the 1919 edition of the dream book, he observed:

Nor can we leave the subject of regression in dreams without setting down in words a notion by which we have already repeatedly been struck and which will recur with fresh intensity when we have entered more deeply into the study of the psychoneuroses: namely that dreaming is on the whole an example of regression to the dreamer's earliest condition, a revival of his childhood, of the instinctual impulses which dominated it and of the methods of expression which were then available to him.[43]

The wishes which were gratified in the manifest dream were wishes and fantasies of an infantile nature. They were contained in the repressed and unconscious part of the mind. The emergence of such wishes in the dream state involves a temporal regression to the mental state of early childhood. This implies not only a retention and carrying over of infantile wishes and fantasies to adult life, but also the persistent activity of such wishes within the unconscious. In sleep, particularly in the dreaming state, such wishes obtain partial discharge or disguised gratification due to the fact that one of the cardinal features of primary process thinking and infantile mental life is that symbolic substitutes or displaced objects can serve readily as surrogates for immediate gratification. A part may substitute for the whole; opposites may be accepted as having the same meaning.

Freud's instinct in turning to the study of dreams was a stroke of genius, for this pattern of mental functioning can be examined most clearly in the process by which the mind translates the underlying latent dream-thoughts into the manifest dream content. He was able to see that similar mechanisms were involved in symptom formation and in dream formation. The basic process involves repression, followed by the partial failure of repression and the return of the repressed. The censor—the repressing agency identified in the repression of dream-thoughts—is not altogether successful in its attempt to repress the infantile wish completely. Under certain conditions, the censor will allow expression and gratification of this partially unrepressed wish—but only in a disguised and distorted fashion. The wish achieves partial gratification and expression through the formation of an hysterical or phobic symptom.

This partial and disguised gratification of the underlying wish falls within the limits of the censor's permissible expression, since it does not permit direct gratification of the wish—which is repressed and therefore presumably dangerous or disagreeable in some fashion to the repressing agency. At the same time the censor allows a partial gratification of the wish by exploiting the capacity of the unconscious and the primary process to accept substitute objects. Both theories—symptom formation and dream formation—rely on the function of concrete, primary process thinking. The operation of the primary process is attributed to the regression from more abstract and reality-oriented thinking to the primitive seeking of immediate gratification by sensory experience.

The Relation of Primary and Secondary Process

In the *Interpretation of Dreams* Freud treated the differentiation between primary and secondary process as being rather sharp and mutually exclusive. In the treatment of dreams and also in his study of the psychopathology of everyday life (1905), he presented the primary process as characteristic of infantile levels of mental organization and as the predominant mode of thought in early development. The secondary process was seen as arising out of the primary process as a result of the bitter experience of the limitations of reality. The function of secondary process was thus conceived of as controlling, directing, limiting, delaying, and detouring thought processes as required by the impact of reality. Freud's interpretation of these shifts from primary to secondary process thinking seemed to rest simply on environmental factors.

Freud also viewed the progression from primary to secondary process thinking as taking place phylogenetically as well. Primitive thought was viewed as largely primary process. Some years later, however, in his

Totem and Taboo (1913), he turned to a more explicit examination of primitive experience. He saw the system of primitive taboos as operating to restrain the expression of instinctual sexual and aggressive forces. He explained this restraining force again by an appeal to historical and experiential factors—the murder of the father by the primal horde. Freud wondered at the time whether in making appeal again to an experiential and real factor he might not be making a mistake similar to his assuming the reality of infantile seduction. He saw the primitive mentality as functioning in a manner similar to the neurotic in its closeness to the unconscious and its tendency to use primary process. The analogy was not complete. Freud observed:

Nor must we let ourselves be influenced too far in our judgement of primitive men by the analogy of neurotics. There are distinctions, too, which must be borne in mind . . . neurotics are above all *inhibited* in their actions: with them the thought is a complete substitute for the deed. Primitive men, on the other hand, are *uninhibited:* thought passes directly into action. With them it is rather the deed that is a substitute for the thought. And that is why, without laying claim to any finality of judgement, I think that in the case before us it may safely be assumed that "in the beginning was the Deed." [44]

Despite this hypothetical appeal to experience as the basis out of which the restraining forces arose, Freud saw the animistic thought system of primitives as having a structure, organization, and coherence which was as logical and ordered as more civilized and developed thought. Moreover, the conception of secondary process organization he offered was somewhat different in emphasis. He wrote:

The secondary revision of the product of the dream-work is an admirable example of the nature and pretensions of a system. There is an intellectual function in us which demands unity, connection and intelligibility from any material, whether of perception or thought, that comes within its grasp; and if, as a result of special circumstances, it is unable to establish a true connection, it does not hesitate to fabricate a false one. Systems constructed in this way are known to us not only from dreams, but also from phobias, from obsessive thinking and from delusions.[45]

The notion of the secondary process, therefore, comes to include the idea of a unifying, connecting, and rationalizing synthetic function. The synthetic function emerges in this treatment as independent from the demands of both instinctual drives and external reality. It cannot be seen as merely a modification of primary process in terms of the demands of external reality. Consequently, Freud's earlier view that secondary process arose out of the primary process under the pressure of environmental demands and limitations was significantly modified. The secondary process not only was independent from both instincts and reality in its development but it followed its own intrinsic development, at least in part. Today we would conceptualize these matters by treating the secondary process and the synthetic function as relatively autonomous ego functions.

Today our thinking about primary and secondary process does not treat them as so sharply dichotomized or exclusive. The development of secondary process is seen much more in terms of the development of autonomous and conflict-free functions of the ego. The question is cast in terms of the development of these autonomous functions rather than in terms of their differentiation out of primary process functions. There is general recognition of a gradation of intermediate steps between the primary process thinking of infantile levels of development and the capacity for higher-level abstraction of the adult. The work of Piaget and other developmental psychologists seems to suggest that thought processes continue to mature until rather late in adolescence, and perhaps beyond. In addition, as we have suggested, we have a much greater awareness of the persistence and continued use of primary process thinking in adult life—and not necessarily in relation to primitive or infantile modes of thinking. Thus the view of primary and secondary process today is considerably more complex and nuanced than when Freud originally formulated them.

The sharp dichotomy that Freud originally made between the thought processes governing the conscious and preconscious parts of the mind and the primary process, which was thought to govern the unconscious, needs radical revision. There is now available a considerable amount of evidence to indicate that certain forms of regression and their associated primary process forms of mental operation are essential to a number of quite sophisticated and highly integrated mental functions. Kris has described some of these regressive constituents under the rubric "regression in the service of the ego." The basic idea is that regressive and primary process thought constituents may be utilized and integrated by the ego in the service of its creative or adaptive purposes. Many original and creative contributions in major areas of human endeavor—in the sciences and the arts—reveal the positive adaptive value of primary process thinking in the creative process.

Even so, despite the importance of understanding the manner in which primary and secondary process thinking can be integrated in various modalities of mental operation, the major differentiation between thought which is based on and oriented to reality considerations, and thought which basically ignores the existence of reality and responds to a drive-derived pattern of organization, remains fundamental. The capacity to test and accept reality and to tolerate the separateness of objects are major functions of the mature ego. Developmental failure in these respects are among the criteria for distinguishing between individuals who continue in their adult lives to live under the dominance of the pleasure principle and individuals whose thoughts and actions are based on a realistic assessment of available goals and means of action.

Adaptation

Considerable emphasis is laid in contemporary psychoanalytic thinking on the importance of adaptation. It is regarded as one of the major metapsychological assumptions of psychoanalytic theory. The assumption is often made that the capacity for adaptation is a function of the level of development of secondary process thinking. In his 1911 paper on mental functions, Freud observed:

This setting-up of the *reality principle* proved to be a momentous step. In the first place, the new demands made a succession of adaptations necessary in the psychical apparatus. . . .[46]

It is frequently assumed that adaptation was only introduced as a primary attribute of mental functions by Hartmann in his *Ego Psychology and the Problem of Adaptation*.[47] But it is clear that Freud not only used the term "adaptation" but that it was implicit in many of his formulations. In the dream book, for example, he made many statements which imply that psychic development included changes which were adaptive in nature.

Freud also dealt with the emergence of secondary process in implicitly adaptive terms. He wrote:

Restraint upon motor discharge (upon action), which then became necessary [due to reality demands], was provided by means of the process of *thinking*, which was developed from the presentation of ideas. Thinking was endowed with characteristics which made it possible for the mental apparatus to tolerate an increased tension of stimulus while the process of discharge was postponed. It is essentially an experimental kind of acting, accompanied by displacement of relatively small quantities of cathexis together with less expenditure (discharge) of them. For this purpose the conversion of freely displaceable cathexes into "bound" cathexes was necessary, and this was brought about by means of raising the level of the whole cathectic process.[48]

This implies that the capacity to delay action and hold an impulse without discharge is a necessary attribute for adaptive thought and action. These statements, taken in conjunction, imply that the mental apparatus develops some structural capacity in the service of adaptive mastery.

The Structural Integration

The structure implied in these formulations does not simply correspond with the concept of the ego which Freud was later to describe in *The Ego and the Id* (1923) and later papers. It does, however, conform to the more general definition of psychic structure proposed by Rapaport. The latter has suggested that a differentiation can be made between mental energy and mental structure. Mental energy as such is free-floating, rapidly shifting, tending to immediate discharge and displacement. It is under the dominance of primary process. Mental structure, however, is characterized by a capacity for the restraint, delay, and direction of discharge, maintenance of tension over time without discharge, and particularly by a relatively slow rate of change. Psychic structures, therefore, can remain relatively permanent and stable over considerable periods of time. According to Rapaport's view, whatever changes slowly and is subject to delay of discharge has structural attributes. It is not clear that this statement of what constitutes structure is adequate. We may have to include some notion of organization and ordering of parts and functions. But this notion of structure neither implies rigid and unchanging permanency, nor does it make any clear differentiation between that part of structure which is conscious and in touch with external reality and that part which remains unconscious. It refers mainly to the fact that some parts of the mental apparatus are able to impose delay or provide constancy to responses which have more or less permanent characteristics for each individual.

Freud's earlier thinking about both structure and levels of consciousness was dominated by his primarily topographical orientation, focusing on the relation of mental processes and functions to consciousness. The structural attributes of the mental apparatus were thus treated almost synonymously with the conscious and preconscious parts of the mind, which employed secondary process thinking. Thus conscious thought organization was contrasted with and differentiated from the free-floating fantasy and primitive thought processes which seemed to characterize the unconscious derivatives. Consequently, in Freud's early thinking the unconscious and the unstructured were regarded as for all practical purposes identical. The structural part of the mind was conceived as deriving its energy from self-preservative instincts. These same instincts were also responsible for maintaining repression and the other defenses. The censor or repressing agency was, therefore, considered to belong to the conscious-preconscious system and was consequently relatively available to conscious introspection.

It was only gradually and in the light of accumulating experience of his patients' clinical resistance that Freud came to realize that the repressing agency was for the most part unconscious. Freud found, for example, that many of his patients would try consciously to cooperate in the work of analysis but would in fact put up strong resistances. Such patients could not understand what or why they were resisting. Thus the clinical evidence gradually mounted to support the conclusion that repression and the related defenses were just as unconscious as the repressed content against which they were directed. In other words, Freud came to recognize that structure and the conscious-preconscious parts of the mind were not necessarily synonymous. He gradually came to realize that he could no longer maintain his earlier dichotomy between the conscious-preconscious parts of the mind as structured and the unconscious as devoid of structural attributes.

As we have previously indicated, our understanding of the organization of cognitive processes would no longer allow us to maintain the assumption that primary process thinking is restricted to the unconscious operations of the mind. We can recognize that primary process thinking plays an important role not only in preconscious thought processes, but that it also plays an important part in conscious thought—in daydreams and reveries, for example. But more importantly, we have become aware of the integration of primary process thinking with forms of secondary process in the more creative and imaginative aspects of scientific and artistic work. For these reasons Freud had to abandon his topographical view of the organization of the mental apparatus. He was forced to review and reconstruct his model of the mind and its structure. The result was the development of the structural hypothesis and the formulation of the structural theory of mental organization and functioning.

[8]

Narcissism and Its Developments: Toward a Structural Theory

Our discussion of Freud's treatment of thought processes in the preceding chapter focused particularly on the developmental aspects of his thinking and on the differentiation of primary and secondary process. We discussed the relation between primary process and the pleasure principle and secondary process and the reality principle. Freud associated primary process with freely mobile and displaceable energies, while secondary process was associated more with bound energy in the form of relatively permanent psychic structures. Thus, for a considerable period in his thinking the unconscious part of the mind was considered to be completely unstructured, and as such was sharply differentiated from the conscious-preconscious part of the mind which was associated with structure.

The Unconscious As Structured

The dichotomy remained sharply drawn and persisted for a long time. Only gradually did Freud come to realize that this radical schism could not be maintained. Not only did his clinical findings force him to recognize that some parts of the unconscious mind had structural attributes, but he also came to see that primary process thinking and organization was not confined to unconsciously driven behaviors like dreams, neurotic symptoms, or the slips and errors that constituted the psychopathology of everyday life. The clinical evidence suggested that not only was the repressed content unconscious, but that the repressing agency was also in part unconscious. It was not, as Freud had originally postulated, totally derived from the conscious and preconscious levels of the mind. Rather the agencies which stimulated and maintained repression and its related defenses were often just as unconscious as the repressed wishes themselves.

Narcissism in the Psychoses

The gradual realization that the unconscious also contained structural aspects and attributes came in relation to a number of other observations, and led Freud to make a number of significant alterations in his thinking about the mental apparatus. He was forced to make fundamental changes in his basic model of the psychic function and also in his basic thinking about human instinctual life. Some of the parallel observations that bore a significant influence on Freud's thinking had to do with the understanding of psychotic mental disorders. Freud had followed out and extended Hughlings Jackson's famous dictum that the understanding of insanity lies in the discovery of the secret of dreams. Freud's discoveries of the nature of dreaming and the primary process inevitably stimulated his interest in the disordered thought processes of psychotic states. He thought of psychotic thinking as a kind of "waking dreaming." But his experience with psychosis was limited. He was not really trained as a psychiatrist; his basic training was in neurology and related sciences. He himself seems to have had very limited exposure to psychotic patients. His most important work on psychosis, in which he boldly applied his theories developed out of his work with neurotics to psychosis, was not even based on direct contact with clinical material or knowledge of the patient clinically. It was based on his reading of a most remarkable document, the *Memoirs* of Daniel Paul Schreber. Schreber was a distinguished jurist and a man of high intelligence who suffered a psychotic state from which he never really fully recovered. Despite his malaise, he was able to write an account of his illness and the delusions and hallucinations that formed the content of it. Freud's analysis of the Schreber case is perhaps the most famous and most influential analysis of a case of psychosis—probably a severe and chronic paranoid schizophrenia—in the history of psychiatry. It is remarkable that it was written by a man who never knew the patient and who had so little experience with mental derangements of this sort.

Other figures in the early psychoanalytic movement, however, did bring to their understanding of psychotic processes a considerable amount of experience. Jung was one of the first to bring to the psychoanalytic movement a rich experience which he gained in Bleuler's clinic. By the time the psychoanalytic movement was formally initiated in 1908, a number of analysts were busily engaged in psychiatric work with seriously ill patients. Among them the names of Abraham, Ferenczi, and Ernest Jones stand out—they were all actively engaged in treating psychotic patients as well as pursuing the psychoanalytic treatment of neurotics. The major pioneer in the application of psychoanalytic understanding to the psychoses was Karl Abraham. His original paper on the differentiation between dementia praecox and hysteria is a classic treatment. His work on the understanding and treatment of manic-depressive psychoses was a pioneer effort in the application of analytic understanding to patients who have suffered overt psychotic episodes.

The observations that these men made in their examination of psychotic patients were of considerable importance. The first observation that was made—a mistaken observation as subsequent experience has demonstrated—was that psychotic patients did not seem capable of developing a transference to the therapist. Certainly it was clear—and this is a valid observation—that psychotic patients do not establish the same sort of transference that one finds in neurotic patients. We know now that psychotic patients do, in fact, establish transferences which are often quite intense. But when these early observations were made, it was thought that the apparent lack of transference reflected the patient's inability to cathect objects. Abraham observed in his descriptions of the differences between dementia praecox and hysteria that the capacity for relating to other human beings seemed to be absent in these psychotic patients. He felt that the sexual interests, which in nonpsychotic patients were directed to objects outside of themselves, seemed in these patients to be directed toward the self. The psychotic withdrawal was seen as a witholding of cathexis from objects and a turning of it toward the self. The self was the object of libidinal investment and not objects in the patient's environment.

Freud also observed that in certain patients who were prepsychotic or in patients whom we would describe today as borderline there was detectable a division in their minds, as though one part of their mind were able to talk to another part. This did not seem to have a gross hallucinatory quality, but Freud felt that it might represent a possible condition which was a precursor of a delusional or hallucinatory state. It was as if one part of the mind were standing aside and observing and commenting on what the other part was doing. Freud also saw that what he observed in this rather gross and manifest form in these relatively disturbed patients was not terribly different from what was observable in the operation of conscience in neurotic and more normal patients. In the operation of conscience, too, there is an implicit sort of communication of one part of the mind telling the other part what it ought to think or do, or presenting it with prohibitions of one or other kind.

War Neuroses

Thus, these original and pioneering observations led to two important conclusions: first, that in these more disturbed states there was a withdrawal of interest or libido from external objects to the self, and second, that there was some sort of structure within the mind which was somehow separated from the rest of the mind and could direct orders and prohibitions to this remainder. All this had come to light before World War I. During the war years the analytic movement was interrupted and communication among analysts was negligible. During the war, however, analysts were naturally enlisted in the study and treatment of war neuroses. Freud, Abraham, Ferenczi, Jones, Eder, and others all made individual and separate contributions to the understanding and treatment of such neuroses. When the war was over, they had the opportunity to begin to compare their findings and conclusions. They found that their results and their conclusions showed a remarkable similarity. The conclusions—arrived at disparately and individually—were quite compatible.

The compatibility of these conclusions not only offered a form of confirmation of the validity of the analytic approach (as we have previously noted), but it led to some important conclusions about the nature and function of the mental apparatus. Working independently, these analysts all agreed that they could not explain their clinical findings on the basis of a conflict between a conscious-preconscious self-preservative instinct on one hand and unconscious object-directed sexual instincts on the other. This dichotomy had formed the basic instinct theory which Freud had originally postulated and which had formed the basis for much of his early thinking. The distinction between self-preservative ego instincts and sexual instincts could no longer be supported. A hint of this difficulty with Freud's dual instinct theory had already been seen in the conclusions about psychotic patients, but it was underlined by the conclusions from the study of war neuroses. We shall return to this point.

The study of the war neuroses revealed the important finding that the major threat which led to the more serious and relatively irreversible disturbances was not the mere fact of being put in a situation in which the loss of one's life became an imminent possibility. The realistic danger to one's life was not sufficient by itself to produce a war neurosis. If that had been the case, we might have expected every soldier who was put in a situation of extreme danger to develop a war neurosis. But such was not the case. One might also have expected that individuals whose prewar personality functioning was relatively neurotic and immature might be expected to be the ones to develop severe and irreversible disturbances. But this also did not turn out to be the case. What seemed in fact to underlie the development of the more severe and difficult cases of war neurosis was that the threatening condition had to do with damage or injury to the individual's self-image, rather than a threat to life itself. These individuals suffered more severe disruption from the threat to their narcissistic image of themselves than they did from a direct threat to their lives. The threat to the self-image, it seemed, could include a disruption and altering of the body image, as in cases where maiming or loss of bodily integrity was closely related to the individual's image of himself as healthy, whole, well-functioning, physically attractive, etc. But it could also include the inner psychological threat to the image of oneself as strong, brave, courageous, able to stand up to and resist any stress or danger.

These empirical observations made at first in the first war were further confirmed a generation later in World War II. To the surprise of many analysts working with the armed forces and dealing with war neuroses, soldiers with known histories of manifest anxiety and/or phobic symptoms seldom, if ever, developed the relatively severe and irreversible form of war neurosis which had been studied extensively in the years between the two great conflicts. They did indeed develop symptoms of anxiety, exhaustion, and tremulousness. Many of them suffered battlefield breakdowns, many came to the attention of military psychiatrists and were even admitted to military psychiatric centers. In general, however, such cases showed a rapid and often remarkable capacity for reconstituion; they were frequently able to return to active duty in a short period of time, and more importantly did not experience any serious impairment of self-esteem or of their capacity to relate meaningfully to others.

There were also a number of patients in the World War II group of war neuroses who resembled a group that had been described by Kardiner in his study of World War I cases. These were patients who developed chronic and irreversible war neuroses. Typically they presented a premorbid history which seemed to be far more normal than the patients we described above. They were often regarded both by themselves and others who knew them fairly well as stable, resourceful, courageous, and well-adjusted people. They frequently were found to have volunteered for active service without any anxiety about the probable dangers or their capacity to handle themselves under such stress. In the actual situation many of them broke down under conditions of minimal stress. Although they usually recovered quickly from their acute anxiety, they were unable to reconstitute their previous self-image. The self-image had been in effect shattered. These men were individuals whose self-esteem had been contingent on the image of themselves as brave, fearless, and capable of taking any amount of stress or danger. The experience of manifest fear and/or anxiety had impaired their self-image to a degree that proved irreversible and resistant to treatment.

Narcissistic Libido

To return to the significance of these findings for the problem of narcissism, Freud had already determined that in the neurotic process sexual instincts were basically directed toward objects. Because of repression, however, the sexual instinct might be dammed up and thus displaced from current objects. The libido that is displaced from objects is not then attached to the self—as it would be in Freud's conception of psychotic withdrawal. In the process of neurotic symptom formation, the libido is displaced to fantasies and wishes having to do with infantile objects. Object investment thus remained a crucial aspect of the neurotic process in terms of fantasy and memory. The investment of libido in past objects which characterizes neurotic patients creates a situation in which they are able during the course of treatment to reinvest their libido and attach it to the analyst as a substitute object or displacement for the original infantile object of libidinal attachment. This is the basic mechanism of transference. Freud's view was that the attachment of libido to the self was such that reattachment and reinvestment in the analyst as an object was impossible or very difficult. He concluded, therefore, that psychotics were incapable of forming a transference neurosis.

Freud's definition of neurosis was not really contradicted by the new conclusions that were arrived at as a result of these findings. Nonetheless, observations of both the psychoses and the war neuroses suggested that even in healthy states or in states of neurotic adjustment there was a measure of libido which remains attached to the self. In our contemporary view of narcissism, we would describe this degree of self-directed libido as a necessary component of adequate self-esteem and a secure self-image. There are, however, pathological degrees of narcissism, as we shall see. One of the difficulties with the concept of narcissism in contemporary psychoanalytic usage is that it has come to be used for a variety of things which may not, in fact, be compatible with each other. A critical question is whether the original meaning in terms of libidinal investment of the self and what we regard as self-esteem are really compatible notions.

In the consideration of narcissism it is important to keep in mind the developmental perspective which was associated with Freud's use of the term. He suggested that the self was the object of libidinal investment at birth and that only very gradually through the course of normal development does the individual attain a capacity for object love. If we put this assumption in the context of pathological regression, we can distinguish several levels. Regression may occur to a limited extent to a level merely of the loss of adult object relations. Or it may occur in a more severe fashion and proceed to an even earlier level of development, a level in which libidinal investment in objects had not yet been attained at all. Regression can thus be evaluated in terms of the degree of capacity for libidinal investment in objects. It may return only to a relatively less mature condition in which the investment in objects is in a sense compromised but not terminated. In the more severe regressions, however, it may return to a level before the investment in objects was a developmental possibility, before the differentiation between subject and object itself had been achieved. From this perspective, the psychoses and probably some of the more severe traumatic neuroses serve as examples of regression in which a considerable amount of libido has been withdrawn from objects and reinvested in the self. The regression, however, in these cases is to a relatively primitive level. In Freud's developmental perspective, then, narcissistic libido undergoes a development which involves a gradual mobilization of libido which is originally invested in the self and passes through stages of direction to objects outside the self. The stages of libidinal development and the organization of libido as object-directed becomes sequentially organized around certain bodily zones and organ constellations in conjunction with the physical and physiological maturation of the body. Thus the stages of libidinal development and of object relatedness can be formulated in terms of oral, anal, and later genital patterns.

The idea of investment of libido in the self does not imply that sexual feelings and fantasies about others can be discharged in the form of autoerotic activity. The concept is more abstract. It implies rather that all instincts, and particularly the sexual or libidinal instinct, are not directed externally toward objects at all at the beginning of life. At the beginning of the child's life experience, there are no objects. He has yet to reach a stage of his cognitive development in which the differentiation between himself and objects around him which are separate from him can be appreciated. Without a differentiation between self and objects, between self and nonself, any libidinal investment in objects is out of the question. Libido is rather invested in the self—or perhaps better it is held within the self. This original possession and self-investment of libido Freud described as "primary narcissism." It is only as the infant becomes aware of objects around him as separate and different from himself that he can begin to direct some of the libido to them. Freud conceived of this fund of primary narcissism as being turned to object libido by directing it toward objects—like an amoeba reaching out its pseudopodia to touch and engulf objects around it. Like the pseudopodia, libido once directed to objects could be withdrawn and taken back into the body of narcissistic libido. Object libido can be reinvested in the self and thus return to a condition akin to primary narcissism. Freud believed that this was clinically observable in conditions of physical illness, in the psychoses, as well as certain other conditions of external and internal stress.

The significance of the maintenance of self-esteem for the capacity of soldiers to recover and restore their ability to function in the face of life-endangering stress and anxiety seems to suggest that a stable self-image and basic self-esteem serve as healthy factors in the adaptive functioning of the personality. In simple terms, the individual who does not maintain respect and esteem for himself is impaired in his capacity to relate to others and in his ability to tolerate stress. In more technical terms, the loss of healthy and appropriate self-esteem leads to a withdrawal of object-directed interest and a preoccupation with self. This pattern of withdrawal and self-preoccupation is a common phenomenon in individuals who are subjected to some form of physical illness. The patient seems to withdraw, lose interest in the affairs of the world, becomes increasingly dependent on others and often demanding, and often becomes quite preoccupied with his illness and even his slightest symptoms. Similar withdrawal and self-preoccupation was also characteristic of those war neurotics who had previously maintained a rather high level of functioning in their relationships with others—prior to their encountering the stressful situation. Such patients manifest a form of narcissistic withdrawal which involves a detachment of libido from objects and a consequent impairment of object relations and a temporary reinvestment of libido in themselves. In Freud's view of the infantile investment of libido in the self (primary narcissism), the increased narcissism and libidinal investment of self seen in physical illness or war neurosis was a form of regression to an earlier developmental level of libidinal organization.

Evolution of Instinct Theory

The development of the idea of narcissism and the clinical evidence which related to it also led Freud to question his original instinct theory. He had originally postulated a dual set of instincts: the sexual instincts and the self-preservative instincts. He had explained inner psychic conflict in terms of the opposition and contrary aims of these sets of instincts. The question of where to put the narcissistic libido forced itself on him. Was it to be included under the sexual instincts? If so, what did it mean to have sexual instinct directed to the self? Was it to be regarded among the ego instincts? If so, what did it have to do with self-preservation? The whole idea of narcissistic libido raised a number of complex and difficult problems. It became difficult to maintain the dual instinct theory, at least in its original form.

Here too other observations of the war neuroses played an important part. Up until the time of the end of World War I, Freud had maintained his theory of the dream as a wish fulfillment despite some serious difficulties. There was difficulty in explaining certain anxiety dreams and dreams in which an instinctual wish was difficult to elicit on the basis of wish fulfillment. A particular difficulty was raised by the repetitive dreams reported by patients suffering from traumatic neuroses. In many cases of war neurosis, there was frequently a recurrent dreaming of traumatic and terrifying situations. In these frightening dreams the patient would typically re-experience the actual trauma again and again without any significant modification or lessening of the traumatic affect. How could one explain this recurrent dreaming of an extremely painful and traumatic experience on the basis of the dream serving as a wish fulfillment? Freud came to the conclusion that these dreams represented an exception to the theory of wish fulfillment. Instead of abandoning the theory of wish fulfillment, however, he began to consider such recurrent and repetitive dreaming in relation to a number of other empirical observations.

In *Beyond the Pleasure Principle* (1920), Freud called attention to the behavior of a young child during periods when his mother was absent. The child of one-and-a-half years was in the habit of throwing his toys away with an expression of interest and satisfaction. He developed a little game of throwing a reel with a string attached to it over the edge of his cot so that it disappeared. He would then retrieve it by pulling on the string and recovering it with obvious delight. The entire game—disappearance and return—was played out again and again in untiring repetition. Freud speculated that the child was rehearsing the painful absence of the mother in this little game and that he had turned the situation of passive and painful loss into a situation of active control which had a pleasurable outcome—the return of the reel and, by displacement, the return of the mother. The child transforms the passivity of his experience into the activity of the game, and works out the mastery of his disappointment in the repetition of the activity.

Freud related the repetition of traumatic dreams and the repetition of elements of loss in the play of children to certain observations in his neurotic patients. He observed that many of his patients would continue to repeat certain neurotic patterns of behavior even after adequate interpretation and insight into the nature of their behavior. He concluded that there was some force motivating and driving this repetitious behavior which could not be simply reduced to the functioning of the pleasure principle. He was thus led to modify his theory of instinct. He moved into a realm of theorizing about highly speculative biological principles which went far beyond the empirical observations that were available to him. He postulated that there was in human beings a fundamental tendency to return to a previous state of rest, ultimately to a state of complete quietude and cessation of all activity—death. Thus he was led to formulate the concept of the death instinct. He tried to explain these repetitive and painful phenomena as due to a repetition compulsion which was ultimately due to the operation of the hypothesized death wish.

Freud's instinct theory had gone through a gradual evolution over the years. The original theory had postulated two sets of instincts—sexual and self-preservative ego instincts—as we have seen. The introduction of the concept of narcissism was the first break in this dual instinct formulation. It introduced a libidinal component into the ego instincts, so that the neat dichotomy of libidinal versus ego instincts could no longer be maintained. But Freud held on to the idea of nonlibidinal ego interests, thus maintaining a certain content for the "ego instincts" but remaining rather noncommittal as to their nature.

A further problem that gradually emerged in the consideration of the instincts was aggression. Aggression had originally been grouped under the ego instincts. Freud's thinking was set in the context of love and hate, where love was conceived in terms of libidinal factors and hate was regarded as a nonlibidinal component of the ego and thus one of the ego instincts. It was only after the formulation of the structural viewpoint and the conception of the ego and superego as separate from the id that Freud was able to revise his view of aggression as an instinct. Aggression could then be seen not as belonging to the so-called ego instincts, but as representing a dynamic component of the vital stratum of the mind which was the repository for instinctual drives. Aggression, therefore, took its place finally as an independently existing instinct of destruction existing along with the sexual instincts in the id. Consequently, the ego instincts ceased to have any independent existence and were seen as deriving from both sexual and aggressive drives.

The result of this segregation of aggression was that the ego was now more clearly seen as having to struggle with and control aggressive impulses. Freud was also taken up with the related problem of guilt and masochism. Aggression, it seemed, could be channeled outward in various forms of hate and destructiveness directed against objects. But in masochism and various manifestations of depression and guilt, it seemed that destructive impulses were being directed against the self. In a way parallel to libidinal impulses, it seemed that aggressive impulses could be directed to objects or directed to the self. Arguing on the analogy of narcissism Freud raised the question of a primary destructiveness—a sort of primary masochism as an analogue to primary narcissism. The clinical phenomena, which did not seem adequately explained by postulating that aggression was turned against the self (how could one understand such a self-destructive wish?), and the methodological pressure to find a parallel to the libidinal theory prompted Freud to assume a self-destructive drive that was somehow operative primarily within the self. The parallels to narcissism were then complete. The aggression directed to objects derived from the primary destructiveness just as object-libido derived from primary narcissism. Moreover, secondary destructiveness or the redirection of aggression against the self (via the superego) was parallel to secondary narcissism in which the libido once attached to objects was reinvested in the self.

From these speculations and formulations, it was only a small step that was required to arrive at the postulation of a more general and abstract set of basic principles which would offer an explanation for these observations and the existence of the postulated primary instincts. In so doing Freud stepped beyond the limits of psychology into an area of biological speculation. He postulated the existence of primal and underived instincts of life and death. In considering his concept of these primal instincts, it is important to distinguish between the abstract biological speculation and the stimulus it provided for his own thought and that of succeeding analysts about instinctual life. The argument over the death instinct has had a certain heuristic value in that it has focused psychoanalytic attention on aggression as a persistent problem in human behavior.

There are still a great many unresolved problems in psychoanalytic attempts to understand human instinctual life and the way in which instincts influence behavior. One of the persistent and unresolved problems involves the nature and extent of native instinctual endowment—in terms of both aggressive and libidinal instincts—and how that might influence the subsequent course of development and the ultimate functioning of the personality. We have gained some understanding of the degree and manner in which instinctual development, both libidinal and aggressive, is modified and directed by the influence of experience. One of the most important periods during which such influences appear to be active is infancy, but it is precisely this period of development that is least accessible to clinical understanding. We are also in need of better understanding of the relationship between primitive sexual and aggressive instincts and the modifications of instinctual energies in the form of neutralization of energies or the binding of energies in relation to structure formation. Such processes modify the availability and channeling of basic psychic energies for more adaptive and conflict-free mobilization in the service of ego functions.

Thus many questions remain unresolved and highly controversial even at present. The important movement, for our purposes here, is that the original instinctual theory of sexual vs. self-preservative instincts was modified and replaced by the theory of primal instincts—the life instincts and the death instincts. Freud regarded these primal instincts as present from birth, as rooted in the basic biology of the organism and vital processes, and as located within the totally unconscious vital stratum of the mind. He separated this vital stratum from the structural parts of the mental apparatus and regarded it as the reservoir of pure instinctual drive energy—the "id." According to his first descriptions of the id which he proposed in *The Ego and the Id* (1923), Freud envisioned the psychic organization at birth as consisting of more or less undifferentiated instinctual energies which were possessed within and directed toward the self. The structural aspects of psychic organization—the ego and the superego—were thus viewed as parts of the id which had been modified as a result of contact with reality. According to this point of view, all mental energy was derived from id (instinctual) energies and there was a tendency, as we have observed already, to regard the development of ego and superego almost exclusively in experiential terms. Thus the structural organization of the mental apparatus was regarded as essentially derivative from or a by-product of the id.

Development of the Superego Concept

As we will see, Freud later modified this view, returning more or less to the positon he had outlined in the 1911 paper on the principles of mental functioning. There, as we noted in the discussion of the developmental hypothesis (see Chapter 6), he made a conceptual differentiation between instinctual development and ego development. He foresaw the possibility that the predisposition to later mental illness might be influenced by impairment in either instinctual or ego development or both. At the time, however, even when he had arrived at his structural model of the psychic apparatus, he gave considerably less weight and emphasis to the development, structure, and function of the ego than we do today. The structured part of the mind to which he gave the greatest emphasis and which he felt to be the most important in understanding psychopathology was the superego. The title of the book in which the structural hypothesis was introduced, *The Ego and the Id,* was misleading; it is really substantially a book about the superego, its origins and functions. At this point in the history of psychoanalysis, the id and the superego were attributed far more importance than the ego, which was included merely as a part of the mind which was responsible for direct contact with the outside environment and was the organ of consciousness.

The development of Freud's notion of the superego came through two important concerns in his work. The first was the problem of narcissism and the second was the problem of mourning. Both of these considerations contributed to the emergence of his ideas on the nature, formation, and functioning of the superego. In his seminal paper on narcissism in 1914, Freud formulated his thoughts about narcissism for the first time. He offered the suggestion that narcissism was modified in the course of development to provide certain structured parts of the mind. He started again from the fact of repression. He observed that an individual will repress instinctual impulses and wishes only if they are in conflict with his own ethical ideas and ideals. Such ideals, in fact, seemed to be a necessary prerequisite for repression. Freud speaks of the "self-respect of the ego." Repression flows from the self-respect of the ego in the sense that impulses become threatening and give rise to anxiety as a signal of danger insofar as they violate an ideal which the individual has set up in himself by which he measures his own actual ego. Content which is not consistent with the ideal is thus repressed.

The ideal which is thus set up in the ego embodies all the feelings of self-love and perfection which the individual felt himself to possess as a child. The child's narcissism is built into this ideal. Freud writes:

The ideal ego is now the target of the self-love which was enjoyed in childhood by the actual ego. The subject's narcissism makes its appearance displaced on to this new ideal ego, which, like the infantile ego, finds itself possessed of every perfection that is of value. As always where the libido is concerned, man has here again shown himself incapable of giving up a satisfaction he had once enjoyed. He is not willing to forgo the narcissistic perfection of his childhood; and when, as he grows up, he is disturbed by the admonitions of others and by the awakening of his own critical judgement, so that he can no longer retain that perfection, he seeks to recover it in the new form of an ego ideal. What he projects before him as his ideal is the substitute for the lost narcissism of his childhood in which he was his own ideal.[49]

If the individual can conform to the demands of this ideal, to that extent he regains some measure of his earlier narcissistic perfection and gratification.

Freud also suggests that since the observing of the ego ideal is so important for regaining lost narcissism, there must be a special psychic agency whose function it is to see to it that narcissistic satisfaction from the ego ideal is ensured. Such an agency would have the capacity to observe the real ego and to compare its behavior and functioning with the ideal standard in the ego ideal. Freud observes that such an intrapsychic agency, whose function was observation and comparison of the ego, would explain the common paranoid delusion of being watched. The ego would in fact be under observation not of a real external observer but of an internal observer which is delusionally projected. Such an internal observer is found in normal life as well as in the conscience. He also identified this internal observer and self-critical agency with the dream censor which carries out the work of repression in dream activity.

Thus, Freud envisioned the formation of the ego ideal as an important step in the development of the ego. It consisted essentially in a departure from the state of the infant's original primary narcissism and a subsequent attempt to recover that lost narcissism. The ideal is imposed from without, through the criticism, prohibitions, and teaching of parents, and these ideals and standards derived from parents are reinforced and sometimes modified by later learning and education. The libido of the original narcissism is displaced to the ideal and recovery of narcissistic satisfaction is achieved by fulfilling the ideal.

The important points in this consideration are that Freud viewed the development of ego ideal as a derivative of primary narcissism and that this process gave rise to another structural component of the mental apparatus. In his original formulations he did not distinguish clearly between these structural derivatives of narcissistic libido and the ego as such. But the process of formation and narcissistic investment of the ego ideal clearly gave rise to a split in the ego and produced a new structure. The relationship between the ego ideal and the repressing agency—the agency of observation and censorship—was also unclear at this point. What was clear, however, was that the splitting of the ego by which these new structures arose was related to the displacement and reinvestment of narcissistic libido.

Mourning and the Mechanisms of Internalization

The next important step in the development of Freud's ideas came in relation to his attempts to understand mourning and depression. His classic paper on this subject was "Mourning and Melancholia." It was not published until 1917, but it is clear that he had worked out some of the basic ideas even before he finished the paper on narcissism in 1914. These two important developments of his thinking, therefore, must be seen as emerging hand in hand.

In this paper Freud draws a distinction between mourning, which is depression due to the loss of an object, and melancholy, which is depression over a sense of worthlessness of the self. Freud saw this self-depreciation of melancholy as representing attacks on the self. These self-attacks were really substitutes for attacks on an object and symbolized such attacks. The attacks were effectively turned against the self by a taking of the lost object into the self so that the attack on the object became an attack against the object-as-self, as a part of the inner organization of the self. Thus object loss is translated into ego loss. There takes place a reconstruction of the object and its setting up in the self by means of identification. Thus the ego becomes the object, and the libido is reattached to the ego by the process of narcissistic identification. Freud puts it graphically: "Thus the shadow of the object fell upon the ego . . ." [50]

By this redirection of libido and narcissistic identification, the object is taken into the ego and becomes a structural part of the internal organization of the latter. Thus the external conflicts that obtained between the ego and the external object now become internal conflicts within the ego between the ego and a split-off portion of the mind. The result, of course, was that aggressive components that were inherent in the original ambivalent relation to the object became intrapsychic aggressions directed against the incorporated object. In this way, Freud tried to explain the attacks against the self which were so characteristic of melancholy.

Freud commented: "We see how in him one part of the ego sets itself over against the other, judges it critically, and, as it were, takes it as its object." [51] The self-reproaches replace reproaches which belong to the lost libidinal object. The narcissistic identification allows for aggressive discharge without a direct attack on the hated/loved object. Writing soon after in the *Introductory Lectures* (1917), Freud observes:

From this we can conclude that the melancholic has, it is true, withdrawn his libido from the object, but that, by a process which we must call "narcissistic identification," the object has been set up in the ego itself, has been, as it were, projected onto the ego. . . . The subject's own ego is then treated like the object that has been abandoned, and it is subjected to all the acts of aggression and expressions of vengefulness which have been aimed at the object. [52]

The split-off portion of the mind which directs this attack against the self was the precursor of Freud's notion of the superego. The result of his consideration of melancholia was that the mental structure that he had envisioned in his earlier consideration of narcissism became more clearly defined as the responsible agency for depression and guilt. The basic elements for his understanding of the superego were thus provided by the conjunction of his thinking about both narcissism and depression.

The Superego As Structure

These currents were not brought into clear focus until 1923 when Freud finally proposed his structural theory. He saw the superego—as he had seen the ego ideal—as a structural modification, a split-off portion of the ego. The superego was a structural precipitate within the ego which came about as a result of the resolution of the oedipal situation. The mechanism for this internal modification by which parts of the oedipal parents were taken in to form the superego was the same one which Freud had defined in the analysis of mourning—narcissistic identification. The superego thus becomes the primary agency for resolving the oedipal conflicts which dominate the genital period of development— the love for the parent of the opposite sex—and the correlative of morality and ethical standards. It was not clear in Freud's own presentation of his thinking what the relation of superego to ego ideal might be. It was not clear whether the superego replaced the ego ideal in whole or in part, or whether he still regarded them as separate entities. The ambiguity still persists in contemporary thinking about these parts of the mind.

The superego, in any case, represented the child's relations with his parents, both real and fantasied. It incorporated their standards of behavior, their prohibitions and moral directives. The superego judges, observes, criticizes, orders, and prohibits the ego—and castigates and punishes it when it does not live up to its imposed standards. As the child once obeyed its parents, so the ego obeys the superego. If it does not obey or fails to meet the superego's imperative demands, the ego is punished by feeling the sting of superego aggression, in the form of depression and/or guilt. The superego possesses a rather archaic and primitive morality. It can be hypermoral and rigid and even tyrannical in its demands upon the ego. But it can also be modified by incorporating the injunctions and standards of other authority figures besides the parents.

Freud applied the mechanism he had developed in relation to the understanding of melancholia to the formation of the superego. He viewed the superego as being formed on the basis of identifications with the parents. The object cathexes directed toward both parents in the oedipal relationships were replaced by identifications. The child thereby makes the parents part of his own inner psychic organization and consequently erects in his own mind the same capacity to restrain the expression of instinctual impulses which the parents previously provided as external agents. Thus, in a sense, the authority of the parents continues to exercise its restraining influence—now as an internal part of the child's psychic apparatus rather than as an outside agency.

The superego, however, is not simply the sum of parental and other identifications. It represents a definite structure within the ego, a consistent organization which is separate from other constituents of the ego. It is a distinct structural entity within the mental apparatus. Beyond its function as a representation and derivation of parental prohibitions and directives, the superego also functions as a channel for the intrapsychic expression of the most powerful drives of the id. The superego has instinctual drive energies immediately available to it and can mobilize them against the ego. Thus the superego is to a large extent unconscious, due to its intimate relation to the id. When aggressive impulses, for example, are not directed outward to an external object, they tend to be assimilated to the superego and directed against the self. This is what happens in melancholy. The aggression which is properly directed against the object is inhibited and controlled, with the consequence that it is diverted to the superego and directed against the self. The fear of the superego's aggression is a reflection of the earlier castration fear that the child experienced in the oedipal situation.

The concept of the superego, once formulated, became a crucial area for psychic investigation for a number of years. Just as the earlier period of psychoanalysis had focused for the most part on dreams and fantasies, in the period of the 1920's and 1930's, following Freud's formulation of the structural theory, the superego occupied the center of attention. One of the major goals of therapeutic analysis concerned the modification of the harsh, punitive superego of the neurotic patient. This was emphasized often to the detriment of other aspects of treatment. The theories of therapy published during this period were taken up almost exclusively with the problems of superego analysis. It was only in the late 1930's—particularly after the publication of Anna Freud's *The Ego and the Mechanisms of Defense* in 1937—that the ego and its defenses began to receive increasing attention.

The superego represented the internalized threats and prohibitions of one's parents. Freud was suggesting that a real fear—real in at least a subjective sense—namely, castration anxiety, could be internalized. The child would inhibit or repress the expression of instinctual impulses and wishes because of his fear of his real external parents and their possible retaliation. In the course of development, however, the external danger becomes converted into an internal threat. It was this internalization, Freud felt, that was responsible for the institution of repression and the other defenses. The child, instead of fearing his father as an external object, internalized the threat that derived from the father. He thus prohibited his own inner instinctual impulses by internalizing the prohibiting parental figure. In this way he made the father figure into a relatively permanent internal structure which had the capacity to inhibit and control the gratification of potentially dangerous and primitive instinctual wishes. According to this view, then, the superego was regarded as the major psychic structure responsible for the institution and maintenance of defenses.

Within the developing discipline of psychoanalysis, there have been —and still are—significant differences of opinion regarding the degree to which the harsh severity of the neurotic superego derives from the actual character of the parents. The superego of the severe obsessional neurotic is far more harsh, far more severe, far more demanding and threatening, than any ordinary parent might be. Many analysts, including Freud himself, recognized that the frightened child might attribute to a parent retaliatory and destructive wishes which were in fact a reflection of his own infantile aggressive wishes. At one extreme some analysts maintain that the actual character of the parents plays the most significant part in determining the quality of the internalized superego. At another extreme, theorists like Ernest Jones and Melanie Klein gave little if any importance to the role of the actual parents, but attributed the nature and quality of the internalized superego to the child's own inner aggressive impulses that were diverted to the superego. Most analysts today would adopt an intermediate viewpoint. Undoubtedly, the character of the parents plays an important part in the nature and quality of the child's earliest identifications. These influence the development of both ego and superego. At the same time it must also be recognized that in certain stages of development the child's capacity to differentiate clearly between himself and others is limited. It is possible, therefore, that he may attribute his own aggressive wishes to one or both of his parents. This tendency must be taken into account in trying to understand the predisposition to certain forms of neurotic dysfunction.

Although in its formation the superego internalized qualities of the real parents, the contact of the definitive superego with reality was limited. It was assumed that the superego formed at the time of the passing of the oedipal conflict was a relatively permanent structure. It was conceived as reflecting the development of the first five years of life, and not undergoing any significant modification after that. The future neurotic, then, would enter life with an excessively harsh and demanding superego which was the heir of his oedipal conflicts. The work of analysis, therefore, was seen primarily in terms of reopening the oedipal conflicts which had resulted in the formation of such a severe superego. The analyst was regarded as assuming the role of a superego surrogate. The work of therapy involved the gradual diminution and softening of the demands and prohibitions which had impeded the neurotic patient's health and happiness.

This point of view was not without value and still has its relevance as an aspect of therapy in some cases. However, the emergence of Freud's views on the ego was followed by a shift in analytic interest from superego to ego. The emphasis in treatment of neurotic patients followed a similar shift from concern with superego dynamics to concern with ego functions and defense. The emergence of ego psychology in the last few years has had a tendency to overshadow superego functions and their role in neurotic processes. The clarification of such functions, their development, and their relation to and integration with ego functions, remains a task for the future of psychoanalysis.

We can see, then, that when Freud became aware of and took up the consideration of the problem of narcissism, he entered on a path that had profound implications for the further development of his thinking and for the shape of psychoanalytic theory. He was led inexorably to the modification of his dual instinct theory. That development led to his reconsideration of the problem of instincts and his ultimate separation of libidinal and aggressive instincts into a separate instinctual compartment—the id. He was also led to consider the vicissitudes and modifications of narcissism in the course of development. He saw that certain modifications of the ego and its functions became the repository for the abandoned narcissism of childhood. The conceptualization of the ego ideal, and later the superego, as portions of the ego which were split off as separate structural components of the psychic apparatus flowed out of these considerations. The structural theory was simply the extension and more systematic schematization of these views which Freud had been fashioning over the course of a decade.

Moreover, through the development of these ideas about structure and structure formation, there was implicit the important factor of the relationship between these processes and the ego's relation to objects. It was through identifications, based on and derived from object relations, that the formation of structure was achieved. This consideration will assume increasing importance in our later discussions—as it has in the post-Freudian development of psychoanalytic theory.

[9]

The Ego
and Its Development

Our discussion of narcissism and its vicissitudes in the preceding chapter focused on the development of the structural viewpoint and on the model of the psychic apparatus which Freud formulated in terms of the structural theory. Freud's working model of the psychic apparatus had undergone significant changes from his original formulations in the *Project* (1895) and somewhat later in the *Interpretation of Dreams* (1900). In the earlier models, there was little room for the spontaneous and active exercise of functions within the ego. The emphasis lay on the relatively passive reception and seemingly automatic transfer of memory traces among the mnemonic systems, rather than on active processing of information.

The Evolution of the Ego Concept

In *The Ego and the Id* (1923), the structural theory separated the elements of energy and structure in the mental apparatus and located the sources of all mental energy in the vital stratum of the mind—the id. The id was thus conceived as the source and reservoir of all psychic energy which was derived from the basic instinctual drives. Both ego and superego were described as structural derivatives of the id, as parts of the id which had been separated from it by the structuralizing effects of the organism's contact with reality. At this stage of Freud's theorizing, the ego was little more than a helpless derivative of id processes, a weak and relatively passive entity which was caught between the conflicting demands of id, superego, and external reality.

Within the next few years, from the publication of *The Ego and the Id* to the publication of *Inhibitions, Symptoms and Anxiety* (1926), Freud's thinking about the ego underwent some significant changes. We have discussed some of these changes briefly in connection with the evolution of Freud's views on anxiety and repression (see Chapter 5), but we shall focus specifically here on the import of these shifts for the conceptualization of the ego and some of their implications for the emergence of ego psychology. The changes were foreshadowed to a certain extent in 1923 but became more explicit in the later work. One of the most important changes, and one that was pivotal for the development of Freud's ego psychology, was the view of the ego as the seat of anxiety and other affects.

The change in point of view which made the ego the seat of anxiety reflected the modification of Freud's view of anxiety. His first view of the latter as a biochemical or physiological alteration of dammed up sexual instinct did not necessarily have any psychological meaning. Anxiety was more or less an automatic and physical phenomenon. The shift toward a view of it as an affect and making the experience of affect a function of the ego not only made anxiety a significant psychological experience, but gave increased recognition to its greater significance in psychic life. It also brought a much different appreciation of the role of the ego in psychic functioning. Even at this point in the development of Freud's thinking, however, anxiety was still defined as a derivative of instinctual impulses. He still felt that anxiety resulted when instinctual impulses which could not be allowed appropriate discharge reached a level of intensity which exceeded the ego's capacity to maintain its established pattern of defense. The shift in viewpoint was nonetheless significant since it was the first time that anxiety, and by implication all other affects, was specifically assigned to the ego. The ego thus became not only the executive organ of the psychic apparatus, but also the seat of affect.

In our earlier discussion of anxiety, we indicated that the development of Freud's ideas about it were closely tied up with the emergence of his ideas about the ego. It is important that the pattern of the development of the concept of the "ego" be understood. Freud's earliest ideas about the ego were rather diffuse and unsystematic, even though the pages of the *Project* reveal a variety of aspects of the ego and its functioning which later took a more systematic place in his thinking. The influence of Herbart and especially of Meynert—the great physiologist whom Freud revered and with whom he studied—on Freud's view of the ego were marked. The ego was described as a group of ideas to which a number of functions were ascribed—perception, memory, thinking, attention, judgment, etc. The most important function of the ego at this early stage, however, was that of defense. The concept of defense and the concept of the ego were linked. The ego was regarded as an organized group of ideas. Certain ideas could be incorporated in this group by association of memory traces, and certain others had to be excluded. The presumption was made that any ideas which were included in this associative mass were thereby made conscious. Any ideas which were excluded were correspondingly unconscious. The "ego" therefore stood loosely for the "person" or the "self," or broadly for consciousness. Defense was conceived of as directed primarily to the memory trace, thus preventing the recall of certain traumatic reality experiences. Consciousness (ego) thus dominated the mass of ideas and the effect of defense was to dissociate the incompatible ideas from consciousness.

The developments in Freud's ego concept as a result of his study of dreaming were not very great. The ego concept remained substantially unchanged, but some important functions related to the dream process were formulated. The ego was held responsible for the wish to sleep, for the exercise of dream censorship, as well as for the secondary revision to which dream elements were subjected. The dreaming ego, therefore, had substantially the same sort of function as the waking ego. The understanding of basic thought processes and insight into the influences on organization of patterns of thinking—primary and secondary process —were important additions. But the ego remained substantially the same—an organization of ideas structured around the basic functions of consciousness and defense.

The break in this line of thinking came with the abandonment of the seduction hypothesis (see Chapter 4). Fantasy moved to the center of the stage and Freud's interest was absorbed with the processes that produce such fantasies. Psychoanalytic theory underwent a period of instinctualization. The instincts and their vicissitudes dominated psychoanalytic interest and theory. Interest in the defenses and ego functions faded. As the concept of defense became more or less global, it was treated as equivalent to repression. The process of repression was thus conceptualized as due to the conflict of sexual instincts as opposed by ego instincts. The ego's defensive function, which had been its predominant characteristic, was thereby reduced to a function of instinctual drives.

At the same time, however, Freud was advancing his thinking on a variety of fronts. He was dealing during these years with the problem of narcissism, as we have seen. The binding of narcissistic libido was seen as resulting in the splitting off of structural elements in the psyche. These elements were at first seen as parts of the ego, implying a separation of ego from id (instincts) and the correlative separation of structured from unstructured parts of the mind. Freud's treatment of narcissism introduced the concept of a libidinal cathexis of the ego. It was not at all clear how this libidinal investment of the ego related to other forms of energy in the ego. The specification of the other ego instincts remained in the dark. In Freud's earlier formulations of the ego, he had placed it in opposition to libidinal drives. In his treatment of narcissism, however, the ego was seen as including a libidinal element. As a result the ego was instinctualized and repression was conceived in terms of the conflict between two instinctual agents. This was a clear departure from his earlier view in which ego and libidinal instincts had been opposed.

Freud was also in the process of developing his ideas about the reality principle and its relation to the ego. The roots of the development of this aspect of his thought lie in the distinction of primary and secondary process thinking. The secondary process came to be seen as related to the reality principle and to the ego's relation with reality. Primary process was linked to unconscious thought, and secondary process was identified with conscious thought and the orientation to reality. While it was not very clear what the relationship between instinctual drives and secondary process might be, the linking of secondary process with the reality principle located these processes in the ego. Thus the basis was established for a conception of the development of ego functions independently of instinctual vicissitudes.

Therefore the evolution of the ego concept was one of gradual separation from instinct and emerging clarification of the role of the ego in drive regulation and control. In *The Ego and the Id* the ego is described as a coherent organization of mental functions. It arises out of abandoned object cathexes by way of identification. Its organization is centered around conscious and preconscious processes, but it is also partly constituted by unconscious structural elements which are responsible for resistance. It is capable of transforming the energies of instinctual drives to its own purposes and objectives. Consciousness, which before had been viewed as coterminous with ego functions, is reduced to a quality of some ego functions.

From Mediating to Autonomous Ego

Even though the ego emerges at this stage as a coherent organization with a genetic history and capacities which are not immediately derived from instinctual drives, the ego does not yet occupy a very strong position. It is still driven by instinctual forces. It went where instinct took it. It was a more-or-less passive mediator between the conflicting influences of id, superego, and reality. The view that Freud paints of this poor ego is rather dismal:

From the other point of view, however, we see this same ego as a poor creature owing service to three masters and consequently menaced by three dangers: from the external world, from the libido of the id, and from the severity of the superego. Three kinds of anxiety correspond to these three dangers, since anxiety is the expression of a retreat from danger. As a frontier creature, the ego tries to mediate between the world and the id, to make the id pliable to the world and, by means of its muscular activity, to make the world fall in with the wishes of the id. . . . It is not only a helper to the id; it is also a submissive slave who courts his master's love.[53]

However weak and derivative this concept of the ego may seem, the latter begins to take on some life and meaning in its own right. More important, however, is the fact that the ego begins to take on certain functions which suggest some implicit shifts in the basic concept of it. Freud attributes to this ego the function of unifying and integrating psychic processes. The addition of this integrative function, which is the forerunner of what we would call the synthetic function of the ego, alters it from a relatively passive organization—the resultant of the operation of other psychic entities—to an organizing force within the personality. Thus the ego begins to look more like a central agency of functional control and integration.

The next significant step in the development of the ego concept came with the publication of *Inhibitions, Symptoms and Anxiety*. Freud moved from a view of the ego as relatively weak and derivative from instinctual drives, to a conception of it as autonomously initiating defense and capable of converting passive anxiety into an anticipation of danger. This marked a definitive shift in Freud's view of anxiety and the functioning of the ego. He recast the relations between anxiety, repression, and symptom formation by returning to the case of Little Hans. Hans was the little five-year-old boy who had substituted a phobic symptom for his fear of castration by his father. Instead of fear of his father he expressed his anxiety in the fear of horses. By this displacement and substitution, he was able to avoid the experience of anxiety in relation to his father, since the phobia was attached to horses and he could avoid them—even if he could not avoid his father. In discussing the origin and development of this phobia Freud reached a new conclusion about the nature of anxiety. Hans's phobia could not be regarded as the result of repression, as Freud had postulated in his original theory of repression. The horse phobia served little Hans as a signal of danger. The avoidance of the external object of the phobia was comparable to avoidance by repression. The anxiety was a signal for the mobilization of defense against an instinctual danger. Thus Freud concluded that anxiety served as a signal by which the ego alerted itself and mobilized its defenses to deal with the threatened danger.

Anxiety and Danger

This revision of the theory of anxiety was crucial for the emergence of the next phase in the development of the concept of the ego. The ego became the seat of anxiety and it became possible then to interpret the varieties of anxiety in terms of the ego's relations with the id, the superego, and the external world. Freud was able to outline a typical pattern for the emergence of and response to danger situations. Thus the idea of anxiety as a danger signal adds a new dimension to the functioning of the ego—its capacity for the use of anticipation in the mobilization of defensive resources. The ego thus assumes a much more active and dynamic role. Freud began to speak increasingly of thought processes and other ego functions as working not with instinctual energies, but with a modified form of energy which he called "sublimated" or "desexualized." Later developments of this basic notion would refer to such energies as neutralized. The ego thus gains the relatively autonomous capacity to modify basic instinctual energies and adapt them by neutralization for its own conflict-free and noninstinctual functioning.

During the period when many of these ideas were taking shape, Freud was engaged in writing his *Introductory Lectures* (1916–1917). In his discussion of anxiety he presented numerous examples of the sorts of things that may arouse fear or anxiety. He points out the differences between realistic danger in which the fear is justified and has a definite object, semirealistic danger in which there is some real danger but the fear is out of proportion to the magnitude of the danger, and neurotic anxiety in which there is no real basis in reality for the fear but the individual is nonetheless frightened irrationally by something that symbolizes an internal danger to himself.

The evaluation of the extent of real danger outside may have a significant subjective component. Freud hints that some of his own attitudes may have been in part a reflection of his own phobic responses. He distinguished, for example, between the fear of mice, which he regarded as irrational, and the fear of snakes, which he described essentially as realistic and unavoidable. Mice were harmless little creatures—"mouse" was in fact a common term of endearment. The fear of mice, then, must be neurotic and due to the fact that the mouse symbolizes something unconscious. The phobic individual is avoiding a symbolized unconscious danger by avoiding the mouse. Fear of snakes, according to Freud, was something different. Snakes were dreadful, horrible, and frightening creatures. Fear of snakes, therefore, was not in the least neurotic since it was proportioned to the horrible and dreadful nature of these creatures. He makes no reference to the fact that most snakes are perfectly harmless. We might wonder whether Freud himself might not have been justifying his own snake phobia, while condemning the fairly widespread mouse phobia that he himself did not share. One man's phobia may be another man's foible. Drawing the line between situations of real danger and phobic situations of inner danger is not always easy.

These examples, and others, were quite useful to Freud—particularly examples of isolated phobias (although phobias are well known to travel in packs, like rats: when you catch sight of one, there are liable to be others lurking in the darkness); they provide good examples of how the ego's use of anxiety as a signal of danger can prevent further symptoms from developing. There are many patients who have more or less isolated phobias, and as long as they are able to avoid these particular phobic situations they are able to function reasonably well. Someone with a fear of heights need not climb the Eiffel Tower. Someone with a fear of subways can manage to avoid that means of transportation. Someone with a fear of flying usually will not choose to fly if he can travel by other means. Such individuals, however, get into trouble when they are forced by circumstances to repeatedly face the phobic situation. In such circumstances, the internal and unconscious psychic dangers which had been externalized in the phobia are remobilized. The result may be the emergence of quite severe anxiety. There was a patient in England during World War II who suffered from a lifelong phobia of subway trains. After the outbreak of the war, gas rationing made it impossible for him to drive his car to work. He was forced to take the subway. Within a short time, he began to decompensate. From a rather well-adjusted and relatively symptom-free young man, he became an extremely phobic and severely anxious patient. His previous phobic anxiety had not been incapacitating and he was able to use the relatively minor degree of phobic anxiety as a danger signal which allowed him to ward off the emergence of a more severe and disabling anxiety.

Primary vs. Secondary Anxiety

This sort of clinical example illustrates several important points about Freud's revised theory of anxiety. First, it suggests that the purpose of the signal anxiety was to prevent the emergence of a far more severe and serious internal danger. The ego can anticipate the threatened danger and mobilize its resources—defensive and executive—to forestall and circumvent the threat. Second, it indicates a differentiation between forms of anxiety. Freud distinguished between primary anxiety and secondary anxiety. Primary anxiety is the kind that is linked with a traumatic state of the ego. Secondary anxiety is signal anxiety, the kind which provides an internal signal that a traumatic state is threatening the ego.

Freud had first introduced the term "primary anxiety" and the concept of the traumatic situation in *Inhibitions*. In this work, as well as in his *Introductory Lectures,* his thinking about the problem of anxiety had been strongly influenced by the work of Otto Rank. Rank had advanced his theory of the birth trauma in his book *The Trauma of Birth,* which was published in 1924, although it seems that Freud knew about his theory before that. Rank had suggested that birth was the prototype of all anxiety situations. At birth the child has not yet acquired a capacity for defense and is exposed to an overwhelming rush of stimulation against which it can erect no barriers and no defense. The ego thus experiences a state of helplessness and of being overwhelmed by forces outside its control. The ego's response to this situation of total helplessness and engulfment was anxiety. And in Rank's view, this situation of primal helplessness lay at the root of all subsequent anxiety experiences.

Freud took up Rank's suggestion, but rather critically and with some reservations. Rank had tried to work out an approach to therapy which was much shorter than the usual psychoanalytic treatment and which attempted to go directly to the birth trauma and to interpret it. Freud accepted none of Rank's views about therapy. But he found the idea of the birth trauma to be quite useful in filling out his own ideas about anxiety. The birth situation might be considered as the prototype of a basic situation in which the human organism is subjected to maximal stimulation, both internally and externally. When this occurs under circumstances in which the individual possesses neither the knowledge nor the capacity to take defensive or protective action, a situation arises in which the ego is overwhelmed by excessive stimulation. There will result a painful and frightening discharge which takes the form of severe anxiety—a fear of annihilation and engulfment—primary anxiety. The situation of excessive stimulation which gives rise to this anxiety is described as a "traumatic situation." The birth trauma thus provides a prototype and model of a traumatic situation which endangers the ego and gives rise to primary anxiety.

If we return for a moment to our discussion of the war neuroses (see Chapter 8), we can place what we discovered there in the context of Freud's revised theory of anxiety. You recall that certain patients experienced little or no anticipatory anxiety before going into battle. When they were exposed to the first situation of real danger—the first exploding bomb or the first experience of being fired at—they experienced a complete loss of control and panic. Such extreme responses serve to illustrate Freud's description of a traumatic situation. The soldiers' response to such an unanticipated threat of external danger was a complete collapse of defensive and adaptive capacities. The patient's ego was literally swamped by his overwhelming affect. In the last chapter, we discussed the predisposition to this type of reaction in terms of the concepts of narcissism and self-esteem. Here it illustrates the differences between anxiety, which serves as a signal which mobilizes defenses, and the anxiety which emerges in a traumatic situation. Certain soldiers, who failed to develop an adequate degree of anticipatory signal anxiety, which would have enabled them to respond more adaptively to the external danger situation, were thus predisposed to a traumatic experience and primary anxiety.

Other cases of war neurosis, however, showed a different pattern of reaction. One typical patient had a lifelong history of neurotic symptoms. He had been anxiety-ridden, nervous, an inveterate nail-biter, and had many feelings of insecurity and self-doubt. He was, however, extremely aware of his own anxiety. He had a great deal of anticipatory anxiety, and when he was confronted with situations of real external danger he became quite frightened and anxious. But his ego was not overwhelmed and the situation was not, therefore, traumatic. Such patients were better able to tolerate their anxiety in the first place. When they did decompensate in the face of danger, they were able to pull themselves back together and return to active duty in a relatively short time.

Looking at these patients from the point of view of the ego as the seat of anxiety, the first type had previously developed defenses so readily in the face of unconscious signal anxiety that they had not experienced anxiety as a subjective affect in response to an anticipated danger. In the second type of case, the individual had been less successful in mobilizing adequate unconscious defenses and had thus learned to experience, as well as tolerate, overt anxiety as a subjective affect. When confronted with a situation of external danger, the ego which had allowed itself to experience no anxiety was able to tolerate the flood of anxiety that came upon it. The ego that had been able to allow itself to experience some anticipatory anxiety was better prepared to deal with the more severe anxiety associated with the real situation of danger, even though it also had difficulty in facing that danger. In the second case, the ego was better able to deal with the resulting anxiety so that the situation did not become as severely traumatic as it proved to be for the relatively unprepared ego.

The Emergence of the Ego

Quite apart from other implications, the ego emerges in this new perspective as that part of the mind which has to make defensive responses to danger and which, when such defenses are not available, is overwhelmed and threatened. Thus the ego takes on a much more important, active and central role in organization, regulation, and adaptation to organism. This view of the ego is a far cry from the earlier view in which the ego was little more than a puppet on a string—subject to the whim and harassment of three powerful masters—without power or energy of its own to speak of. As soon as the ego was put in the position of being the part of the mind which not only experiences anxiety as an affect, but also sets up and maintains defenses and organizes and directs the action of the organism by its executive functions, it became clear that this ego was a central element in the intrapsychic drama and that it was perhaps the most important part of the mental apparatus for the internal and external adaptation of the personality. The implications of this revised view of the ego and its functions has dominated psychoanalytic thinking and investigation ever since.

Freud continued to develop this notion of the ego in his later writings. As he added to the capacities and functions of the ego, it became apparent that its stature in psychoanalytic thinking was growing. The direction of his thinking was toward greater autonomy and independence of the ego in relation to other parts of the psychic apparatus. The initiation of defense through the use of anxiety as a signal was an autonomous function of the ego—and from this point of view was a conceptual breakthrough. Although Freud did not develop the idea of ego autonomy directly, he provided the basis for it which would be enlarged upon by later theorists. He pointed out that the ego had certain constitutionally given constituents which included perceptual, cognitive, and affective mechanisms. The ego was, therefore, in part relatively independent in its development from instinctual sources. In his *Analysis Terminable and Interminable* (1937) he quite explicitly suggested certain inherited characteristics of the ego. He also pointed to an epigenetic principle in the development of the ego which involved the gradual capacity of the ego to convert passive ego responses to active ego-initiated processes. The ego, therefore, had inborn roots, intrinsic maturational factors, and a course of development which was parallel to but independent of the course of instinctual development.

We have previously traced the development of Freud's instinct theory. The basic presumption that operated through most of his early thinking was that the instincts in one way or another served as the source of psychic energy. In his early treatment of defense, in order to deal with the fact of opposing forces within the psyche and in order to explain the phenomenon of defense, he had to attribute a source of energy to the repressing agency. Thus his instinct theory took shape along the lines of a basic division between sexual instincts and ego instincts, and the opposition between them gave rise to conflict and defense. We have seen that this view underwent changes with Freud's gradual coming to grips with both the problem of narcissism and the problem of aggression. This movement culminated in a separation of both aggressive and libidinal instincts and their assignment to the vital stratum of the mind—the id.

This raised a further problem. If the sexual and aggressive instincts were assigned to this separate structural division of the mind, where did the energies come from which the structural parts of the mind, the ego and the superego, had at their disposal? The problem was less difficult for the superego, whose functions in large measure reflected instinctual influences. The problem was more acute for the ego, however, since it was the agency of defense, operated in terms of the demands of reality, and in general exercised control of and directed countercathectic energies against instinctual pressures and wishes. The problem became more intense as the status of the ego improved and it became a stronger, more active, and more autonomously functioning structure within the psychic economy.

With the emergence of the ego Freud came increasingly to assign it energies that were qualitatively different from instinctual energies. He sketched a picture of the ego in one of his last writings, *An Outline of Psychoanalysis* (1940):

Here are the principal characteristics of the ego. In consequence of the pre-established connection between sense perception and muscular action, the ego has voluntary movement at its command. It has the task of self-preservation. As regards *external* events, it performs that task by becoming aware of stimuli, by storing up experiences about them (in the memory), by avoiding excessively strong stimuli (through flight), by dealing with moderate stimuli (through adaptation) and finally by learning to bring about expedient changes in the external world to its own advantage (through activity). As regards *internal* events, in relation to the id, it performs that task by gaining control over the demands of the instincts, by deciding whether they are to be allowed satisfaction, by postponing that satisfaction to times and circumstances favourable in the external world or by suppressing their excitations entirely. . . . The ego strives after pleasure and seeks to avoid unpleasure. An increase in unpleasure that is expected and foreseen is met by a *signal of anxiety;* the occasion of such an increase, whether it threatens from without or from within, is known as a *danger.* From time to time the ego gives up its connection with the external world and withdraws into the state of sleep, in which it makes far-reaching changes in its organization. It is to be inferred from the state of sleep that this organization consists in a particular distribution of mental energy.[54]

If we compare this statement of the ego and its position relative to the other parts of the psychic organization with the picture presented even as late as 1923 in *The Ego and the Id,* it becomes clear that in Freud's mind the ego and its interests takes predominance—or in the normally functioning mind, should take predominance—over the aims and objectives of id or superego. It is the ego which controls other psychic agencies and orders them to the demands and limitations of reality. In order to accomplish this, it remains questionable whether the ego can function solely on the basis of energies derived from instinctual sources.

One of the important problems that had influenced Freud's development of a modified instinct theory had been the problem of love and hate and the conflict between them. Freud had returned to this problem again and again in the course of his writings, although it was only gradually that the role of aggression came more into focus. Its place as a full-fledged instinct came only with the revision of his theory in 1923. He observed repeatedly that love can be turned into hate. Instincts can be turned into their opposites. It is a common clinical observation that patients express what appears to be hatred as a means of defending themselves against the recognition or admission of feelings of love. You will recall that in the dream, "My friend R. is my uncle," Freud observed the change of hostile feelings of rivalry into feelings of affection. Again in Freud's analysis of the case of the Rat Man, the patient's severe obsessional neurosis provided clear indications of his conflicts over love and hate. The Rat Man's obsessional difficulties reveal the tremendous difficulties and conflicts which arise from ambivalence, the direction of love and hate simultaneously toward one and the same person. The mastery of ambivalence remains one of the central and crucial developmental tasks of the ego. As Freud's view of the ego emerged, the resolution of ambivalence was one of the basic functions of the ego. How it was to accomplish this balancing and directing of instinctual forces was not immediately evident, although it was clear that the ego alone was in the position to apprehend the internal and external factors in terms of which the conflict might be resolved.

Freud came to the idea of neutralized energies placed at the disposal of the ego through a consideration of the change of love into hate—or the case of rivalry changing to homosexual love—which seemed to represent the transformation of one instinctual drive into another. He assumed that there was an underlying ambivalence and that the apparent transformation was accomplished by the addition to one aspect or the other of a displaceable energy, which was neutral in itself and completely at the disposal of the ego. He regarded such neutral energies at first as derived from the narcissistic reservoir of libido which was stored in the ego. Freud was never able, however, to really resolve the conceptual tension that was created by the emerging concept of an autonomous ego with independent functions and the basic persuasion that all energy available to the psychic apparatus somehow derived from the vital stratum of the mind.

It must be said that the hints and basic roots which Freud could do little more than suggest have flourished in the years since his death, and that the problems of the ego and its functions have become the primary focus of psychoanalytic thinking and development. Of particular importance to that development has been the whole question of the ego's relation to reality. The role of reality, as Rapaport has indicated, was quite significant in Freud's early thinking, but under the influence of the discovery of the importance of fantasy and the correlative abandonment of the seduction hypothesis, the role of reality was more or less ignored and discounted. It was only with the re-emergence of the ego and the realization of the importance of the reality principle and the ego's relation to it that the importance of reality began to assert itself—but now on completely different terms and in ways much more central to the theory.

The Role of Identification

One of the important developments in Freud's thinking about the ego was the gradual development of his ideas about identification. The notion of identification had been present in his thinking from very early, but it was restricted to a merely representational function as a form of consolidation in dreaming or it was applied to the analysis of symptom formation as a mechanism in the formation of hysterical symptoms. Thus Freud spoke of hysterical identification as underlying hysterical symptoms—as with Dora's identification with her father in the development of her physical symptoms.[55] It was again Freud's reflections on narcissism and the nature of the modifications in ego organization that related to the vicissitudes of narcissistic libido that pointed his attention to the mechanisms by which such modifications took place. The problem of mourning and the analysis of depression provided the next important stimulus. Identification became the central mechanism in explaining how aggressive impulses originally directed against the lost object became turned against the self. The lost object became taken into the self and the self was conceived to have become the object of aggressive impulses by reason of its identification with the lost object. The self was thus modified by a narcissistic identification. Freud was thus able to say that an object cathexis was replaced by an identification.

Thus the basis was laid for his later development of the theory in *The Ego and the Id.* There identification became the primary mechanism of ego development. He wrote:

We succeeded in explaining the painful disorder of melancholia by supposing that (in those suffering from it) an object which was lost has been set up again inside the ego—that is, that an object-cathexis has been replaced by an identification. At that time, however, we did not appreciate the full significance of this process and did not know how common and how typical it is. Since then we have come to understand that this kind of substitution has a great share in determining the form taken by the ego and that it makes an essential contribution towards building up what is called its "character." . . . It may be that this identification is the sole condition under which the id can give up its objects. At any rate the process, especially in the early phases of development, is a very frequent one, and it makes it possible to suppose that the character of the ego is a precipitate of abandoned object-cathexes and that it contains the history of those object-choices.[56]

Thus, it is in terms of the mechanism of identification that the reality principle and the ego's basic orientation toward reality take on added significance. The ego's relation to reality becomes significant for its own inner development, since the pattern of that development is derivative from the significant object relations and object choices that the ego makes. It also brings us to the awareness, which was a dawning realization for Freud, that the significant reality in terms of the ego's development and ultimate capacity for adaptation is other human beings, the objects which the ego relates to and ultimately internalizes through identification.

Anxiety and Ego Development

Freud did not extend his thinking to a specifically object-relations theory of the growth and development of human psychic structure. He did, however, propose the basic roots out of which later theorists were able to develop the elements of such a theory, as we shall see. In his attention to the developmental process and to the factors that seemed to facilitate or inhibit personality growth, Freud was continually conscious of and felt the necessity for integrating the influence of reality factors. The development of the ego was regarded for most of his career as due to the interaction with reality, and it was only gradually that he was able to admit nonexperiential developmental influences for the growth of ego. Much of Freud's approach to this problem was influenced by his concern with anxiety and its developmental role. He described this role of anxiety in a number of contexts. He suggests, for example, that situations in which children tend to become anxious usually contain elements of realistic danger. The birth trauma was the outstanding example. At birth the infant is placed in a situation of maximal stimulation both internally and externally. He possesses neither the structural nor the adaptive capacity to respond with any sort of defensive action. Through most of the child's infancy, in fact, as Freud saw it, the child was not equipped to deal with the amounts of stimulation to which it was exposed, and consequently the child was in a relatively vulnerable position throughout most of its early infancy. The child's responses in this situation were the sort of responses that are elicited when an individual is subjected to stimuli which are beyond his capacity to master and integrate—the "traumatic situation."

Later in his development, Freud observed that the infant is confronted with a different threat. He suggested that in the later months of infancy the child is really justified in the fear that he might lose the all-important object on which he depends for sustenance and relief of his inner tension and distress, namely his mother. The fear is justified by reason of his extreme dependence on her, which is quite real. Freud saw the resulting anxiety—which we could now regard as separation anxiety —as based on real considerations.

Another crucial developmental situation in which Freud saw the child's fear as based on reality was the oedipal situation. During this period, the child's fear that his father would possibly castrate him were he to express his oedipal wishes toward his mother is more or less justified. Freud describes the castration fear of the oedipal child as a realistic danger—a point which is open to discussion. The individual even later in his life cycle is subject to real dangers and fears. It was Freud's view that adult individuals were justifiably afraid of the recriminations and accusations of their own superego. They are also justified in fearing the loss of approval from the significant individuals around them from whom they seek respect and love. In all of these cases, Freud is focusing on the realistic justification for the anxieties which lead to the development of defenses against the individual's own inner, innate impulses —whether in the development of the child or in the adaptation of the adult.

In discussing these anxieties and their role in the development of the ego and its defensive capacity, Freud makes the following statement:

Among the factors that play a part in the causation of neuroses and that have created the conditions under which the forces of the mind are pitted against one another, three emerge into prominence: a biological, a phylogenetic and a purely psychological factor.

The biological factor is the long period of time during which the young of the human species is in a condition of helplessness and dependence. The intra-uterine existence seems to be short in comparison with that of most animals, and it is sent into the world in a less finished state. As a result, the influence of the real external world upon it is intensified and an early differentiation between the ego and id is promoted. Moreover, the dangers of the external world have a greater importance for it, so that the value of the object which can alone protect it against them and take the place of its former intra-uterine life is enormously enhanced. This biological factor, then, establishes the earliest situations of danger and creates the need to be loved which will accompany the child through the rest of its life.

The existence of the second, phylogenetic, factor is based only upon inference. We have been led to assume its existence by a remarkable feature in the development of the libido. We have found that the sexual life of man, unlike that of most of the animals nearly related to him, does not make a steady advance from birth to maturity, but that, after an early efflorescence up till the fifth year, it undergoes a very decided interruption. . . .

The third, psychological, factor resides in a defect of our mental apparatus which has to do precisely with its differentiation into an id and an ego, and which is therefore also attributable ultimately to the influence of the external world. In view of the dangers of (external) reality, the ego is obliged to guard against certain instinctual impulses in the id and to treat them as dangerous. But it cannot protect itself from internal instinctual dangers as some piece of reality that is not part of itself. Intimately bound up with the id as it is, it can only fend off an instinctual danger by restricting its own organization and by acquiescing in the formation of symptoms in exchange for having impaired the instinct.[57]

Thus the inherent developmental problem of mastery of anxiety is intrinsically linked to the child's capacity to form and sustain meaningful relations to the significant and sustaining objects in his environment. It is as though by reason of his relatedness to objects he can make up for the lack of native endowment with which he begins life. The significant objects supply the nurturing and protective functions which he does not possess and which he needs for survival. His attachment and relatedness to them are the guarantors of his capacity to master anxiety and thus adapt to reality.

The measure of the infant's increasing capacity to accomplish this twofold objective of inner mastery and outer adaptation is the measure of his growth. The infant, however, cannot remain dependent simply on external objects to sustain these functions. In the course of his development he must acquire by gradual accretion the capacity to perform these important functions for himself. He can only do this by developing the capacity to tolerate the absence, the separateness, and ultimately the loss of the important objects on which he once depended. In so doing he can acquire in his own right the capacity to carry out these vital functions of mastery and adaptation. We can say, then, that the human individual's growth to maturity has a dual involvement in object relations. From a positive point of view, the human organism depends on and needs meaningful object relations in order to satisfy its own inner needs and capacities. In the infant, dependence on significant objects is essential for survival; in the adult, meaningful relatedness to the world of objects is important for the maintenance of self-esteem and identity. From a negative point of view, however, it is the ability to tolerate the absence, separateness and loss of significant objects which allows the individual to develop the basic strengths which underlie his mature adaptive capacities.

In discussing instinctual development, ego development, and even up to a point the development of reality testing, we have focused primarily on intrapsychic processes. We have been concerned mainly with what goes on within the mind of the developing child. When we speak of instinctual development, for example, we have suggested that as the child develops and matures he normally shows an increased capacity to tolerate delay of gratification or frustration. If we approach this same capacity from the point of view of ego development, we can point to the emergence of a psychic structure which has the capacity to impose delay and control. Freud's original approach to this problem was based on the differentiation between the pleasure principle and the reality principle. As he viewed it, the child had to apprehend the absence of an object for immediate gratification, had to be able to tolerate this absence realistically and to delay the impulse for immediate gratification—and only then was he in the position to begin to make the appropriate adaptive actions to achieve realistic gratification.

We can suggest, therefore, that each developmental step rests on an essentially negative experience. As the child grows he learns to wait, to delay. He learns that he cannot always—if ever—pursue immediate gratification of his wishes. He learns to follow a more indirect and roundabout course to gain satisfaction. Progress in development comes to mean—in a very primary and basic way—the capacity to learn how to tolerate the postponement or absence of gratification. This point is of primary importance and we cannot stress it too strongly. Growth in human psychological development occurs through an increasing capacity to tolerate absence of gratification and loss.

If we recall Freud's original definition of thought, he regarded thought as a form of experimental action in which the individual does not act externally but substitutes a trial action in his mind. He thus is able to delay the immediate translation of his wishes into external action and waits until he has thought through the proposed action. This allows him to take into account the difficulties, contingencies, and consequences of the proposed action, thus making it more congruent with the demands of reality. Hence the capacity to tolerate disappointment, delay, postponement of gratification, frustration of wishes, anxiety, separation from and loss of loved objects appears to be an essential requisite for the development of emotional maturity and psychic health.

Thus our discussion has carried us to the point at which we can meaningfully ask: What are the factors that contribute to and determine this capacity? How does it develop? Freud saw clearly that the child's biological dependence made the quality of his relationship with the significant objects in his environment an essential part of the problem. Our task, then, is to understand the meaning of the child's relationship to these important persons in his world and to understand their role in the development of the emerging ego capacities and strengths we have been discussing.

[10]

Factors in
Early Development

The course of our discussion thus far has brought us from a consideration of the basic problem of anxiety through the various aspects of Freud's thinking about the nature and development of the psychic apparatus. Our considerations of the development and formation of the superego and of the ego have brought us to a point in our discussion where the question of object-relations and their influence on development of the psychic apparatus assumes a central importance. Freud's remarks in his *Inhibitions, Symptoms and Anxiety* (1926), which we cited in the last chapter, make the centrality of object relations quite clear. He refers to the child's biological dependency and to his relationship to the important caring and feeding persons in his environment as central to his early adjustment and development.

Elements in Growth

We also pointed out that each significant developmental step that the child makes can be viewed as the result of his increasing capacity to deal with and master painful experience. The child's progressive development seems to depend to a high degree on his capacity to learn how to tolerate postponement of gratification, frustration of wishes, and separation from significant gratifying objects. The capacity, therefore, to recognize and tolerate painful affects like depression and anxiety—the affective responses to frustration, loss, separation—would seem to be one of the essential prerequisites for the development of emotional maturity and mental health.

We are at the point, therefore, in the development of our argument at which we can meaningfully begin to ask ourselves how and in what way these essential capacities develop. Since Freud himself placed so much emphasis on the biological factors which contribute to the child's basic dependence on his objects, we can usefully examine the implications of the relationship between the young infant and those who care for him and fulfill his basic biological needs. We can thereby shed some light on the influence of this interaction on the emergence of the basic strengths we have been discussing.

The first point that needs to be emphasized is the following: If, as we have suggested, growth and development are derivatively dependent on the capacity to recognize and tolerate frustration and loss, this would inevitably imply that a positive experience or gratification must have preceded the recognition of absent gratification or frustration of the wish for gratification. The concept of fear of loss or the toleration of the painful affect of loss becomes somewhat meaningless unless we presuppose a previous experience of gratification and a valuing of what is wished for or lost. Despite the fact, therefore, that each developmental step is based on and includes negative components, we must necessarily assume that acquisition must somehow precede loss and that the experience of gratification must somehow precede the pain of frustration or loss.

Primary Narcissism

In the maturational perspective that Freud proposed, he described the neonatal and very young infant in a state of libidinal self-embodiment which he referred to as "primary narcissism." All of the infant's libido is invested in himself, contained within himself as in a reservoir of libidinal potentiality. It is only gradually and as a consequence of the experience of and attachment to objects that he begins to direct some of this reserved libido outward and to invest it in objects. On the other hand, Freud's statement of the basic biologically determined dependency of the child implies something that might be paraphrased as follows: The helpless infant begins life with the sum total of his libido wrapped up in himself. But in fact he is utterly helpless and entirely dependent for survival and the satisfaction of his basic needs on the people in his environment who look after him and care for him.

There is something analogous in this situation to what we observe clinically in our examination of severely disturbed, and particularly schizophrenic, patients. On the one hand, the child or the schizophrenic gives definite evidence of a high degree of investment of libidinal interest in himself. The schizophrenic entertains illusions or fantasies of omnipotence. The infant enjoys a state of fulfillment of needs which approximates omnipotence. Under these conditions both the very young infant and the very sick and regressed patient will tend to believe that wish and gratification are synonymous. Both infant and schizophrenic in their respective ways come to interpret the gratification of the wish as something to be attributed to their own omnipotence. On the other hand, if the wish should not be gratified, both the child and the schizophrenic are sooner or later confronted with their own total and complete helplessness.

Clinically we often see in our sicker patients the attitude that they are either fully omnipotent or totally helpless. They can envision their situation only in terms of extremes of power or powerlessness, capacity or incapacity, etc. Their position is one of "all-or-none." They can see nothing between the alternatives of impotence and omnipotence, thus omitting or ignoring the whole range of human potency. Their thinking is dominated by the unrealistic expectation of immediate gratification or its negation in the lack of gratification. The concept of realistic delay of gratification seems to play little or no role in their thinking. Their attitude is split between omnipotent "having" and impotent "not-having" —with no room for the possibility of "having-after-delay." It is precisely in this middle ground between the alternatives of omnipotence and impotence that our understanding of the impact of object relations on the early development of the child's psychic apparatus must focus.

Freud's hypothesis of primary narcissism—that all libido at birth and in the early phase of infancy is invested in the self—remains a useful construct. Keeping in mind Freud's developmental model and the levels of regression, it is helpful in understanding the excessive investment of the self and the all-or-nothing responses we often see in our sicker patients. The theoretical presumption in such cases is that this behavior represents a regression to early narcissistic developmental levels and manifests infantile omnipotence. Despite this usefulness, however, the concept of primary narcissism needs some modification in the light of contemporary knowledge and understanding. If one assumes that all libido is invested in the self at the beginning of life, this implies a correlative assumption to the effect that there is a self in which the libido can be invested. Thus the concept of primary narcissism presupposes the existence from birth of some ego or self which can serve as the object of investment. This presupposition is doubtful at best. Most contemporary psychoanalysts would seriously question the capacity of the newborn infant to have any concept—however vague and undifferentiated—of himself as a separate individual. He is not, in fact, capable at birth—or for that matter for the first several months of his postnatal experience —of knowing where he ends and where objects in his environment begin.

Our task, therefore, is to try to understand the developmental steps which precede and lead up to a level of growth and maturation at which the human infant is capable of differentiating between himself and his objects. If we use the term "primary narcissism," we need to understand that it refers to a period in the infant's development which precedes the emergence of a separate concept of the self or of a real ego with any sense of self-awareness. As we would reconstruct the infant's experience from our more contemporary understanding, the young infant whose hunger is satisfied by the mother's breast does not see the breast as a separate feeding object—even a part object—but rather sees it as indistinct from himself, as an extension of his own body. He is unable to discriminate where his own body ends and the body of the feeding mother begins. The development of the sense of self as distinct and different from others is contingent on the child's reaching a growth level at which he becomes capable of this crucial and essential differentiation.

Innate Instinctual Endowment

When Freud proposed his structural theory in *The Ego and the Id* (1923), he tended to assume that the human infant is born with his full instinctual endowment. The infant at birth was thought to be more or less pure id, with the full complement of libidinal and aggressive drives. The subsequent course of development was thought to involve modification of this given id as a result of experience. This point of view is also one which we would question today. In the last score of years—largely as a result of Freud's hypotheses and guided heuristically by his formulations—there has been a considerable amount of data accumulated by way of the long-term longitudinal observation of infantile development. The results of such studies generally indicate that the child's instinctual responses at birth are quite diffuse and undifferentiated. It is not really until he is about three months old that his responses are sufficiently differentiated to permit the emergence of behavior which is sufficiently focused around the oral zone to allow us to describe it in terms of orality, as we understand it today. In the newborn infant, however, there is a more diffuse responsiveness to a wide variety of stimuli

—tactile, thermal, gustatory, etc.—and other forms of instinctual behavior which are characteristic. The patterning of instinctual behavior thus would seem to undergo a specific development which is to a considerable degree contingent on the interaction with experience. The emergence and patterning of instinctual responses, therefore, follows a phase-related and phase-specific pattern of development which is partly the result of intrinsic maturational factors and partly the result of the interplay with the infant's experience of gratifying stimuli.

To understand the developmental hypothesis as we now view it, and to understand its relationship to innate endowment and innate maturational factors, we must make a new assumption. There is a great deal of evidence to suggest that at every stage of growth optimal development is limited by innate maturational factors. Newborn infants are far from being identical. Even at birth they show remarkable and often striking differences. They are not always born at a comparable level of development in different functions or capacities. There are differences in degrees of prematurity. The child who is born prematurely will be less ready or able to produce a sucking response than a child who is born at full term. The child who is born after a prolonged and difficult maternal labor or who comes into the world under the influence of a variety of forms of fetal distress—cerebral anoxia, excessive cranial molding in delivery, injury from forceps, fetal effects of anesthesia, various syndromes affecting fetal functioning, etc.—may have a harder time getting started than the child whose birth has been essentially normal and uncomplicated.

There are many differences between individual children which may reflect the relative level of development attained at birth, but might also be indicative of innate differences. Some children are regarded as easy and happy babies right from the start. Other babies are more easily upset and disturbed by all sorts of stimuli, not only during birth but for a considerable period after birth as well. We are thus forced to recognize that the perceptual sensitivity, the reactiveness, the restlessness, and degree of distress shown by infants in response to different kinds of frustration or discomfort reveal significant individual differences from the very beginning of life. Similar differences are also evident in the child's capacity to suck with pleasure, in his capacity to develop satisfactory sleep patterns, and in his ability to respond to positive as well as negative stimuli.

Experiential Factors

Given these innate differences, we must also take into account that the degree to which each infant develops to his optimal level within each phase of his developmental course depends to a considerable extent on the degree to which he is provided with suitable experiences which are appropriate to and intermeshed with his present maturational level. Along with the epigenetic emergence of maturational phases as a result of the elaboration of intrinsic factors, there is a matching sequence of phase-specific experiences and responses—primarily taking place between the child and his significant objects—which maximize the developmental potential of each phase. Of primary importance in the earliest months of life are the experiences which take shape in the interaction between the child and the primary caretaking person—the mother.

The point we are making here can be illustrated graphically by referring to the work of one of the English psychoanalysts, one who has contributed some extremely important observations regarding the influences between mother and child which determine the developmental progress of the child. The analyst is D. W. Winnicott, whose work on developmental problems is well known. Winnicott began his career as a pediatrician, and only later became interested in psychiatric problems and trained as an analyst. Some years ago he was in charge of a pediatric clinic attached to one of the large children's hospitals in London. The clinic was essentially a well-baby clinic, but because of Winnicott's interest in emotional difficulties he received a large number of referrals from other pediatricians who would send children with a variety of such problems. Winnicott developed a routine for examining such children which proved to be quite revealing.

The children were for the most part quite young, babies of four months of age and older. Whenever he saw these patients for the first time, he would see the mother and the baby together. He would ask the mother to hold the baby on her lap while he took a history. On the desk next to the mother and within easy reach of the child, he would place a spatula or spoon. As he talked with the mother and took the history from her, he would pay little attention to the child. Other members of his staff would carefully observe the child's behavior. Normal, healthy babies would inevitably begin to look at, take an interest in, and try to reach out for the spoon. During the course of the fifteen or twenty minutes during which the interview took place, most of these babies would be able to reach the spoon, pick it up, and then put it in their mouths.

During this process it was possible to observe not only the behavior of the child, but the reactions of the mother as well. One could learn a great deal about the baby, about the mother, and about the baby's development from the simple reactions which were displayed in this setting.

There were very few of the healthy and well-developed babies of six months or better who were not able to accomplish their objective—namely of getting hold of the spoon, putting it in their mouths, and having a nice time playing with it. There were a wide variety of reactions to this situation. Delay in performing the operation, excessive anxiety on the part of the mother or of the child, ignoring of the spoon on the baby's part, or the mother's frustration or anger when the baby dropped the spoon, or her getting upset and either performing the operation for the child or apologizing to the doctor for the baby's naughty behavior in trying to pick up something from the doctor's desk—all of these types of reactions suggested trouble. Such behavior was almost always confirmed by the subsequent identification of one or other form of developmental failure. If some difficulty were revealed in this simple play situation, there were—almost without exception—other difficulties in the child's behavior and development. These would take the form of feeding problems, sleeping problems, problems in elimination—usually constipation—irritability, or a variety of other problems. These difficulties were found even though the clinic was not one for sick or obviously disturbed babies. These children were nearly all well within the range of normal development.

Interaction of Innate and Experiential Factors

This simple play situation provides a convincing demonstration of the objectively verifiable relationship between well-developed, orally focused activity on the part of the baby and an essentially positive mother-child interaction. The theoretical interpretations of these observations are quite divergent. If, as the early analysts tended to believe, focused oral (instinctual) activity is regarded as present from birth, then we would have to conclude that the behavior of disturbed babies reflected some form of interference—whether internal or external—with the baby's native intellectual endowment. In other words, instinctual oral activity was held to be present from the beginning of life and subsequent developments were thought to inhibit or interfere with the operation of this instinctual mode of expression. Such developmental difficulties have been explained in a number of ways. Some theorists, for example, have attributed them to the unduly strong aggressive drives and destructive instinctual elements in the baby, thus providing an instinctual force within the child which requires the institution of strong inner defenses against the external expression of these forces, even at the tender age of six months. Psychoanalytic reconstructions which are based on the presumption that instinctual activity is innate, powerful, and present in nearly the full extent of its endowment from the moment of birth on, would imply that the baby who is unable to express and satisfy his straightforward oral impulses—even at six months—is already showing a regressive interference with a relatively mature and developed instinctual drive. This sort of reconstruction is implicit in the Kleinian approach.

Without underestimating the importance of aggression and its influence on the internal instinctual economy of the child, one could also approach the interpretation of these observations from a quite different perspective. Let us suppose, as more recent evidence seems to suggest, the development of orality as a focused instinctual activity is much more complex than had previously been appreciated. We can suggest that patterns of instinctually derived behavior must be elicited by appropriate and proportional stimulation. If the specific eliciting stimulation is not available—in the appropriate measure and in the appropriate phase of instinctual development—the pattern of instinctual activity may not emerge in a focused manner or, for that matter, as a pleasurable and gratifying activity for the child.

We might also suggest that the child's successful negotiation of Dr. Winnicott's spatula implies not merely a certain level of instinctual development but also the availability of certain definite ego functions. The vignette of the healthy child getting, grasping, manipulating, and enjoying the spoon provides an excellent illustration of Freud's first definition of the reality principle as emerging in the service of the pleasure principle. What the child seeks is oral pleasure. In order to obtain such gratification, the baby must be able to recognize the spatial relationship between itself and the spatula, he must have developed sufficient hand-eye coordination and fine motor coordination to enable him to grasp the spatula and direct it into his mouth. These activities imply a considerable amount of autonomous ego functioning organized and directed on the basis of reality perception. These functions are organized in the service of obtaining pleasure, the pleasure in the present instance being one which is available and permitted to the child. The healthy child feels free to explore, reach out to take the spatula, and to take charge of it and put it to his own instinctually prompted uses.

Mother-Child Relationship

It is in this dimension of the process that the quality of the mother's interaction with the child becomes particularly significant. The detailed study and examination of infants over long periods of time have demonstrated that the early mother-child relationship and the pattern of interaction between them are decisive for the development of all of the attributes of the psychic apparatus which we have been discussing—the dynamic, economic, adaptive, and structural dimensions which constitute the basic dimensions of mental organization and functioning. The early mother-child relation is decisive for determining the development of the capacity to tolerate frustration and delay, the development of early ego functions, the development of the capacity to distinguish between oneself and external objects, and the capacity to perceive and adapt to the external world. It is a major contributing influence to the development of the capacity to relate to another human being as a whole and separate individual in a meaningful one-to-one object relationship.

From the very beginning of their association, mother and child are involved in a continual process of active and mutual influencing. Both mother and baby are trying to influence and accommodate to each other in a wide variety of ways, some quite subtle, some not so subtle. Erikson has called attention to the process of mutual regulation that occurs in the successful mother-child unit which is so important for the course of the child's development.[58] One of the crucial achievements of the earliest phase of the mother-child interaction is an intermeshing of the mother's mothering and caring activities with the child's needs and capacities. Conversely, there must come about a successful adapting and responsiveness in the child to enable him to receive the mother's mothering and to find gratification and pleasure in it.

At the very beginning of life, in the period immediately after birth, there is an initial phase of mutual adaptation between mother and child. This is the beginning of their career together. It provides the first of several discriminable phases of their progressive interaction. These progressive phases are organized around specific developmental issues which lay the groundwork—each in its turn—for future developmental steps. Each of these issues becomes the focus of a real interaction process between mother and child. The success with which they are able to resolve any one of the earlier issues influences the pattern of the child's development as it becomes organized around that particular issue and also influences the relative success of the resolution of future issues.

As mentioned, the initial period of adaptation between mother and infant focuses on the primary task of establishing a suitable meshing of mothering activities with the baby's needs and inner states. The infant emits certain signals which serve as cues to his inner states of distress and need. These signals are crucial because their correct reading by others and their response to them are matters of survival value to the infant. We have already discussed Freud's view of the newborn child as utterly and biologically dependent on others for his survival. The infant is not a self-sufficient organism. He depends in critical ways on the mothering activity of others both for sustaining life and, more to the point, maintaining the homeostatic balance of his natural bodily functions and needs which provides him with a sense of well-being and security. The inner balance of physiological states is necessary to avoid the internal tension and distress which give rise to unpleasurable and anxious states. Only if this balance is maintained will the child be able to thrive.

Thus mother and child are caught up in a continual process of mutual interaction and negotiation over matters of basic and vital concern —feeding, eliminating, sleeping, and waking. The successful resolution of these matters is normally achieved during the first few months of life. The success of this process is reflected in the extent to which the child establishes a stable and comfortable rhythm of such activities. This stable rhythm of vital processes takes the form of regular and easy feeding, regular and satisfying elimination, and a regular pattern of sleeping and waking. The child also develops a certain capacity for discrimination in his responsiveness to handling by the mother. He is more responsive to her and quiets more readily when she picks him up than with anyone else. From the mother's part, the success of the relationship is reflected in her growing assurance that she knows her baby and understands him in a way that no one else does. It will also be reflected in a considerable decrease in her anxieties about accepting the responsibility for providing these life-sustaining ministrations for the child.

Mutuality must be established in this earliest phase of the interaction. The mother must be sensitive to and responsive to the cues that the child is able to emit. An essential aspect of her healthy responsiveness is the balance that she must maintain between her empathy, with what she feels to be the child's needs, and her objectivity, in viewing him as an independent unit apart from her own thoughts, feelings, and fantasies. A certain measure of objectivity is essential if the mother is to be able to pick up the unique functional qualities that characterize individual infants from the moment of birth and to which she must learn to adapt her mothering activities. If the mother is unable to maintain this balance, she fails to respond to the child's cues and runs the risk of responding more to her own inner thoughts and feelings, which she may begin to mistake for the child's.

The working out of this mutual regulation in this earliest period of development serves to establish certain basic life issues. The most striking dimension of the whole process is that, for the basic regulation and control of inner states and the balancing of vital processes, the infant must depend on another human being—the mother. He must learn to depend on that other for the control of inner states which cause him distress and discomfort. The degree to which he can count on that other person, rely on her availability and presence, find assurance that she is a constant and reliable object for him to relate to and depend on, and particularly the extent to which he comes to know her as sensitive and responsive to his inner needs, are vital aspects of this early interaction. Homeostatic regulation and the maintenance of a sense of well-being in the child are at this level intimately tied to and dependent on the mother's mothering responsiveness. The child's primitive and vaguely undifferentiated sense of wholeness, goodness, and internal security and comfort are a resultant of this interaction. This can be viewed as the basis for what Erikson has referred to as "basic trust." The baby's trusting is reflected in his ease in feeding, in the confidence that what is being taken in from another is good and comforting, in the depth of sleep which can be entered into with the assurance that the needed and sustaining person will be there when he awakens, and in the ease and pleasure of elimination. The infant's familiarity with the mother becomes, as Erikson puts it, "an inner certainty as well as an outer predictability." [59]

Basic Trust

This process of mutual regulation and adjustment leaves a fundamental residue in the emerging personality that will exercise a profound influence on the child's basic orientation toward other persons in his environment. The rudiments of basic trust or its opposite, basic mistrust, are described at this level, and the direction of the child's further development is biased by the resolution of this issue. The capacity to trust is basic to any kind of human relatedness and the extent to which that capacity is impaired will determine much of what later passes for psychopathology and the disturbance of interpersonal relations. Its severest defect is seen in schizophrenic or autistic states in which all human relationships are permeated with dread and the threat of destructive engulfment. Even at best one cannot speak of perfect trust; every human being carries with him a residue of mistrust that reflects the partial breakdown in the mutual regulation between mother and child. The process is bound to have its slip-ups, as all human interactions do. But there is a delicate balance struck which gives a basic resolution to the polarities of trust and mistrust and lays the foundation for the future capacity to enter into trusting and mutually rewarding relationships with other human beings.

Erikson adds a significant note to these considerations. He writes:

But let it be said here that the amount of trust derived from earliest infantile experience does not seem to depend on absolute quantities of food or demonstrations of love, but rather on the quality of the maternal relationship. Mothers create a sense of trust in their children by that kind of administration which in its quality combines care of the baby's individual needs and a firm sense of personal trustworthiness within the trusted framework of their culture's life style.[60]

The child's trusting is a response to and flows from the interaction with the mother's own inner sense of trustworthiness. The infant's inborn capacity to take in by mouth must mesh with the mother's capacity and desire to feed him. The breast-feeding situation is more or less a prototype of the mother-child interaction at this phase of development. As Erikson puts it: "At this point he [the child] lives through, and loves with, his mouth; and the mother lives through, and loves with, her breasts." [61]

While this immediate mouth-breast contact is important, we should keep in mind that it is only representative of a whole series of interactions between mother and child in which the mother is responding to the child's needs and is caring for him. Trust is built out of this matrix constituted by countless acts and responses of both mother and child which create in the child a sense of comfort, security, well-being, and a sense of his own inner trustworthiness—that the discomforting sensations and states of inner disorganization are manageable and that states of inner tension can be relieved. There must develop a sense of inner stability which allows the child to build a sense of trust in himself and to find a sense of trustworthiness in himself. As his own inner capacities for even physiological regulation mature, the sense of security and stability that has been provided by the ministrations of the mother becomes increasingly the child's own.

If we look at all of this from a common-sense point of view, these findings seem simple and almost self-evident. Freud described the biological roots of the infant's dependency. The human infant comes into the world in a less developed state than other animals. This would imply that the care of the infant by the mother is essential—at least biologically, if not psychologically as well. The biological aspects of motherhood are manifested not merely in physiological functions, like lactation, but also in a recognizable subjective experience that mothers have in regard to their offspring. The healthy and adjusted mother of a very young infant is tuned in to the child's inner needs in an intuitive way that other people are not. The normal relationship between a mother and her young infant is really one of close symbiotic union. The gradual growth and development of the child must inevitably involve an increasing separation from this primal symbiotic union. The child must gradually emerge from it as a separate and unique individual—a process Mahler describes as separation-individuation.

The Development of Instincts

From the point of view of instinctual theory, however, the problems are complex. The assumption of instinctual drives and energies remains one of the fundamental hypotheses of psychoanalytic theory. In Freud's original conception, he ascribed instinctual energies entirely to innate, inborn biological sources. In view of the accumulating evidences, however, we must account for the fact that instincts do not seem to possess fully at birth the characteristic that Freud assigned to them. At birth instincts do not seem to have a clear and definite source, aim, or object. These were elements that Freud had laid down as the defining characteristics of instincts. Rather, as we see the process now, it is only as a result of a lengthy process of development that the source, aim, and objects of instinctual drives become relatively defined.

This view is perfectly compatible with the developmental hypothesis. It is reasonable to suggest that just as the human infant at birth is immature in so many of its physical attributes, it has also not yet acquired the full complement of its instinctual endowment, in both a quantitative and qualitative sense. The instincts do not seem to have the strength, direction, intensity, and nature that they develop in later life. We need not consider the infant at birth as having the same endowment of libido and aggression that he will have as an adult. In addition, the optimal development of these dynamic factors, both quantitatively and qualitatively, cannot be understood merely in terms of individual intrinsic maturational factors. Even when they were assumed as biological givens, the instincts were never viewed as predetermined in the same sense as, for example, the organization and development of the eyeball. The appearance, development, and mastery of instinctual drives is contingent on the process of mutual regulation and interaction that takes place between two human beings—mother and child.

This approach to development does not make the process any less biological. It does make it more complex and more hazardous. The baby must in the first place be capable of responding to appropriate external stimuli and of emitting suitable signals of inner states to the mother. Some babies are less well endowed than others. Assuming that a given baby is adequately endowed with the needed capacities to respond at the appropriate time, it is still necessary that the proper stimuli be given and that their timing be right. Study of infants raised in institutional settings over significant periods of time have shown that at a certain level of development these children will develop age-appropriate capacities and behaviors. They are able, for example, to focus on objects, become interested in them, and try to reach out to grasp them. If the adequate stimulus is not given or not continued, the capacity seems to recede or to extinguish. This pattern of response suggests that the development of many functions which are usually regarded as relatively autonomous ego functions does not simply occur spontaneously or automatically. In order to develop these capacities, the baby has to receive appropriate stimulation, in the appropriate dosage and with the appropriate timing. Hartmann has pointed out these aspects of development in terms of the emergence of what he calls "structures of primary autonomy" as related to the "average expectable environment."

Developmental Failure

From our observations of disturbed adults we can often see that there has been something wrong with the developmental process—that there has been a developmental failure. It is not always a simple matter, however, to determine how far these defects in development can be attributed to something that was innately wrong with the patient at birth or how far the failure is attributable to external events and influences. For example, a patient may show a deficient capacity to tolerate frustration, but we do not know whether this reflects a lack of innate endowment or a lack of developmental experiences which would allow him to develop this capacity. A capacity for such tolerance may have begun to emerge early in his development but may not have subsequently been reinforced, and so it might have withered and died away. This sort of thing has been demonstrated grossly in institutionalized children who have been subject to severe deprivation. Many of these children seem to be mentally defective, but they were not born with defective mental endowment. They did not receive the appropriate and proportional environmental stimuli which would make it possible for their mental capacities to develop. The cause of such severe developmental failures is not always apparent.

This problem, of course, is simply another way of posing the old dichotomy of heredity vs. environment, nature vs. nurture. Here the environment is specifically that provided by the maternal mothering activities. What is in question is something very specific and concrete. What is at issue is whether this particular mother or mother substitute has provided this particular baby with the appropriate perceptual experiences, continuity of care, timely relief of his distress, responsiveness to his inner needs, and sensitivity to his developmental progress which will facilitate his maturational course. If this mutual regulation and responsiveness is achieved, the conditions are set for the optimal development of the child's instinctual endowment, his ego and its functions, his capacity for reality testing and especially for object relations. In contrast, if the mother—whether wittingly or not—keeps the child in a state of partial sensory deprivation, or of real deprivation and frustration, or of excessive stimulation, or subjects him to erratic and inconstant mothering, the child's developing capacities will be impaired with a variety of residual defects that may contribute to personality dysfunction and neurotic difficulties in later life. Where the child's basic capacity to differentiate between self and object and his capacity to form a perception of the mother as a whole and separate object are affected, the rudiments of basic trust are disturbed and the consequences for his later development and adjustment would be expected to be much more severe.

All of this implies an important conceptual shift which has particular relevance for contemporary studies. Several longitudinal developmental projects are investigating the relationship between the innate endowment of individual children and the emergence of specific characteristics contingent on facilitating types of experience. These studies have approached the problem over a broad range of both animal and human behaviors. The results of these studies seem to support the conclusion that the interaction between the infant organism and the material organism is an essential determinant of optimal maturation. We can briefly remind ourselves of Harlow's important experiments with baby monkeys raised with terry-cloth-and-wire inanimate substitute mother figures. The babies could receive food from the milk bottles built into these "mothers" and could cling to the terry-cloth skin. No other mothering functions were available, certainly no responsiveness to inner states and needs. Harlow traced the subsequent developmental difficulties of these monkeys. The deficits in the areas of socialization were particularly marked, especially in the areas of sexual behavior and subsequent mothering behavior in relation to their own offspring.

The Developmental Process

We would find it difficult in the light of these and other studies to ignore the increasing importance of perceptual experience as a factor in development. We must try to correlate this appreciation with a theory of the development of mental life, and with an understanding of its progression, regression, and its forms of deviance and illness. This understanding must include the hypothesis that the mind possesses basic energies which can be subject to quantitative variation. This implies both a dynamic and an economic hypothesis. The dynamic attributes of the mental apparatus can be either expressed directly in the form of instinctual behavior or—as we have seen in our consideration of repression —they may not find direct expression at all, but be retained in a vital and active form in the unconscious. Here they continue to exercise an influence, dynamically seeking pathways of discharge and determining the individual's capacity to obtain instinctual gratification.

We can remind ourselves of the continuing operation of instinctual drives by recalling the changes that take place at puberty. At the beginning of puberty there are certain phase-specific biological modifications —hormonal and gonadal developments—which lead to a marked upsurge in sexual energy. The biological changes of puberty are accompanied by changes in the mental economy which have a considerable influence not only on the experiencing and expressing of sexual interests and feelings, but also on almost every other area of mental life. The instinctual drives which had been hidden during the years of latency development once again assert their active and dynamic presence in the appropriate developmental context.

We have multiple evidences to the effect that instinctual wishes can be repressed, distorted, and displaced. These are the evidences that Freud struggled with in trying to understand symptom formation, repression, defense, dreams, and the psychopathology of everyday life. Nonetheless, we need to raise some questions about the extent to which the individual human being is born with a specific instinctual endowment which he will retain throughout life. The possibility must be considered that the emergence and development of these very basic dynamic properties are in part contingent on environmental-experiential factors. We are still confronted with the problem that Freud raised in his postulating of a complemental series in the process of development.

We can say that at birth the baby must have the potential equipment to respond to suitable environmental stimuli if he is going to develop in a healthy manner. The situation is more complex, as we have suggested, since it is not merely a matter of the environment providing an adequate stimulus, but also of the infant's capacity to elicit a response by emitting appropriate signals of his inner needs and of successfully negotiating the developmental issues with his caretaking and mothering objects. The process is one of mutual regulation and responsiveness which reflects the combined influence of intrinsic and experiential factors.

This pertains particularly to the development of the basic psychic equipment that the child acquires in the first months and years of life, well before the onset of oedipal involvements and conflicts. During this period of relative dependence, the child's development is contingent on the successful achievement of one-to-one relationships. We have not paid much attention to the child's developing relationship with his father, but it too has important developmental implications as we shall see later. We can feel fairly certain that, unless certain developmental steps are taken during this crucial early period, the prognosis for later mental health and functioning will be relatively poor. It is thus important for the child to be able to engage in meaningful and positive one-to-one relationships both with his mother and with his father—or their substitutes. The success with which the child will be able to move on into the oedipal situation and to resolve its conflicts in a healthy way depends on the quality of the one-to-one relations that he brings with him to the triangular context.

[11]

The Primary Relationships

In the preceding chapter we discussed the significance of the earliest object relations and their implications for the age-old question of the relative influence of hereditary vs. environmental factors on the course of individual development. We discussed the accumulating objective evidence which seems to point to the importance of experiential factors in eliciting the optimal developmental capacities of the individual child. These findings are fully compatible with a developmental approach to human mental life which takes into consideration intrinsic maturational factors. The fact that the early mother-child interaction seems to be so crucial is compatible with a biological understanding of the importance and function of mothering activity. The fact, however, that human growth and development are contingent on shared experience introduces a number of complexities.

Influences on the Mother-Child Interaction

We should point out that, up to this point, we have been focusing mainly on the actual perceptual experiences of the young infant from birth up until the development of the capacity for self-object differentiation. We can say that the importance of the mother-child interaction is biologically understandable. Human beings, after all, are animals, and the birth process is a biological phenomenon. It is generally believed that a mother will show innate instinctual responsiveness to her child, unless inhibiting factors come into play. In other words, unless the mother's psychological conflicts interfere, she can be expected to respond to her child in a reasonably healthy and adaptive manner. The adaptation is a basically instinctual relationship between mother and child. It includes the mother's responsiveness to the child's inner needs and states. It also includes her responsiveness to the progressive developmental changes in those inner needs and states. It implies her responsiveness to his growing autonomy. His needs shift from a state of almost pure passivity at the beginning of life to an increasing activity. During the second half of the first year of life, and on into the second and third years, the child begins to show an increasing capacity for tolerating delay and frustration. He also begins to show increasing needs for independence and autonomy. The mutual adaptation between the child and his parents—at first the mother, but then also increasingly the father— are crucial factors in the resolution of each of these developmental steps.

The development of a human baby is influenced by the fact that its mother is a complicated human being herself. It is more difficult than is often appreciated for a sophisticated, relatively intellectual, and often somewhat neurotic mother to respond to the needs of her baby in an instinctively adaptive and spontaneous way. Breast feeding, for example, is an enormous achievement for many women in our more advanced Western societies, whereas it is by and large taken for granted in more primitive societies where it often has survival value. It is only in recent years, moreover, that we have begun to appreciate the importance of child-rearing practices for the patterning of personality development. There is a large body of evidence to suggest that even in primitive societies the manner in which child care, weaning, and toilet training are carried out has important effects on more or less typical character traits within the specific cultural context. Erikson in his *Childhood and Society* (1950), for example, has marshaled some of the significant evidences to illustrate the degree to which important differences between the adult characteristics of primitive tribes may be related to child-rearing attitudes and practices embedded in the culture of the tribe. The sort of treatment the child receives at birth, in early feeding, in weaning, in toilet training—and more significantly the attitudes and values reflected in these practices—have a definite impact in shaping the child's future character and manner of adaptive functioning. We must not fail to appreciate that these modes of providing a specific quality of perceptual experience, including the experience of frustration, are patterned after and supported by a consistent cultural system and have a decisive influence on the shaping of the psychic equipment of the individual, not merely in eliciting the structural organization of the psychic apparatus but in shaping it to the needs and dimensions of the culture within which it develops and lives.

In the contemporary social setting, we need to remind ourselves that the experience which any individual mother provides for her child will be largely determined by her own psychological makeup. This includes her own inner conflicts about her femininity, her sex role including the fact of motherhood, her sense of self-esteem, the quality of her relationship and interaction with her husband, as well as his capacity to accept and adjust to the demands of fatherhood and paternal responsibility. Young fathers—not uncommonly—respond to the birth of their first child with a degree of anxiety and even jealousy which may complicate or even interfere with the mother's capacity to provide a good mothering experience for the child and to adapt to the child's needs and inner states. Thus environmental influences are not simply reducible to the question of whether the mother loves the child or not, or whether she wants him or not. The influences are considerably more complicated. They involve the fact that human beings are so complicated that the number of subtle factors interfering with the mother's mothering capacity and performance may be nearly infinite. The process of mutual regulation and sensitive and adaptive responsiveness within the mother-child relation is very precarious and easily disturbed. Despite the complexity of these problems, we can gain some significant understanding of them by examining the process.

In this connection it is important to keep in mind that the reason why certain experiences occur or do not occur is far less important than their actual occurrence. Whether a potentially good mother is handicapped by physical illness, external interferences or distress, or inner turmoil and conflict during the early months of her interaction with her baby is far less relevant to the development of the baby than the actual experiences and quality of interaction which she is able to provide the child during this crucial period. These difficulties may affect the mother-child interaction, but they need not. A mother may be quite severely handicapped in a variety of ways, and still function as a good mothering object. An extreme case, for example, is provided by some of the evidence about schizophrenic mothers and their mothering capacity. There is good evidence to suggest that chronic schizophrenic women, who would usually be regarded as poor candidates for motherhood and as relatively incapable of managing the roles and functions of adequate mothering, may in fact undergo the experience of pregnancy, childbirth, and nursing and caring for a young infant in a quite positive and adaptive manner. The baby's experiences during the first six months of life may, in fact, be better with a schizophrenic mother than they might be with a healthier, intelligent, although neurotic, mother who is afraid to touch or pick up her baby and feels terribly anxious about handling him because of her own inner conflicts.

Thus what is crucial in the earliest months of life and extremely important for the baby's development is the actual experience and interaction that is achieved between himself and his mothering figure. Quite clearly, this mothering figure need not be the child's own biological mother. We might find that the infant whose own mother is absent for some reason during the first six months of life and who is cared for during this period by a really loving and adequate mother substitute, may be provided with better mothering experiences than he might have received from his own mother. Such might be the case, for example, where the mother suffers from a relatively mild postpartum depression. Such a mother might well recover and be able in time to assume the responsibilities of the mothering task, but during the period of her illness, which may last months, she might subject her infant to inconsistent care and would be inadequately responsive to his basic needs. Such a child would experience alternating frustration and overindulgence, sensory deprivation and overstimulation.

Gratification and Delay

The types of experience with which we are dealing have to do, first, with the development of satisfactory instinctual activity, particularly in the feeding situation. As we already discussed in the last chapter, this not only is important for the development of instinctual drives, but also is related to the emergence of early ego activities. We noted in discussing the behavior of healthy children in getting and playing with Dr. Winnicott's spatula that not only was instinctual satisfaction involved as a motivating factor, but that the behavior expressed the operation of a number of ego functions. Optimal development is not merely a question of positive gratification of instinctual drives; more is required. In addition to gratification, it is essential that there be enough experience of delay and frustration so that the developmental influence of the reality principle can find a balanced and proportional interplay with the working of the pleasure principle.

The child requires sufficient continuity, sufficient consistency, and sufficient perceptual stimulation to facilitate and elicit those maturational steps which will result in a focused and integrated pattern of orally directed behavior during the second three months of life. Repeated experiences of gratification, delay, and gratification seem to be crucial.

When and how such experiences are laid down in the memory bank, or when and to what extent they become part of the infant's awareness and remembered experience are difficult to determine. There is good evidence, however, that memory traces are being continually laid down well before they reach any level of explicit and conscious remembering. If we observe the normal and healthy baby of about four months, we can already see a patterning in his behavior. When he wakes up in the morning, he does not immediately begin to cry. He will often chatter rather contentedly to himself for a while. When his mother comes to greet him and feed him she is welcomed with a warm and winning smile. The smiling response—although it usually does not reach its height until well into the second half of the first year—occurs earlier and indicates the child's assuming some initiative in the social exchange with his mother. It also suggests that even though the baby may not be consciously remembering and associating to past experiences of gratification, there has nevertheless taken place somewhere in his mind a gradual integration of a pattern of repeated experiencing of hunger, satisfaction, sleep, and waking, with a gradual emergence of a vague awareness of rhythmic patterning.

When the child has reached this stage of development, his psychic apparatus is already manisfesting discernible dynamic, economic, structural, and adaptive capacities. The optimal development of these capacities is contingent not merely on the passage of time and the expression of intrinsic maturational factors. It is also contingent on what the patterning of experience has been during this period. The patterning of experience may be deficient, excessive, inconsistent, or intermittent. Time alone—given the infant's capacity to survive—would very likely allow for a certain amount of maturational progress. But in the absence of adequate stimulation, the expression of maturational factors is likely to be severely impaired. The absence of adequate stimulation, however, can have rather serious and severe effects. The work of Spitz on anaclitic depressions in institutionally deprived children is well known. Such children may in fact not survive—they become apathetic, stop feeding, and die. More often they show severe developmental retardation and impairment of fuctioning.

Either gross defectiveness in the innate equipment of the infant, or alternatively, gross traumatic experience can severely affect and interfere with the development of focused orality and the early emergence of ego functions. Such grossly deviant patterns are easily recognized but are rarely seen. Winnicott has suggested that in the interaction of the ordinary baby and the ordinary mother, however, there is included a wide range of developmental patterns. Within this range the child whose endowment will allow for reasonably healthy development, and the mother who despite her conflicts falls within the normal range, will be able to achieve some degree of mutual adaptation. The child's object-directed impulses will be able to develop. He will experience a certain proportional gratification when his wishes are met. He will also experience periods of distress and rage during periods of delay or frustration when his wishes are not being met.

Self-Object Differentiation

When the infant gets to be about six to eight months of age, he reaches the level of development at which he normally becomes capable of self-object differentiation. The child begins to form some idea of where he ends and of where nonself—the world of separate objects—begins. We do not know, of course, at this early period just how much the infant's mind is really aware of. But there seems to be an increasingly integrated recognition, developed through repeated experiences of frustration and delay of gratification, that he is not the source of his own gratification. This vague and increasing awareness becomes more definitive when he becomes capable of self-object differentiation. At this point the preponderance of positive as against negative experiences during the period of this developing awareness seems to be a matter of decisive importance. At one extreme—the positive extreme—the infant who is excessively gratified, who has not been allowed to experience a certain amount of delay between his crying and distress and the appearance of the mother, has not been allowed a sufficient amount of negative experience for him to be able to gain recognition of his dependence on a separate object. Conversely—at the negative extreme—the child who has been exposed to excessive deprivation and frustration will be much less likely to be able to experience positive anticipation when he first becomes aware of the absence of the needed object. His sense of security and trusting expectation will be undermined.

We can also look at this process from the point of view of the object-directed experience within the mind of the baby. We have pointed out that the earliest relationship between mother and child is essentially symbiotic. In trying to reconstruct the development of genuine object relations in the child's mind we are assuming a minimal distinction between the baby's self and his objects in his earliest experience. The gradual achievement of some capacity for delay plays an important part in the development of memory functions and in the development of self-object differentiation. The increasing ability to tolerate delay is accompanied by an emerging capacity to recall prior sequences of delay followed by gratification. Tolerance for delay is supported by an increasing assurance of satisfaction after delay. Tolerance for delay, therefore, serves to foster the emergence of memory functions, and the development of memory functions has a reciprocal influence on the increasing capacity for delay. The capacity for delay in a similar manner contributes to and is fostered by the ability to differentiate between self and the gratifying object. Tolerance for delay is abetted by the increasing reassurance that inner distress will be responded to by the absent but recurrently available object.

In this early period, however, the infant may not be explicitly aware of the fact that the source of both pleasurable and painful experiences derives from an external object. He may not be aware that the experiences of pleasure and unpleasure derive from the same object, or that they derive from a whole object rather than from a breast, or a bottle, or voice, hands, smell, etc. Objective evaluations of infant perceptual organization indicate that the baby cannot really organize his sensory input into a percept of a whole person much before the age of six months. Long before the development of such organizational capacity, however, the normal and healthy child has been able to accumulate experiences and memories of the repeated and reliable rhythms of distress and relief, of need and gratification, of waking and sleeping, of feeding and eliminating. To some degree, then, one must assume that past images, however dim and vague, of gratifying and frustrating objects have been accumulated and in some sense internalized, thus providing a basis for further developmental elaborations.

The First Objects

Formation of a genuine object relationship implies that these primitive experiences have been integrated into a perception of the mother as a whole and separate person. It is difficult to delineate the actual steps by which such an integration and differentiation are achieved. There is also a problem in sequence in the development of such cognitive organization. In one sense it does not make much sense to speak of an object relation until there is a self to share it. If there is to be a relationship it necessarily involves not only an object but a subject as well. But, on the other hand, we have reason to believe that a gradual acquisition of a sense of self depends on the internalization of what is experienced in the object relationship. Freud began to explore this relationship in his effort to establish identification with objects as a mechanism of ego development. The differentiation of objects is correlative with the differentiation of self. The genuine relatedness to objects must, therefore, reflect a genuine sense of self. How this crucial developmental step occurs we do not really know. We do know that when it occurs in an optimal manner the child develops in parallel the ability to tolerate frustration, disappointment, and anger. He is able to integrate the experience of pleasure and pain and associate them with the same object. He can hold affects of both love and hate for the same object—which is both gratifying and frustrating—without feeling that they are exclusive. He gains the capacity to have the same object as the recipient of contradictory emotions at one and the same time. He thus becomes capable of tolerating ambivalence in his relation to significant objects.

For this important developmental goal to be achieved and for the capacity to deal with ambivalence to emerge, it seems vital that good experiences outweigh bad ones in the period preceding the differentiation of self and object. From the point of view of the object relation itself it is important that love should be stronger than hate. A balance in favor of love offers the assurance that the relationship will persist and not be destroyed. A similar principle applies to the balance of instinctual forces with which the child progresses to further levels of development. The greater the experience of and feeling of love, the more will the libidinal aspects of the child's instinctual endowment play the predominant role. The greater the experience of and feeling of anger and frustration, the greater is the likelihood that aggressive and destructive impulses will have a determining influence in the course of later development.

Mahler has described this aspect of the developmental process in terms of the conditions of the mother-child symbiosis and the mother's "holding behavior." If these conditions are optimal, the infant is enabled to "hatch" from the symbiotic relation with the mother more readily and easily. The child is thus better equipped to separate and to differentiate his own self-representations from the previously fused self-and-object representations of the symbiotic union.

If we accept as a basic premise the notion that the very young, instinctually satisfied infant makes little if any distinction between himself and his object, we would conclude that the infant whose every wish was immediately gratified would not have the necessary stimulation to be able to recognize that wish and gratification involve two distinct steps. This basic recognition is equivalent to Freud's description of the initiation of the reality principle. This provides the starting point for the later differentiation of primary from secondary process thinking. It is implicit in primary process organization that wish and gratification be synonymous. In the most basic sense of the term, however, secondary process includes at least an implicit recognition of a distinction and separation of wish and gratification. It implies at least a two-step process in which wish is followed not by immediate gratification, but by delay, and that only after delay is gratification achieved.

Some frustration in the infant's experience is inevitable. Even in the most ideal situations gratification cannot be total and immediate. There is always some element of frustration, some waiting, some delay; and satisfaction is rarely if ever complete. These negative aspects of experience enable the child to build up a capacity to tolerate frustration. Many theorists feel that the potential capacity to tolerate frustration and delay is one in which constitutional factors may play an important role. In his Farewell Address, for example, Ernest Jones suggested that the development of this capacity was related to having the physical equipment which would enable the organism to hold an afferent stimulus without an immediate efferent discharge. This would enable the organism to postpone the gratification related to the discharge of excitation.

The development of object relations involves carrying the appreciation of the separation of wish and gratification a further step, to the recognition that gratification is dependent on another person. For this to occur, the infant must be able to recognize that he has a wish which is not immediately gratified and at the same time he must be able to remember previous experiences of similar delay followed by satisfaction as a result of the presentation of another whole person. The child must combine a positive wish with the absence of a gratifying object. For this to be experienced as pleasurable anticipation rather than simply as intolerable frustration, there must be a recollection of positive experiences in which delay was followed by gratification. The attachment of such pleasant recollections to the person of the gratifying object make it possible for the development of adaptive self-object differentiation to be tied to the beginnings of object love. Thus it becomes possible for a good, early object relation to be initiated, and this can help to set the conditions for the earliest ego identifications. This is intimately related to the inner security which derives from the external reliability of the gratifying object that Erikson places at the core of the infant's trusting relatedness to his significant objects.

The role of the mother in determining the course of this development is central. The experiences she provides the child will have a significant influence on a number of important attributes of the future adult's psychological makeup. Further, the actual instinctual endowment that the child carries over into later developmental stages is profoundly influenced by the balance of good and bad experiences in earliest infancy. There is considerable controversy over these matters, particularly in regard to the aggressive instincts. At one extreme, the Kleinian position holds that there is an innate death instinct and that most of the early developmental problems are due to the child's defenses against his own innate aggression during the early months of life. At the opposite extreme, Bowlby and others maintain that there is no such thing'as innate aggression or a death instinct. They see aggression entirely as a response to frustration or deprivation.

Most contemporary psychoanalysts, however, believe that there is some form of innate active and aggressive drive in the organism. How clearly this basic drive can be identified with aggression or hate, as we are able to identify them in more adult forms of expression, and how far it is directed toward and concerned with active mastery are controversial questions. Even so, there is rather general agreement that whether or not aggression is an innate instinct, it is certainly increased and intensified during the first years of life by negative and frustrating experiences. Some analysts, therefore, are now inclined to think that just as the ego is not really present in a differentiated form at birth, so too the basic instinctual endowment is present in an undifferentiated form. Consequently, the more differentiated affective states of hate and love cannot be identified at the beginning of life. We can conclude, in general, that the early object relations have several crucial developmental effects. They serve to elicit optimal instinctual activity and to induce the proportional focalizing of instinctual behavior. They effect the initiation of relatively autonomous ego functioning which begins to emerge in relatively diffuse and undifferentiated manner even before the acquisition of self-object differentiation. They contribute to the quality of self-object differentiation which serves as a basis for earliest identifications and the subsequent establishment of object love. They also contribute to a basic motivation toward mastery which will significantly influence the capacity for later adaptation.

Separation and Individuation

In the beginning of the child's developmental course, the mother is for all practical purposes the sole object for the child. The first six months, more or less, are given over largely to the working out of a basic pattern of interaction between mother and child. The mother's anxieties about providing her infant with life-sustaining care gradually diminish and she becomes increasingly able to indulge in the more and more delightful and playful experience of stimulating and responding to the child. The child's smiling behavior gradually emerges and represents his first assuming of initiative in the social interaction with the mother. More and more he takes on the function of stimulating her to respond to him. One of the basic questions for the infant's continuing development is the extent to which these initial efforts will be successful in eliciting a rewarding response from the mother, particularly the extent to which his initiative can bring about a mutually enjoyable and reciprocal exchange with her.

As the child's role becomes increasingly active in the exchange, other important developmental issues are joined. The range of the child's initiative is slowly extended. His efforts are directed toward focusing the mother's behavior to meet his needs. He accepts feeding more easily from her, seeks her lap for comfort and security, etc. The success of these focalizing attempts serve as the anlage for the child's emerging sense of autonomy. He gradually develops a sense of his own capacity to control and bring about responses in the significant caring persons. His ability to focalize the mother's responses to meet his needs gives him a sense of inner resourcefulness and control over the discomfort and tension that arise with unfulfilled needs. He becomes increasingly aware of himself as capable of inner regulation and as capable of influencing the predictability of significant others on whom he has learned to depend. Not only can he find a familiar trust in the reliability of caring figures, but he can to some extent succeed in bringing about those trustworthy responses as a result of his own initiative.

This is the beginning of the process of separation-individuation. The child begins to achieve a sense of separate functioning, but still in the presence of and with the continuing emotional availability and support of the mother. However optimal the conditions of this separation, the nature of the process continually poses the threat of object loss. The child is enabled to overcome the separation anxiety embedded in each new step toward separate functioning by the pleasure derived from his newfound capacity and by the mother's continuing approval and support. There is a spurt in the emergence of the child's developing autonomy which is bolstered by the development of ego functions and by a flux of developmental energy. The child's emerging autonomy is reinforced and extends into the period of negativism that attends the anal phase of development.

Emerging Autonomy

Somewhere in the second year, this process reaches a climax. The child possesses an expanded sense of his own magical power and omnipotence—even though in large measure this sense of power is still dependent on his sense of sharing in the power of the mother. But he is also caught up in dealing with a sense of physical separateness from the mother. As he separates from the mother and his dependence on her, he becomes increasingly vulnerable, and the rudiments of his sense of self and self-esteem may be damaged. The emerging autonomy begins to qualify some of his sense of magical omnipotence and opens the way to more realistic adjustment. As individuation proceeds, the processes of internalization are set to work and the conditions provided for the development of true ego identifications with the parents.

The prototypical situation in which certain of these developmental issues and their related conflicts are displayed is that of toilet training. Much has been written and much mythology has been generated about toilet training, but we should not lose sight of the fact that it coincides with a developmental phase in which some of the most basic aspects of the child's emerging personality are being worked out at large in the child's experience. The maturation of his body with the gradually increasing control over the operation of muscle sphincters gives him the capacity to hold on to or to let go of feces in terms of more voluntary control. This provides a natural ground on which many of these developmental issues can be joined. The same issues are joined in many other and diverse contexts of the interaction between the child and his parents—so that we cannot attribute any magical significance to the struggles over the toilet.

As the child enters the second year of life, he comes into a period of self-assertion. The phenomenon of negativism at this stage is something that every parent knows quite well. The child learns the word *no* and begins to exercise it in many directions as an expression of his increasing assertion of himself as against everything else. He seems at times almost driven to carry out his own intentions and to extend the area of his manipulation and control. Before this his initiatives had been more or less for eliciting supportive responses, at first from the mother, but gradually including his father and later other important figures in his environment. Little by little, however, he begins to try out his initiatives even in the face of the opposition of these others. A contest of wills emerges. The important issue to be negotiated at this stage is whether the child can establish his self-assertion in these interactions and in what areas. He must gain some sense in this process that he can to some extent have his way and that his having his way is acceptable to the important others, particularly his mother and father.

The mutual regulation between the child and his parents is crucial at this stage as well. The child still needs the support of outer controls and the reliability of external predictable and trustable adults. If the external controls are too rigid or too early, they may deprive the child of the opportunity to exercise his own control. If the child's attempts to control his own functions are interfered with, he may develop a sense of powerlessness that forces him to resort to earlier regressive patterns of behavior or to progress prematurely to a pretended and fragile autonomy. He may regress to begging, whining, and demanding behavior or to forms of oral behavior like thumb-sucking. Or he may become hostile and willful, assuming a pretended autonomy that includes a wish not to depend on anybody. There is a basic conflict between willingness and willfulness.

The development of a genuine and proportional autonomy both extends and depends on the earlier development of a sense of basic trust. The child must learn that his sense of trust in himself and in the world will not be jeopardized by his emerging wish to have a choice and to exercise his own willingness or willfulness. His potential willfulness and destructiveness must be met by parental firmness, which can both protect him from the internal threat of his own destructive wishes and can guide and support him in dealing with his wishes to hold on to and to let go of with appropriate discretion. Otherwise the child runs the twofold risk of stubbornly holding on to or of letting go of without control. The external support and guidances thus continue to serve a homeostatic function in helping the child to balance his inner states. The failure to achieve such balance would prejudice the development of real autonomy by the child's developing a sense of shame or of self-doubt.

The objective of this stage is to help the child establish a sense of self-control without loss of self-esteem. As Erikson puts it:

This stage, therefore, becomes decisive for the ratio between love and hate, for that between cooperation and willfulness, and for that between the freedom of self-expression and its suppression. From a sense of self-control without loss of self-esteem comes a lasting sense of autonomy and pride; from a sense of muscular and anal impotence, of loss of self-control, and of parental overcontrol comes a lasting sense of doubt and shame.[62]

If the child is encouraged to stand on his own feet, he must at the same time be protected from experiences which threaten him with either doubt or shame. The child not only tests his own capacity for self-assertion, but gradually begins to test the extent to which he can carry out destructive and aggressive wishes—especially in the mother's or the father's presence. The manner in which the parents respond to and treat these assertions are crucial for the development of autonomy. If the child's aggression is treated with too much permissiveness, he may develop a sense of his own dangerousness and the dangerousness of his impulses which neither he nor the powerful others can control. If his aggression is treated in an overly controlling or punitive manner, the child will develop a sense of his own inner wickedness and destructiveness and come to feel that the inner destructiveness needs to be guarded against and dreaded. In either event he falls prey to shame and self-doubt.

Metapsychological Assumptions

Let us try to rephrase some of these developmental observations in terms of our basic metapsychological assumptions. These include the dynamic, economic, structural, adaptive, and developmental hypotheses. By the time the young infant has reached the level of self-object differentiation, his psychic apparatus has acquired these basic attributes. As a result of the interaction of maturational and experiential factors, his development has progressed to a new level. The adaptive hypothesis implies in this context that each developmental level has an optimal mode of adaptation that is more or less phase-specific. In the period preceding self-object differentiation the emergence of structural attributes does not imply that the infant possesses a definitive ego or superego with relatively permanent structural attributes. Rather it means that we can discern structural attributes in certain areas of functioning—an increased capacity for delay, the emergence of hand-mouth coordination, and the gradual integration of memory traces essential for the emergence of self-object differentiation. As we have suggested, no child can develop beyond the limits imposed by his innate endowment. The nature of his early experiences, however, will substantially affect the degree to which at any level of development he is able to approximate the optimal mode of adaptation.

It is also clear at the end of the first year that the infant's psychic apparatus is endowed with dynamic attributes which function in terms of economic properties. In the simplest terms, he is capable of both positive and negative impulses toward the objects in his environment. The relative strength of these loving and hating impulses and the relative balance between them will be substantially influenced by the degree to which earlier experiences have been positive, negative, consistent, or inconsistent. Whatever one's persuasion about native instinctual endowment, there is widespread agreement that frustrating and other negative experiences during the early months of life, especially if present in excess, will tend to increase the amount of aggression which the infant carries over to later developmental phases.

From Primary to Secondary Identification

Even though the young infant is unable to distinguish between himself and his object, we can nevertheless describe a primitive precursor of an internal process that will develop into one of the most important ego mechanisms. The infant's most primitive form of relation to the object is one in which he does not recognize any boundary between himself and the object, but rather includes the latter as part of himself. It is not even accurate to speak of this phenomenon as if objects were perceived as part of the self, since the self has not yet been established. The infant's global awareness does not yet make such precisions; it is simply that the boundaries between self and objects have not been established as yet and the lines between inner and outer worlds not drawn.

Freud spoke of this primitive way of relating to objects as "primary identification." It is clearly different from the types of secondary identification which serve a critical function in the developmental process not only from infancy through adolescence, but even further into adult levels of personality integration. The distinction between primary and secondary identification can be linked to the related distinctions of primary and secondary narcissism, of primary and secondary anxiety, and even further with the distinction of primary and secondary process. Primary identification is intimately related to the state of primary narcissism, both of which precede self-object differentiation. It is only after such differentiation is achieved that the ground is laid for the rudiments of ego formation. Only after the self is delineated from objects does secondary identification and the direction of libido to objects become possible. Secondary narcissism, therefore, is dependent on the development of the distinction between self and objects and on the mechanisms of secondary identification. It is only then with the emergence of ego structures that the capacity for secondary anxiety and secondary process thinking becomes possible.

One can indicate certain of the young infant's activity as reflecting elements of primary identification. Many young infants imitate their mothers' movements or expressions. This has been described as "mirroring activity." This activity is more imitative when it is observed after the level of self-object differentiation. But before that level is reached, such activity suggests not that the infant is imitating the mother's behavior so as to be like his mother, but rather that he experiences no difference between himself and his mother. His smiling is her smiling, over and above the rewarding response elicited by his smiling. Similar patterns of imitative activity can be observed in severely disturbed psychotic patients. The boundaries between self and object become undifferentiated and the patients seem to believe that if they do what the doctor does they thereby become the doctor. Such psychotic identification can be regarded as regressive forms of primary identification.

After the differentiation of self and object has been achieved, however, the infant can begin to initiate his first genuine identifications with objects. These are qualitatively different from the mirroring activity of primary identification. They are motivated by the desire to become like the object. The quality and stability of these early identifications are significantly determined by the kind of object relation the baby has developed during the first six months. The quality of this earliest object relationship, then, influences both instinctual development and structural development of the ego—in both a qualitative and quantitative manner. Both these developments determine the adaptive capacities, both active and passive, which the child will carry with him into later crucial periods of development.

Positive vs. Ambivalent Identifications

The child whose early mother-child interaction has been on the whole positive will have had an experience in which the balance of pleasure outweighs unpleasure. He will have had a sufficiently consistent experience so that he can relate to objects with positive anticipation rather than with negative fear. He has acquired an image of the mother as more accepting than rejecting. He will thus be able to achieve an essentially good object relationship. This will foster positive early identifications. The child's wish will be to become more like his mother—or later like his father. In contrast, if the object relationship has developed in a setting of inconsistent experiences in which the ratio of negative, frustrating, and punitive events has approached, equaled, or exceeded the positive and gratifying experiences, then the capacity for positive and growth-promoting identifications will be impaired.

Even under such circumstances—unless there is some sort of gross pathology—the child will be able to achieve a level of self-object differentiation and will to some extent identify with the mother. But then it is identifying with an object which it perceives as frightening, rejecting, demanding, and aggressive. The child cannot identify with such an object without taking defensive measures. One of the typical defenses which the newly emerging ego adopts was described by Anna Freud. She called it "identification with the aggressor." The child will defensively identify with the aggressive aspects of the object and by making the aggression his own thereby make the object less terrifying. He may even imitate the threatening or aggressive behavior of the object. He is thereby enabled to achieve some mastery over his own anxiety and aggressive impulses. The mechanism really turns the passive fear of the object into an active adoption of the threatening attitude or behavior. For example, the frightened child who is terrified by a visit to the doctor will turn around and play "doctor" in relation to his playmates.

In the developmental context, the more ambivalent the child's relationship to his early objects, the more probable does it become that his earliest identifications will contain marked aggressive components. These components will contribute in the child's later development to an increased tendency to defend against objects by the use of identification with the aggressor. The introjection of such aggressively colored objects at certain critical stages of the child's development can have severe implications for the development of the emerging superego. We shall return to this aspect of development shortly.

Let us return to the question of the influence of early experience on instinctual development and the way in which experience influences the instinctual equipment which the infant carries into subsequent periods of psychic development. We can consider first the baby who has enjoyed a good relationship with his mother, whom he perceives as good and loving. We can then compare him with the baby who has been exposed to a more ambivalent relationship and who sees the mother in more aggressive and rejecting or frustrating terms. We have already suggested that there would be important differences in identification between them. But it is also extremely probable that there would be related differences between the impulses and affects that each of these babies would experience in relation to their objects. The baby who has had a good relation is likely to feel more love for his objects and less hate. In the light of a basically loving relation toward its objects, there will be less threat in acknowledging its ambivalence and greater motivation toward mastering its inevitable and unavoidable ambivalence. The child who has had a more ambivalent relation, by way of contrast, will experience considerably more anger and hostility and possibly greater hate toward its objects. It will experience less love toward its objects. In this setting aggressive and destructive impulses become much more dreadful and threatening. The child will be less able to acknowledge his ambivalence and feel greater need to defend himself against his aggression. Mastery of his ambivalence thus becomes much more difficult and problematic.

In a more ambivalent object relationship the early ego identifications are less stable and less secure. These early identifications are closely linked to the development of basic trust. It is through these early identifications that the external reliability and predictability of a trustworthy mothering figure are internalized and become inner certainty, an assured reliance on the object, and an inner sense of trust—both as to the object and trustworthiness of the self. The ambivalent object relation interferes with these early identifications and tends to push the child in the direction of identification with the aggressor. It increases the aggression and anger that the child feels toward his objects, and basic trust is undermined. The roots of a lasting mistrust are established. Whatever the innate differences in the child's instinctual endowment, we can conclude that the relative distribution of instinctual impulses—the balance of aggressive and libidinal impulses—with which the child approaches the level of self-object differentiation is substantially influenced and determined by the nature and quality of its early experiences.

Innate factors play an undeniable role, but the crucial aspect of the developmental process remains the mother's capacity for adaptive and sensitive responsiveness to the child's inner needs in the carrying out of her mothering. Mutual regulation and reciprocal responsiveness are essential. Certain mothers, who are able to respond quite intuitively and adaptively to their first babies, may find that similar patterns of response to subsequent babies are unsuccessful and unsatisfactory. Such mothers lack a certain flexibility in the mothering situation. Often success in the anxious experience with the first child increases her confidence in dealing with a second child, but the confidence seems to rest on a repetition of learned behaviors. The failure of the second child to respond in the same way certainly seems to suggest that innate endowment expresses itself in many aspects of the developmental process, influencing not only dynamic and economic properties, but also the chosen modes of adaptation which emerge as the child develops and acquires psychic structure. Where the mother fails to tune in on and fails to respond to the subtle clues that the child emits to communicate its inner needs and states, her mothering fails to be adapted to the child and their interaction suffers. Consequently, even though the child's innate endowment can influence his capacity for signaling and interacting, an essential element is the mother's capacity to respond to whatever the child presents.

In general we can say that the more the mother finds the baby's modes of activity congruent and compatible with her own, then the better will she be able to adapt spontaneously to the baby's signals. When such a fit between infant needs and maternal responsiveness is achieved, it makes it possible for the child to achieve a predominantly positive object relation with the mother. Consequently, at the time of self-object differentiation probability of positive ego identification is increased. Ernst Kris, for example, offered the suggestion that when it turned out that the defensive patterns of the mother were compatible with the individual makeup of the child, positive identifications between the child and the mother were more likely. The mother's defenses in such a case may be more or less neurotic, but if the pattern of interaction is such that the relation is more positive, the child's identification may include such patterns of defense and be able to integrate them into his own adaptive ego functioning. By way of contrast, where the mother's mode of reaction differs radically from the child's, her responsiveness may lack spontaneity, and she may try to impose her patterns of regulation and control on the child. Identification in this instance will be relatively impaired; what the child internalizes from the mother will be poorly integrated, and his identificatory tendencies will progress more in the direction of identification with the aggressor—as noted above. The pattern of development may thus be set on a definitely neurotic course, with the likelihood that the child will progress toward forming a rather severe, rigid, primitive, and punitive superego. Such superego introjects remain unintegrated with the ego and persist as the preferred intrapsychic agency for channeling aggressive impulses against the ego (self).

Obviously the mutual adaptation between mother and child can never be perfect. Normal development, however, can tolerate a considerable range of differences. The early experiences and mutual adaptation have widespread developmental influences. They influence the development of instinct, of object relations, the emergence of early ego functions, and help to set the pattern for early ego identifications. They also affect the precursors of the superego and the ego ideal. The more the child is able to attain a sense of inner trust and self-esteem, the more likely is he to develop a reasonable and realistic ego ideal. This in turn increases his capacity for mastery and adaptation. The more ambivalent his early relationship, however, the less will he have a sense of inner trust and value, the more will his basic self-esteem suffer, and the more will he tend toward identification with the aggressor. This course leads to the formation of a relatively harsh and punitive superego—at the expense of the development of a relatively positive and reasonable ego ideal.

[12]

The Development
of Object Relations

In the preceding chapters we have been dealing with those factors, both innate and experiential, which influence the development of the basic psychic equipment of the individual human being. Both innate maturational factors and experiential factors play a decisive role in determining the child's early sense of self and in his capacity for achieving object relationships. This involves the quality and stability of the first ego identifications which are intimately related to the rudiments of what will later become the adult's basic sense of self-esteem. We also suggested that both the dynamic and economic attributes with which the child approaches later developmental tasks will be significantly influenced by the balance of positive and negative experiences during the first months of life.

Developmental Issues

The basic sense of self involved in object relatedness is a crucial and important component of that self-esteem which the child carries with him into later developmental phases. The provision of a suitable environment within which it is possible for a basic sense of trust to develop is the first essential prerequisite for the development of good object relations. Basic trust implies that the infant is able to develop a positive object relationship with the first object he is able to perceive as a whole person, namely, the mother. For this initial and crucial object relatedness to be achieved, it means that the child's environment must not be so gratifying that the stimulation for his realizing the separation of self and object is inadequate. It means that his environment must not be so frustrating that when the absence of the object is experienced the balance of the child's recollected experience is negative, rather than positive. The balance is critical, since the relative proportion of basic trust and basic mistrust that the child carries away from his earliest experience of objects remains a fundamental determinant of the quality of his future involvement with and relatedness to objects around him.

These conclusions may be reconsidered in the context of the development of psychoanalytic theory which we have been considering in these pages. When Freud first introduced his structural theory in *The Ego and the Id* (1923), he made certain basic assumptions about the mental apparatus which need to be modified in the light of our current understanding. First, he assumed that the human infant was born with its full instinctual endowment—which Freud separated in his mental model and located in a vital stratum of the mind, the id. Second, he described both the ego and the superego as id-derivatives, as parts of the id which were differentiated out of the id-matrix. These were modifications of the instinctual drives resulting from the organism's contact with the outside world. Both of these assumptions proved to be extremely useful constructs with considerable heuristic value for the later emergence of ego psychology. Neither assumption, however, represented a final formulation or basic assumption of psychoanalytic metapsychology as we understand it today.

Freud's views underwent a gradual and important revision. As you will recall, a crucial factor in the rethinking of his views about the ego were the changes in regard to his theory of anxiety. The emergence of the concept of anxiety as a signal and as the motive for defense (see Chapter 5) led to an increased respect for the capacities and functions of the ego. Freud had originally seen it as relatively weak and ineffectual, buffeted about and subject to the pressures from id, superego, and reality. The revised analysis of anxiety, however, put the ego increasingly in the driver's seat. It became the agency of control, the agency for direction of energy, the regulator of drives, the executor of defenses, and the architect of adaptive functioning. In our discussion of innate developmental factors, we noted that the individual child may possess preferred modes of reaction which influence his choice and patterning of defenses. This is closer to the view of the ego which Freud held in his later years. In *Analysis Terminable and Interminable* (1937), for example, he no longer regarded the ego as a modified part of the id. Rather he suggested that just as the instincts were based on intrinsic maturational factors and underwent a process of development, so too the ego was not simply a part of the id, developed through contacts with external reality. It was a separate part of the mind which had its own intrinsic, innate factors and went through its own separate but parallel course of development. This suggestion has been picked up and elaborated by later ego theorists. There has been an increasing tendency in analytic thinking to regard the ego as developing in relatively autonomous fashion. Hartmann, Kris, and Loewenstein have presented a theory of the ego as developing not out of the id, but both id and ego differentiating gradually out of an originally undifferentiated state. The ego, moreover, is derived from intrinsic maturational factors which give rise to structures of primary autonomy within the ego. The independent derivation of the ego is accompanied by the emergence of sources of energy available to it which are essential to the capacity for autonomous functioning.

The optimal development, however, of both ego functions and instinctual drives is more dependent on experiential factors than Freud believed in his earlier approach to these problems. We should also keep in mind that most of his original hypotheses were derived from evidence obtained through the analyses of adult patients. His conclusions about development were consequently reconstructions from later developmental attainments to earlier levels. In his own clinical work he tended to stress the importance of the oedipal period, with particular reference to castration anxiety in the boy and penis envy in the girl. His treatment of early identifications in *The Ego and the Id,* for example, would not be acceptable today. He maintained that the child's first identification was with the father. There was of course little known about such early relationships at that time and in general Freud tended to underestimate the importance of the early mother-child relationship as an influence in development. He was able to appreciate the infant's prolonged dependence as crucial in the developmental process, but he never really appreciated the role of the early object relationships as a crucial factor in ego development. We should remember, however, that the importance of the mother-child interaction and their mutual regulation and relation has only been demonstrated in recent years.

Our considerations of the early mother-child relationship have important implications for the understanding of the adaptive hypothesis as well. The idea of adaptation can be traced back to quite early in Freud's thinking; the term, for example, was first employed in his *Formulations on Two Principles of Mental Functioning* (1911). He suggested that the initiation of the reality principle in mental processes involved a series of adaptive functions. The nature of these adaptive processes requires closer examination, particularly in regard to activity and passivity as modes of adaptation. As we have seen, the infant's basic trust and his earliest identifications occur at a level of development at which the balance of his experience is rather passive than active. The infant is more in the position of passively tolerating delay and separation as a preliminary to the gratification of wishes, rather than having the capacity to elicit gratification by activity. This emerging capacity to tolerate delay, frustration, and separation provide the rudiments for the later development of the adult capacity to tolerate psychic pain and loss, particularly in the capacity to bear anxiety and depression. Even though the infant's early experience is predominantly passive, very early the healthy infant begins to show certain active capacities to initiate and achieve its own gratification. The young babies who succeeded in taking possession of Dr. Winnicott's spatula were clearly initiating active adaptive efforts with the goal of achieving instinctual gratification.

We might wonder what the behavior of these children might have been if Dr. Winnicott, instead of having the babies sitting on their mother's laps, had sent the mothers out of the room. We can guess that the result would have been very much different. The behavior of infants in the second half of the first year begins to show many of the characteristics that will become more marked in the second and third years. In these years, healthy and happy children show tremendous adaptivity. They play happily; they explore; they show an increasing capacity for and degree of mastery. Curiosity becomes insatiable. Everything in their environment is examined and nearly everything possible is put into their mouths. Margaret Mahler has described this attitude of the healthy toddler during the second and third years in a felicitous phrase; she describes it as "a love affair with the world."

Separation

We might ask ourselves, however, whether these children are as independent as they might seem. Often they give the impression of having little need of the adults around them. They can play happily in one corner, almost completely ignoring the presence of the mother in the room. But if the mother were to disappear for any substantial period, these same children usually show signs of acute anxiety and distress. Their apparent autonomy and mastery is still strongly contingent on the availability of the mother and is quickly lost in her absence. She remains essentially a home base to which the child can return from time to time to renew the assurance of his basic relationship with her. He can also bring her the reports of his achievements to reassure himself that his increasing autonomy does not mean the mitigation or loss of his dependent relation to the mother. He needs to reassure himself that his adventures and achievements in the direction of increasing autonomy and independence do not meet with her disapproval, or at least do not result in the loss of her availability and supportiveness.

During this period the mother's task in adapting to the child's needs is obviously different from her role during his early infancy. On the one hand she must allow the child to explore, to test out his initiatives, to experience and find satisfaction in his increasing autonomy and to develop his adaptive capacities. But on the other hand, it is important that she should not mistake his apparent independence for a real independence—for his not needing her support at critical points and for his not being substantially dependent on his relationship to her for the maintenance of his increasingly autonomous functioning. His autonomy has not yet become an internal achievement and possession. Optimally, during this phase of development, the child can learn to tolerate longer periods of separation from the mother. In part he is able to do this by an increasing capacity to form secure and confident one-to-one relations with other significant figures. His ability to do this is sustained, however, by the maintenance of basic trust—the continuing reassurance and confidence in the mother's reliability and the assurance that she will return even when she has been absent for extended periods.

Researchers who are engaged in longitudinal studies of child development are putting an increasing emphasis on the importance of the second and third years of life for the definitive integration of the basic ego qualities which emerge initially at the time of self-object differentiation. We can consider how the child combines and consolidates these developmental achievements before the onset of the genital oedipal situation. This level of integration involves the child's relatively passive acceptance of dependence and limitation in the areas of his continuing reliance on external objects. It also embraces an increasing capacity for initiating and sustaining active mastery in certain areas of gradually increasing autonomy. These objectives are clearly initiated during the period of instinctual development preceding the emergence of the genital oedipal situation. Thus, in terms of instinctual levels of development, this process covers later periods which involve the primacy of oral activity, the anal period, and the early period of genital primacy, namely, the phallic narcissistic period which immediately precedes the onset of a genuine triangular oedipal constellation.

The Capacity to Tolerate Loss

The period of the second and third years of development is marked by a considerable amount of back and forth movement. It is distinguished by rather radical swings between periods of relative activity and apparent independence, along with an apparently rebellious autonomy on one hand, and the sudden re-emergence on the other hand of feelings of passivity and fears of separation and rejection. Over the period of many months which seem to be necessary for the gradual integration of these achievements, the child must undergo repeated experiences of activity and passivity, of frustration and gratification, of dependence and self-reliance. The recurrent pattern of frustration and delay offer the child the continuing opportunity to expand his capacity for tolerating frustration, separation and loss. The objectives are similar to those discussed in connection with the developmental experiences of the first months of life. But there are qualitative and quantitative differences. The differences are analogous to the differences between Freud's notion of primary anxiety, which was related to overwhelming traumatic experience, and the notion of secondary anxiety, which reflects the capacity for active mastery of threatening danger based on the previously developed capacity for tolerating painful affect. In the latter case, the ego's capacity to use anxiety as a signal for further mobilization of defenses depends on an already developed capacity to tolerate such anxiety and to use it adaptively. Similarly, the child in the second and third years meets the experiences of frustration and separation with a relatively developed capacity to tolerate such experiences and to begin to use them more constructively and adaptively.

To illustrate this difference, we can consider two rather brief accounts of similar observations reported by the mothers of two little boys who were between one and two years of age. The first little boy provides an example of acute primitive distress comparable to the mixed state of anxiety and depression often seen in adults. This little boy was about eighteen months old. His father had gone on a week's vacation, leaving the child and his mother at home. The child—who was not very talkative—kept repeating "Daddy" over and over, and at the same time eagerly looking at pictures of his father. This child had been able to establish good positive one-to-one relationships with both parents. During the father's absence, he seemed relatively happy and contented during most of the day. But, as the week wore on, he began to show more and more periods of rather acute distress around the time when his father usually came home from work. On one occasion a male friend of the mother who was well known to the child came to visit just at the time when the father usually came home. The little boy suddenly showed an acute distress in which anxiety, rage, and misery all seemed to have a part. He screamed loudly and threw himself into his mother's arms sobbing uncontrollably. The mother found it impossible to comfort and reassure him. It seemed that the father's repeated failures to return at the expected time were stirring up severe anxiety and rage with a significant depressive component. The intrusion of a man who was not his father at the crucial time of day epitomized the child's frustration, separation, and loss. In this particular case the child's distress rapidly disappeared as soon as his father came back on the scene, and the previously reliable and positive relationship was re-established.

The second illustration reflects a somewhat different and somewhat greater capacity for separation and possible loss. The circumstances were practically identical. The child was the same age. His father had gone away on a trip. This child also showed little or no distress during the course of the day. But he began to show some sleep disturbances and experienced considerable distress and anxiety during his waking periods during the night. As in the first example, a friend came to visit the mother. This friend bore a certain resemblance to the child's father. As this man came into the room the child looked up, and thinking for a moment that it was his father, the child's face lit up in expectation and delight. But as the man came closer the child realized that this was not his father and his expression changed to one of severe disappointment and obvious distress. At this point he almost burst into tears, but in fact held them back. His inner struggle was apparent both to the mother and the friend. After a minute or two the little boy turned to the friend with an expression of friendliness and resigned disappointment. It seemed that he was saying, "You are not the one I was hoping for, but I do know you. You are a nice person and I like you. It isn't your fault that my daddy isn't here. You are still a friend and I will make the best of a bad situation." This child was able to master his disappointment and distress, and to tolerate the separation from his father. Although his persistent nocturnal disturbances indicated that his distress over his father's absence was still operating, during the day he was nonetheless able to make progress toward mastering his frustration and toward dealing adaptively with the limitations of reality. Instead of screaming in anguish about not having the father he wished for, he was able to make a positive move toward relating to and dealing with the objects that were available to him.

These examples—like Freud's example of the child's game of loss and recovery in *Beyond the Pleasure Principle*—are all examples of reactions occurring in the second year of life. They are quite typical of reactions in this period. Reactions of loss of this type are all contingent on the previous establishment of object relations. In each case the child is separated from and misses someone he cares about. Neither of these two children was in any way deprived of affection and loving care in the absence of the father. Both the anxiety and the sadness which developed after the father's absence were reactions to the fact that an essentially positive and important object relation was threatened. The continuing separation posed the threat of loss of the significant object. The first child expressed his distress primarily in the form of an explosive rage with acute feelings of anxiety. This was expressed as a time-limited, all-or-none type of reaction. He responded to the visitor who was not his father in a totally negative and rejecting manner. The second child, however, seems to have made a further step. He was able to feel and show his disappointment, to master it, and turn to the substitute object in a friendly and realistic manner. His reaction was neither total nor negative. He did not surrender his wish, nor did he deny his longing for the father. He did not reject the substitute, nor did he accept him as a complete one-to-one replacement for his father.

Both of these two-year-olds had attained a level of development in which self-object differentiation had been established and the capacity for genuine object relations had been acquired. They both responded with anxiety and distress in a situation of separation and threatened loss. Their manifest distress included components of anxiety and depression. But the qualitative difference between their respective reactions is of fundamental importance. It points to the difference between a traumatic situation of loss, which would be closely related to Freud's notion of primary anxiety and separation anxiety on the one hand, and the initiation of a capacity to tolerate separation and loss, along with the sadness and depression which follow upon significant loss, on the other. The response of the second child was much more mature than the acute separation anxiety shown by the first. The second child's relatively developed capacity to tolerate the separation from his father sets the stage for him to move relatively successfully from a stage of one-to-one relatedness to a more advanced stage of triangular relatedness involving both parents.

Both of these children had achieved relatively successful one-to-one relationships with each of their parents. They were both at a level of pregenital or preoedipal instinctual development. Both of them showed manifest anxiety and distress in the absence of an important object. Nonetheless, there was a significant difference in the degree to which these little boys were able to tolerate the affects of sadness and disappointment in the face of object loss. There was also a significant difference in the degree to which they were able to direct, in the face of disappointment and loss, positive responses to the realistically available objects around them.

In neither case is it a question of anxiety as a signal for internal defense. Rather we are dealing with the child's increasing capacity to tolerate frustration of wishes and the separation from significant external objects. Signal anxiety may be a relatively late acquisition in the course of development. In any case, it may be easier to understand the developmental process in terms of a progression from one-to-one relationships to the more evolved and complex situation of triangular relationships and their related conflicts. As the child moves into the third and fourth years of life, he enters into the level of triangular involvements and triangular conflicts. These conflicts are intimately linked to the child's emerging sexuality and his own sense of sexual identity. It is at this level that the child enters into the instinctual period of genital primacy and genital interest.

Initiative

One of the developmental parameters closely linked to the emergence of sexual interests is the whole question of initiative, in the Eriksonian sense of a developmental crisis. The rudiments of initiative really lie in some of the earliest negotiations that the child undertakes in dealing with his environment and particularly with his caretaker. The basis for self-assertion reaches to the earliest levels of human development. At the most primordial level the issues are centered around the question of the degree to which the infant can succeed in controlling and focalizing the mother's caring activities. It is therefore closely involved with and dependent on the establishment of basic trust, and is also correlative with an emerging sense of autonomy.

Initiative does not really become a central issue, however, until about the third or fourth year, correlative with other developments which introduce the child to the oedipal context. The emergence of initiative as a central developmental issue parallels the maturation of a number of aspects of the child's functioning. He seems to become more integrated both physically and physiologically. Locomotion is no longer a skill to be acquired or a task to be mastered. It becomes a capacity to be unconsciously assumed and relied on. The child can begin to explore the limits of his walking and—later—running capacity. He begins to propel himself into space and begins to assert his growing mastery over distance and time. At the same time his use and mastery of language develop to the point where he can begin to exploit it in the seemingly endless asking of questions. His curiosity becomes insatiable; his mind becomes as curiously intrusive into the world around him as his growing body has become in relation to space.

Along with this process there is a development in the child's imaginative capacity. His imagination expands and comes into play in the form of fantastic stories and an interest in fairy tales. Imagination runs riot, and the child's world takes on an animistic and magical coloration which is often at once fantastic and terrifying. The whole constellation has a quality which Erikson describes in terms of the intrusive mode.

The *intrusive mode,* dominating much of the behavior of this stage, characterizes a variety of configurationally "similar" activities and fantasies. These include the intrusion into other bodies by physical attack; the intrusion into other people's ears and minds by aggressive talking; the intrusion into space by vigorous locomotion; the intrusion into the unknown by consuming curiosity.[63]

There are two important aspects of this phase of development which deserve special notice. They involve the development of the child's instinctual life. The intrusive character of the child's activity is related to the mobilization of considerable aggression. The basic issue for the child's growth in initiative is whether he can undertake such aggressive intrusiveness on all of the many fronts of its expression without incurring the risk of guilt. The contest of wills that took form in the joining of the issue of autonomy in the earlier years is continued and extended in the child's increasing efforts for self-assertion and initiative, even in the face of parental wishes to the contrary. The child's insistent intrusiveness can provoke parental frustration and anger. It is important that the child's aggression be met with firmness and acceptance in the setting of limits, rather than angry retaliation or punitive restriction.

Perhaps the most significant aspect of this phase, as we have already suggested, is the sexual. The child's all-consuming curiosity extends at this stage to the sexual sphere. He becomes curiously preoccupied with bodies—his own, his mother's, his father's, his siblings', especially those of the opposite sex. The interest becomes centered on the genitals of both sexes. In boys, particularly, the phallus becomes a focus of sensations, feelings, and interests. Erections may have occurred earlier, but they now become more specifically associated with sexual feelings and wishes, rather than with states of diffuse arousal. There is an increased wish and impulse to engage in sex play and to seek out means of sexual investigation. Children at this age become increasingly aware of sex differences and sex roles. Erikson places an emphasis on the notion of "making" in the twofold sense of goal-oriented and pleasureful competition, and in the slang sense of being "on the make." For boys this takes on a more active and intrusive quality. For girls it takes on a more passive quality of making oneself endearing and attractive. For both sexes there is an emerging sense of sexual initiative that is distinctive for each sex.

The child's emerging sexual interest sets the stage for his growing awareness of his similarity to the same-sex parent and his dissimilarity from the opposite-sex parent. This provides a stimulus to the realization that he can be like one parent and at the same time that he must find a basic style of relating to the other. Such holds the promise of growing up to be like father or mother, and provides the stimulus and motivation for crucial identifications that organize and structure his own personality and contribute to the emergence of his own sexual identity. At the same time it gives rise to significant threats with which the child must deal. The emergence of sexuality brings with it the increase of sexual wishes which are incestuous and forbidden. The increase of the child's own powers and his magical beliefs fosters terrifying fantasies and the fear of his capacity to carry out the forbidden wishes. This sets the stage for the emergence of anxiety as the signal of internal danger, and anxiety thus serves as the stimulus for the establishment of internal defenses. The internalization of parental prohibitions, which serve as the core of the emerging superego, also have a defensive function and contribute to internal regulation and control.

The entire complex of interlocking phenomena gives rise to the development of conscience. The child acquires a sense of a need of internal controls and regulation to contain these threatening impulses and wishes. The origins of conscience take shape around the parental prohibitions. These prohibitions are at first simply extrinsic; yet little by little the child takes them in and begins to make them his own. The gradual internalization is prompted and sustained by the child's increasing need to carry on his emerging sense of initiative and to extend his own capacity as the source and master of his own activity. The necessity for making parental prohibitions his own is related to his need to guarantee that his increasing initiatives are carried out in such a way as to find acceptance and approval from the important and influential figures around him. His initiative, involving as it does the expression of both aggressive and sexual interests and impulses, runs the risk of disapproval, punishment, and the possible threat of abandonment. Initiative thus runs the risk of loss of love.

Oedipal Identifications

The child's gradual internalization of parental attitudes and prohibitions also serves to make him more like his parents. These identifications are crucial for the patterning of his more mature personality. They also form a major contribution to the child's emerging superego. Where parental prohibitions are excessive, punitive, hostile, or restrictive, they create a sense of inner danger, inner insecurity, and a sense of inner evil. The child develops a need for caution and control of his own impulses. This sets the stage for the emergence of anxiety as the signal of internal danger and for the establishment of definitive ego defenses. He comes to distrust and fear his own instinctual life. Not only aggressive but also sexual feelings and emotions become frightening. The result is that his capacity to pass on to more mature levels of functioning at which such impulses must be used and integrated is impaired. The more severe the parental restrictions and prohibitions, the more archaic, punitive, and constricting will be the child's own inner attitude toward himself and the control of his impulses—in other words, the more severe and harsh will be his superego.

As we have already suggested, the resolution of this developmental issue depends not only on the quality of the child's current object relations but also on the residues of previous developmental accomplishments. The conditions which promote the establishment of basic trust and allow the acquisition of firm and positive ego identifications in earlier developmental phases will contribute to muting of superego aggression and build a substratum for continuing self-esteem and a sense of competence—rather than guilt and shame. The balance of positive ego identifications as against identifications with the aggressor is crucial in this regard. Where the balance is in the direction of negative earlier experience and identification with the aggressor, initiative will come in the first instance to represent the threat of internal instinctual disruption and excess. There comes about, therefore, an insistence on control, restraint, organization, and prohibition which extends not only to the direction and organization of one's own inner life but also to the direction and organization of one's environment. Such efforts can be seen clinically in obsessive personalities who suffer from the severity of their own superegos—and also in authoritarian styles of functioning.

The development that takes place in this period differs for boys and girls. In the context of the one-to-one relationship which precedes the oedipal phase, there are important developmental tasks for both boys and girls, and the way in which these are mastered differs less in the pregenital and preoedipal phase than later. Even so, much of the evidence suggests that sex differences are quite apparent even before the onset of oedipal involvements. These differences are in some degree due to biological influences and in some degree may be the result of intrafamilial relationships. The interaction between father-son, mother-daughter, father-daughter, or mother-son can have significant effects on the little boy's or little girl's self image even before the development of genuine oedipal genital feelings.

As we have suggested, the child's entrance into the oedipal period is accompanied by genital feelings and genital interests in both sexes. This may often be expressed in an increase in genital masturbation, but is always reflected in a change in the relationship to and reactions to the two parents. As the child grows into this period of his development— into the period of genital sexuality—there emerge instinctual impulses which can be neither fully gratified nor done away with. The child develops genuinely sexual feelings and fantasies in respect to the parent of the opposite sex. He develops feelings of rivalry and competition with the parent of the same sex. Neither of these sets of feelings and their associated wishes can be fully gratified or dismissed. These wishes and fantasies are object-directed and therefore tend to alter the quality of the child's relationship with both of his significant objects—his mother and father.

The Role of Signal Anxiety

The situation that arises differs significantly for boys and girls. This means that we must take into account that there are significant differences between the developmental tasks confronting the little boy in the genital level of development and the developmental tasks confronting the little girl in the same period. This developmental change in the child's pattern of relationship to its significant objects is accompanied by an increasing necessity for the child to relinquish or repress certain wishes. It is at this point that the concept of anxiety as a signal of internal danger becomes meaningful and plays a role in our understanding of the child's developmental task. The impulses which arise in the child in this period are exciting and enticing to it, but they are also frightening and threatening at the same time. The attraction and sexual wishes for one parent are accompanied by fears of attack or rejection from the other parent. The wishes to have one parent incur the threat of losing the other parent. The child is not only threatened with the retaliation and fear of attack from the same-sex parent, but the mobilization of the child's own aggressive impulses calls up the further fear of hurting or destroying that parent. Thus the conflict of the child's inner ambivalence is intensified. The parent is both loved and feared or hated. In the case of a little boy, for example, we can easily see that the child may be terrified by the idea that the father would retaliate against him and punish him for his genital wishes toward his mother—the well-known castration fears; but the child's fear and anger at the frustration of his wishes produce wishes to destroy his father, whom the child at the same time loves and on whom he depends.

In the accounts of the two little boys whose fathers were absent, their anxiety and distress occurred in a developmental period which considerably antedates the emergence of genital oedipal rivalry. But their distress at the possibility of losing the father was quite real and intense. The father was very much a loved and needed parent for these boys. Moreover, insofar as the boy is beginning to be aware of himself as a boy and insofar as the father treats the little boy and responds to him as a boy, the father begins to serve as an object of identification for the child. Thus the loss of the father, or his threatened disappearance— even before the onset of the oedipal situation—confronts the child with his loving dependence and need for his father. Even at this level of development the child's love and dependence on the parent makes the loss of that parent extremely threatening to the child.

When we think of the child's loving relation to both his parents at a level in which he is still dealing with separate one-to-one relationships, we can begin to envision the intrapsychic conflict and struggle which will arise when he begins to be aware—however vaguely and diffusely—of the emergence of impulses which would mean the threat of competitive and destructive urges and the possibility of losing or destroying one of his beloved parents. The resulting intrapsychic conflict gives rise to the development of anxiety which serves as a signal for defense. The wishes to hurt and destroy the beloved parent are frightening and provide an internal danger signal against which the child must erect intrapsychic defenses. Thus the developmental potential of the oedipal situation derives not only from the changed quality of relatedness to objects, but from the stimulus to internal elaboration of defenses. The latter aspect of the child's psychic development continues and extends his gradually increasing capacity for the toleration of painful affects: in the present circumstances, the toleration for the threat of separation and loss, the emerging resource of utilizing the painful affects of anticipatory anxiety and depression in the interest of defense, and the mobilization of intrapsychic resources in the interest of adaptation.

The emergence in the triangular context of the child's genital and aggressive wishes depends on both the dynamic and economic hypotheses. Despite the difficulties in formulating the development of instincts in early mental life, we cannot account for or gain understanding of the nature of these intrapsychic conflicts without appealing to these basic hypotheses. We have to account for the fact that the relatively healthy child can be confronted with severely distressing and frightening impulses which by their very nature—if acted on and translated from fantasy to reality—might lead to an unwished for and painful event—the death of the beloved parent of the same sex. It is this which provides the major motivation for the mobilization of intrapsychic defenses in this period. This emergence of such disruptive and distressful impulses —the operation of ego-alien or ego-dystonic impulses—can only be understood by postulating a component of active and dynamic instinctual striving which functions in relative independence of ego control and which stimulates the ego to defense. This is essentially the basis of the dynamic and economic hypotheses.

Resolution of the Oedipal Conflict

At the oedipal level the child is confronted by much more than simply the difference between himself and his objects. He is also confronted with the complex task of mastering his hostile impulses toward the parent of the same sex and at the same time of dealing with and controlling his prohibited sexual wishes toward the parent of the opposite sex. These wishes cannot be allowed expression in their direct, immediate, and primitive form. The optimal mastery of these impulses and wishes and the resolution of the conflict which they generate result in the establishment of adequate and rewarding object relations with both parents. The extent to which this can be achieved depends in large measure on the quality of the object relations established with each parent in preoedipal levels of development. If those relationships have been essentially positive and satisfying, the probability of retaining an adequate relationship in the oedipal triangular context is increased. If those earlier relations have been essentially negative, the role of aggressive elements is increased and the adequate resolution of oedipal conflicts becomes less likely.

The balance of these early affects and relationships determines the pattern of the child's development in the oedipal situation. Where the child's relationship has been trusting and positive, and the early relations have resulted in relatively positive ego identifications, the oedipal rivalry with the parent of the same sex becomes less intense and less difficult to manage. The rivalry becomes less important than the identification with this parent. The balance in the oedipal conflict is shifted from a threatened loss of the beloved parent to a wish to become like that parent through identification. This pattern of positive identification allows the child's ego to gain in stature and to gain in mastery by becoming more like the strong adult parent. The child's superego emerges as less aggressive and destructive, allowing for the emergence of a more positive ego ideal and more realistic superego attitudes. The further integration of superego functions with ego functions becomes more likely, with the promise of continuing healthy personality development and functioning. The child's capacity to master and renounce his sexual wishes for the parent of the opposite sex is increased by his increased potentiality for positive identification with the same-sex parent. The identification offers the future potentiality of having a relation with a member of the opposite sex who will be an available and permissible sexual object—just as the parent with whom the child identifies in fact possesses such an object.

But where the child's earlier preoedipal object relations have tended to be more ambivalent or negative, the elements of hostile rivalry and destructive wishes in the triangular relationship are intensified. The tendency for the child's development to follow the path of identification with the aggressor sets up a situation in which his emergence into the oedipal situation intensifies the conflicts involved and makes the successful resolution of these conflicts more difficult and problematic. The child's own aggression is intensified and the upsurge of destructive impulses makes the threat of loss and separation more difficult and terrifying. The resolution of the oedipal conflicts is thereby more precarious. The patterns of identification are disturbed and tend to be less positive and adaptive. The superego incorporates and builds on earlier aggressive components, and what is internalized relates more to the aggressive aspects of the parents than the positive aspects. The superego tends to assimilate these aggressive elements and becomes relatively harsh, punitive, and demanding. Positive ego identifications are impeded and weakened. The basis for further healthy and positive identifications is undermined and the potential for future ego growth is thus correspondingly limited.

If we turn back for a moment to the little boy who was able to tolerate in some degree the absence of his father and to accept an available substitute, we can see in his accomplishment a sort of precursor of what the child must accomplish at the later oedipal level. He must renounce his ties to the object; but in the oedipal situation he is called on to renounce direct sexual wishes toward the parent of the opposite sex. For the little boy, he must renounce his sexual wishes for mother because mother belongs to father and not to him. Although mother is unavailable and forbidden as an object of sexual wishes, the child may still feel internally permitted to look for someone like mother at some time in the future when he will be like father. The child cannot be father, but it is essential that he feel internally free to wish to be like father in ways that appear desirable and offer promise of future fulfillment.

The healthy resolution of the oedipal conflict, therefore, results in a modification and redirection of oedipal wishes along paths which point toward the child's future developmental potentialities. The healthy child will modify his rivalry with the parent of the same sex in the direction of a wish to become like that parent—with the promise of the future attainment of that wish. Similarly, the healthy child modifies his genital wishes for the parent of the opposite sex in the direction of wishing to be liked by that parent—with the future prospect of being liked by and loved by other heterosexual objects. The parent of the same sex thus becomes more of an object of identification, and the parent of the opposite sex becomes an object for warm and affectionate interaction and relationship.

The situation is more complex, of course, since the resolution of the oedipal situation involves a pattern of identifications with both parents. As we have suggested, the child's earliest identification is with his first and closest object in the early stages of development—the mother. This would apply to both genders. The earliest primary identifications do not imply that the child wants to be like, or thinks he is like, the parent; rather, in the child's undifferentiated awareness in which the boundaries between self and object are not established, he becomes the parent and vice versa. In the later secondary identifications, the child is aware of the separateness and difference between himself and his object, but assumes the qualities of the object as a result of a positive feeling and wish to be like the object. The resolution of the triangular conflict and the extent to which the child feels permitted and encouraged to identify with the parent of the same sex are crucial determinants in the maintenance and development of the child's sense of self-esteem. The emerging sense of self-esteem must come to include a positive image of oneself as male or female. This is another way of saying that self-esteem depends in part on the formation of a healthy and positive sense of sexual identity. We must recall that the child's emerging sense of identity —including the sense of sexual identity—is the result of an integration of identifications derived from both parents. A healthy integration reflects the primacy of the identification with the same-sex parent.

[13]

Toward Identity

We have thus far traced the path which the developing ego must follow in order to set itself on the way toward healthy and mature adulthood. We have discussed some of the more significant aspects of development which occur optimally between the achievement of self-object differentiation and the emergence and resolution of the triangular oedipal conflict. We have emphasized the central role in this process of the child's preoedipal one-to-one relationships with each of the parents. In each of these two important relationships the child not only establishes confident object relations but also internalizes certain crucial identifications.

The Oedipal Resolution

In the process of interacting with and relating to objects the child is continually confronted by the need to tolerate his own limitations. This tolerance is facilitated in the first instance in a context of trusting dependence on the object. The tolerance thus emerges at its origin in a context of passivity and dependence. But it does not remain such. In the course of healthy development the child's increasing capacity for tolerance is inextricably interwoven with its increasing activity and the emerging capacity to achieve autonomy in certain areas of functioning. With diminishing dependence and increasing autonomy the child also becomes more capable of establishing other relationships, beyond the assured context of firmly established relations to both parents and family. He can begin to explore beyond the world of the family and to broaden the range of his involvement and relationships to human beings. The important conclusion from this consideration of ego development is that the more the child is able to achieve and integrate the capacity to internalize in the preoedipal years, the more capable will he be of significant adaptive mastery during succeeding developmental periods and life crises.

We have traced this development up to and through the triangular oedipal situation. We have seen how oedipal involvements and attachments are modified in the healthy course of development into significant identifications and object attachments which offer the future possibility of development in an adaptive and adult direction. We have also seen that one of the primary influences on the quality and success of the oedipal resolution is the nature of the preoedipal identifications. Thus the developmental process forms a continuum and a continuity that remains unbroken. Earlier strengths form the basis for the attainment of later ones, and earlier deficits form an impediment to the resolution of later developmental tasks.

We would like to carry the process forward at this point—at least in the broad outlines of its developmental schema—and examine briefly the course of normal development beyond the oedipal resolution into the latency period and further into adolescence. The successful resolution of oedipal conflicts has three noteworthy effects. First, it brings about a modification of the intensity and disruptiveness of instinctual components. This allows the child to come to terms more readily with instinctual derivatives and to make greater amounts of energy available for other tasks and demands related to the outside world. The original notion of the latency period as a developmental phase in which libidinal urges were relatively diminished or repressed is based on this postoedipal phenomenon. Second, the successful resolution of the oedipal conflicts establishes relatively comfortable and meaningful relations with both parents without the pressure of threat or disruption of the relations because of the imminence of oedipal wishes and impulses. These crucial object relations are stabilized and consolidated. They are also modified in the direction of a more realistic and reasonable perception of the parents by the child. The quality of the relations is based more on the real characteristics of the parents without the necessity for projective distortions or fears. And third, successful resolution of the oedipal conflicts sets the stage for an emerging pattern of identifications which will allow for the gradual modification of earlier patterns of identification and their elaboration in increasingly more mature and adult directions. Identification becomes a major process by which the ego develops and approaches a realization of a fuller sense of identity. The child continues to identify, and the identifications which mold and structure his emerging character and personality are based on postoedipal identifications with both parents—now less contaminated by instinctual derivatives—and more and more, as the child matures and extends the range of significant relationships, on identifications with other adult objects.

The Latency Period

The latency period, then, is one of consolidation on one front and of elaborating certain specific ego capacities which the developing organism requires for the successful working through and resolution of the reorganization of personality that will be experienced in the adolescent years. As the child emerges from the oedipal situation he achieves a relatively more differentiated and organized psychic structure that provides the inner strength and resource for effectively channeling and dispersing instinctual energies. The original view of the latency period as one devoid of instinctual urges must now be regarded as a fiction. We know now that instinctual impulses are a significant portion of the latency experience, but that their expression is mitigated. The child's structural attainments provide a resource for the diversification and redirection of instinctual energies. Sexual impulses, for example, are expressed in a variety of masturbatory, exhibitionistic, voyeuristic, or sadomasochistic activities or fantasies. But the child begins to develop ways of diverting and diffusing such impulses without having to experience them simply as distressing and threatening intrapsychic tension. Similarly, aggressive impulses can be increasingly diverted into a variety of active and competitive channels without having to experience them as simply threatening and potentially destructive.

One of the significant aspects of the normal development of the latency period is the growing control and stabilization of both ego and superego functions over the child's instinctual life. There is generally a pattern of inhibition of instinctual derivatives. During the latency period, as an aspect of relatively normal development, one can expect to see an upsurge in the level of obsessive and compulsive behaviors. These patterns of activity emerge in the interest of establishing greater control of libidinal and aggressive impulses. Within the limits of normal development, the increasing capacity for inner control is employed adaptively in dealing with some of the tasks of development in this period. Obsessive and somewhat compulsive behavior can be useful for gaining mastery of some of the tasks of learning and in the development of skills to which latency-age children are often put. The emergence of superego functions contributes an internal source of control and resourcefulness which allows the child to begin to emerge in relative autonomy from his essential dependence on his parents.

Perhaps the most significant development of this period is the child's increasing capacity for identification. The crucial identifications that are acquired in the resolution of the oedipal situation are consolidated and modified in countless ways. The major intrapsychic work of the latency period consists in the gradual modification of postoedipal parental introjects and their integration into relatively consistent and more or less stable patterns of identification. In addition the child is increasingly motivated to internalize aspects of other significant adult objects with whom he comes into contact directly and indirectly. The child's entrance into the world of the school and the community introduces him to teachers, public figures, movie stars, sports heroes, etc. His increasing awareness and his emerging skills for acquisition and processing of information offer him significantly greater amounts of data which become organized around these images. These identificatory inputs tend to blend into the pattern of identifications which is shaped around earlier ones, and particularly the oedipal derivatives.

As a result of this process, there is a consolidation of ego functions and an increasing resistance to regressive pulls of various kinds. The child becomes less and less dependent on parental approval and support for his sense of worth and self-esteem. He increasingly derives his self-esteem from his own mastery and the measure of achievement providing him objective recognition and social approval. The child's inner resourcefulness and sense of mastery become the primary regulators of self-esteem. At the same time, in parallel with these other aspects of development—and presumably linked with them—the ego's cognitive functions of perception, learning, memory, and thought are emerging and becoming better established. They become more reliable and increasingly available as resources for the ego to employ in dealing with inner and outer perplexity. They are also less subject to instinctual influences and are able to operate increasingly in the area of conflict-free functioning. Thus higher functions of the ego and superego become increasingly autonomous and function in a secondary process modality, and less and less in primary process modes as a result of regressive instinctual pulls. This is not merely a result of the emergence of ego functions as relatively more autonomous, but is due primarily to the increasing consolidation and integration from positive identificatory processes of the organization and structure of the ego itself and of its gradual integration with superego elements as a result of the same processes.

Latency Tasks

Erikson has aptly called attention to the importance of the child's latency-age experiences in the development of his ego and its correlative strengths.[64] The important areas are those of play and work. The latency-age child's play is an important area of his life experience. Play is childhood's manner of exploring the world of space-time and material things, as well as exploring the world of objects around oneself. It is also the child's ground for exploring his own imaginative potentialities for adult roles and adult behavior. Children's games, whether they be war games, cops-and-robbers, or playing house or doctor, are calculated attempts to draw the adult world closer to themselves by vicarious imitation, and to draw themselves closer to the adult world in playing out often wishful fantasies. Play thus allows the child an area of free play of his imagination and his resources, making an important contribution to his sense of mastery, and perhaps more significantly to his sense of pleasure and enjoyment in mastery. This has particular relevance to the mastery of inner conflicts. Child psychiatrists know very well how the child expresses his inner conflicts through play outlets. In play he expresses and often experiments with tentative solutions to these conflicts. But perhaps more usefully in developmental perspective, the child learns that play is play, that it has a place, and that the exploitation of his own resources and capacities in play is pleasurable. This child who learns to play and to enjoy play can become an adult who can allow himself the pleasure of play and relaxation and perhaps enjoy himself in such idleness without loss of self-esteem.

The world of work for the latency-age child is school. He learns to win acceptance and acclaim by producing things. He learns the value of effort directed to a goal. He learns the value of knowing and being able to do and make things. The child achieves a sense of being useful or being able to be useful. Erikson describes this as a sense of industry. The child's identifications can take shape around those in his world who know things and who know how to do and make things. His increasing capacity to know and do brings him closer to his adult objects, unites him more intimately with the adult world, and serves to facilitate his capacity for identification with productive and adaptive models. As the child enlarges his capacities he gains an increasing measure of self-esteem, of a sense of himself as a valued contributor to his community, as one who has the capacity to learn and to do, which holds for him the promise of adult capability and productivity.

The danger in this phase of development comes in the form of a sense of inadequacy or inferiority. This may arise from regressive pulls due to an inadequate resolution of the child's dependence on his parents. He may still prefer to be the baby at home and to cling to his mother and her protectiveness, rather than to face the challenges and demands of the school. He may retain a sense of oedipal fear of his father, resulting in a continued sense of guilt for oedipal wishes and/or a sense of inferiority in the rivalrous comparison with the father. Family life in the form of overprotectiveness or oversolicitousness may have inadequately prepared him for meeting and dealing with the less protective environment and competitiveness of the school yard and the classroom. The child's school experience, then, instead of providing the opportunity for growth and mastery, becomes a reinforcement of his sense of inadequacy and worthlessness. The increase of self-esteem that one could expect from learning and producing is short-circuited and the child acquires a lasting sense of inferiority and relative lack of worth.

This consideration brings us back to one of the essential aspects of development to which we have pointed in our previous discussions. This concerns the child's capacity to tolerate separation and loss. The oedipal-age child must be able to tolerate the loss of his parents as oedipal objects in order to progress beyond the oedipal involvement and reach a more mature level of relationship with both parents. The latency age builds on and extends that capacity of the child. The gradual shift during latency from a dependence on external objects to increasing inner control and resourcefulness depends on the child's increasing capacity for tolerating separation from significant supporting objects. The trend in latency is toward increasing internalization. Through this process the internal organization, integration, and structuralization of the ego and superego take place. That internalization, primarily through identification, cannot take place unless the child allows himself to surrender external objects and to surrender his dependence on them. If he is unable to suffer that separation, to abandon his dependence on parents or their substitutes, and to tolerate that loss, then he carries through his latency and on into the further adjustments of the adolescent period an enduring sense of inadequacy, of incapacity, of inferiority, and of the failure of a sense of mastery and self-control. That separation and loss is an essential prerequisite for the emergence of the sense of inner competence and capacity and inner regulation and resourcefulness which the child brings with him into the vicissitudes of adolescence. These same qualities and strengths form the basis for a successful negotiation of the turmoil of adolescence and for the ultimate emergence of adult maturity.

We can add briefly that the developmental tasks of the latency period are somewhat different for boys and girls. For the latency-age boy, his mastery and industry have a more phallic thrust than in the girl. The social models for productivity, activity, mastery, and accomplishment are more available to the boy and show him more clearly the path to performance. Such models are culturally less available to the girl. The models generally proposed to her are based more on passivity and center around mothering activity and homemaking. Productivity for her is more closely linked to sexuality and less in terms of more displaced and sublimated activities. This dichotomy has been blurred in recent years with the increasing emergence of women into professional and more public roles. The impact of these emerging social patterns on the relative development of the sexes is not as yet clear, but its importance should not be overlooked.

While the boy's sexuality is marked by activity and mastery, the little girl's sexuality must be marked by relative passivity and receptivity. This is originally developed in the oedipal relation to her father, but during latency it must be modified by her identification with her mother. The other side of this important development, however, is that a positive identification with the mother in the pregenital period serves as a stimulus to healthy independence and autonomy in relatively normal little girls. The identification with the mother thus serves to promote rather than hinder the gradual emergence, development, and finally renunciation of relatively passive genital wishes toward the father. The identification with the mother in the latency period thus supports the resolution of genital oedipal wishes for the father. If the latency-age girl, however, is forced to gain approval by means of active achievement and accomplishment, the passive oedipal goal will remain, and the resolution of the oedipal situation may be impeded. The result may be a reinforcement of penis envy in the form of an aggressive and achieving exterior which hides an underlying depressive character structure and passivity. It is only in terms of this crucial identification with the mother that the little girl can overcome her penis envy and the impulse for compensatory phallic striving. Her identification with a phallic mother, however, can stand in the way of her acceptance of her feminine position and role. The basic feminine identification is the basis on which the girl's successful achievement of femininity will hinge. The latency task, then, is to consolidate that feminine-maternal identification and to integrate with it the other developmental tasks which we have described above.

For the girl the problem is one of achieving a sense of mastery and industry as compatible with and integral with a basic receptivity and passivity of the feminine identity. For the boy the problem is to achieve a sense of masculine identity—linked with the masculine ideal of mastery and purposeful productivity—without undercutting or eliminating a capacity for affective sensitivity and tenderness. The latter qualities are more feminine, but are essential for healthy adult object relations. For both sexes, then, the latency task is to consolidate a basic sense of same-sex identification, while reaching some effective integration of opposite sex qualities. This preliminary integration is partial and incomplete at this level, but provides the ingredients which are reworked and reintegrated in the adolescent experience.

Adolescence

The changes in bodily growth and the upsurge of hormonal titers usher in the dramatic and often conflictual changes of puberty and the adolescent period of development. As a developmental phenomenon, adolescence is marked by a reopening and a reworking of earlier developmental conflicts and fixations. The adolescent upheaval is anticipated in the closing stages of the latency period by demonstrable, if transient, shifts. The preadolescent typically enters into close and rather idealized friendships with members of the same sex—an intensification of the latency pattern. The capacity for sustaining sublimated interests and work capacity seems to ebb rather than flow. There emerges a somewhat confused, often oppositional, searching for different interests, goals, and values that seems to reflect a dissatisfaction with the present rather than a reaching out to the future. These changes announce the transition to a developmental phase that will be considerably more active and tumultuous than the relative tranquillity of latency.

As the child enters adolescence, there is an upsurge of instinctual drive intensity with which the ego must deal. The mastery of these instinctual drives and their derivatives is one of the major developmental tasks of adolescence. The increase of drive pressure induces a regression in the functioning of the ego which reactivates the basic unresolved conflicts from earlier levels of development. Adolescence confronts the developing ego with the necessity and the opportunity of reworking these conflicts in a more definitive way. The individual has a second chance in a sense—the opportunity to modify earlier childhood experiences or traumata which remain unresolved and which may threaten his present and future capacity for continued growth. The regression of this period permits a reworking of earlier developmental defects and a consequent remodeling of the psychic apparatus. The adolescent enjoys a new capacity for and opportunity for meaningful identifications which can provide a major direction and organization for the remodeling process.

Thus adolescence has a marked developmental potential. More and more, the attitude toward this difficult period has shifted from viewing it as an upheaval or a disruption of the developmental program to viewing it as a normative crisis. It has become increasingly accepted as a period of normal growth which is marked not merely by conflict and regression, but as a period which reveals a remarkable growth potential. The infantile conflicts and exigencies are reworked in entirely different ways which give rise to a new organization of the personality, incorporating and interacting in complex ways with the social and cultural influences of the larger society into which the adolescent must move and within which he must take his definitive place. The more definitive resolution of basic conflicts has a double-edged potentiality. They may be resolved and stabilized in more structured and characterological forms, or they may be reopened only to be solidified into more stable symptom forms or character defects. Adolescence offers the potentiality for both positive and negative consolidations.

Second Individuation

Part of the adolescent development is what Blos has referred to as a "second individuation." The first individuation takes place in the first two years of life in the child's achieving of self-object differentiation. The individuation of adolescence is far more complex and leads ultimately to the establishment of a sense of identity. The adolescent process is one of gradual self-definition. The adolescent must search for and experiment with his identity. His self-awareness is at first fragmented and disjointed. He must struggle to achieve some sense of self in the first instance by opposition to what he wishes himself not to be. The rejecting, opposing, contradicting, resisting, and rebelling of the adolescent are driven by this underlying need. He must also test himself in a variety of roles and positions, often finding it necessary to push his experimentation to the limits of excess in order to clarify his inner confusion and uncertainty. These strivings and excesses have their positive value in the contribution they make to self-awareness and self-definition. The negative delineation of self fosters the essential individuation that is a prerequisite for a more mature sense of identity and at the same time enables the adolescent to grow in a sense of relative autonomy.

The difficulties of such individuation for the adolescent are multiple. As he becomes more an individual by separation from significant objects and structures around him, he becomes more and more at risk. He is overwhelmed by feelings of loneliness, isolation, and confusion. He is confronted with the futility and unreality of childhood dreams and fantasies. He becomes increasingly aware of the limits of his own existence as well as of the need for and irreversibility of commitments. He is faced with the inevitability and finality of the end of childhood. He is called on increasingly to surrender his reliance on and dependence on significant adults and to assume increasing responsibility for himself and the direction of his life. It is not surprising that many adolescents find this aspect of growth threatening and try to prolong their adolescent posture by clinging to dependent positions. One of the major problems in our contemporary society is the prolongation of adolescence and the reluctance to accept adult responsibilities and roles on the part of so many of our young people.

One of the primary adjustment problems of the adolescent period has to do with object relations. In the child's earlier experience his development was closely linked as we have seen with objects. In the earliest stages there was the crucial capacity for self-object differentiation. His optimal development in the first two years of life depended vitally on the quality of his relationship with his mother, on his trusting reliance on her mothering activities and on his emerging capacity to tolerate her absence for increasing periods of time. Object relations for the preoedipal child are concerned with establishing meaningful and mutually rewarding relationships on a one-to-one basis with both parents. If the child has been able to accomplish these adaptive goals in the preoedipal years, when he comes to the triangular oedipal involvements in which he must relate to both parents simultaneously in the oedipal situation, his capacity to resolve these relationships and their accompanying conflicts is correspondingly improved. He can establish less threatening and more comfortable relationships with both parents by reason of a patterning of identifications based on the relative strengths of both parents. Even through the postoedipal and latency years the parents remain the predominant objects in the child's life, although the broadening of his object-relation involvement has already begun during this period. Teachers and others significant adult objects begin to play a meaningful role in his development.

When the child enters adolescence, however, object choice and object involvement take a decisive turn away from the parental objects. The major developmental task of adolescence is the establishment of a capacity for heterosexual object choice on a genital level. An essential part of this process is the renunciation of the primary objects—the parents or parental substitutes. The child must surrender the parents as its love objects. The changes in the quality of parental relationships which were brought about in the resolution of the oedipal situation and the subsequent modifications of the latency involvement with parents must give way to a decisive renunciation. The necessary relinquishing of these important objects leaves the adolescent with a marked object hunger. Abandonment of parental objects and the seeking of new and appropriate objects give rise to important inner shifts of cathexis which strongly influence both object representations and the representation of the self. There arises an inner lability of cathexis which makes the adolescent's sense of self all the more uncertain and confused. His capacity to carry through this important developmental step rests on the extent to which he is capable of tolerating the insecurity and loss that are implicit in the separation from and renunciation of the parents as love objects. That capacity reflects previous developmental achievements.

Libidinal Shifts

During adolescence the libidinal economy becomes organized around genital impulses. Preoedipal and oedipal attachments to parental objects are replaced by nonincestuous attachments to heterosexual objects. The translation from one phase to the other is attended by other shifts in instinctual alignments. The quality of object relations shifts subtly and gradually from a need to be loved and taken care of to a progressively manifest need to love and take care of. The child's dependence on parental objects and relative passivity are gradually translated into relatively more independent self-direction and activity. The polarity of activity and passivity which was elaborated in earlier interactions with the parents re-emerges in adolescence as one of the crucial issues that must be decisively resolved. The struggles over renunciation and finding objects as well as the crisis of activity and passivity provoke a recrudescence of ambivalence. The adolescent becomes overly sensitive to the currents of love and hate that are stirred up within him, and he may often vacillate confusingly and confusedly back and forth between them. He does this both with his relationships with his parents which he both rejects and clings to, and with his newfound objects whom he both hungers for and reviles. The resolution of these conflicts culminates in the normal course of development in relatively nonambivalent object relations and in an ego-syntonic balance of activity and passivity which consolidates into a characteristic pattern.

The renunciation of parental objects and the attendant loss of object libido have a number of important consequences. The loss of parental objects leads to a transitional narcissistic phase which is intermediate between the attachment to parents and a more definitive heterosexual object involvement. Libido is withdrawn not simply from the external parent or parental object representations, but from the internalized parent as well. The superego, as we have seen, arose from the internalization of parental representations in the resolution of the oedipal situation. The superego, together with the ego ideal, thus became the primary agency for intrapsychic regulation and for the maintenance of self-esteem. The shifts in cathexis bring about a weakening of superego functions so that the adolescent is left with less effective inner controls and feels the directives of conscience to be less compelling. There are many social and cultural influences which reinforce this weakening of the superego. In renouncing the parents, the adolescent also withdraws from the internalized parental equivalents which reside in the moral evaluative standards of the superego. This has its risks for future development and for the adolescent's adaptation to the world around him, but as Erikson has pointed out so clearly, these inner developmental shifts provide the continuing potential for reformulation and revivification of the values and beliefs, not only of youth, but of the community at large.

The adolescent's withdrawal from the familiar objects of childhood leads to a narcissistic overvaluation of the self. He becomes increasingly aware of his inner processes. He becomes self-absorbed, self-concerned, and self-centered. This may lead to a narcissistic withdrawal and disturbance of reality testing. The adolescent often resorts to narcissistic defenses to defend against the disappointment and disillusionment of his meager position in reality. He may find it difficult to give up the gratify-

243

ing parent on whom he has come to depend—especially if that parent has been overly protecting and solicitous—and face his own limitations and inadequacies. He may be afraid to take responsibility for his own abilities and their consequences, as well as not want to be faced with the demands of adult responsibility.

In this way adolescent conflicts can be prolonged for a considerable time. It becomes easily understandable that the reluctance to renounce dependence on and love of parents often is not simply an adolescent issue, but that it has its roots in the child's previous developmental history. This sort of process was manifest in a young man who graduated from law school but was terribly conflicted about applying for a position with a law firm. He wished desperately that his father would find a position for him in one of his friends' firms. His wish was to be taken care of and to thus preserve his position as a defective and therefore special child. This young man's conflicts over dependency and passivity related to a lifelong pattern of being taken care of and oversolicitude on the part of his mother. And this in turn was related to her excessive concern and guilt centering on an early heart defect—which was never serious and which was corrected at an early age. The process of detachment from parental objects or their substitutes can go on for a very long time, and even in the normal course of development continues on through adolescence into the postadolescent period. Only when the individual enters upon and can accept responsibility for adult tasks and commitments is the relationship to the primary objects finally decided and resolved.

The withdrawal of libido from parental objects disqualifies the parents as sources of libidinal gratification, and the adolescent is then beset with a hunger for objects. This hunger is reflected in the marked adolescent propensity for shifting, labile, superficial, and transient attachments and identifications. This is the adolescent's way of preserving his ties to the outside world and avoiding a complete libidinal withdrawal. The lability of this internal situation makes the ego susceptible to regressive pulls. The relatively stable identifications acquired in the preceding developmental phases lose their stability and consolidation to a certain extent. They are subject to regressive influences, and the pattern of relationship to parental objects becomes a matter of more primitive forms of internalization. The relations to the parents are based more on the interaction of introjection and projection. As had been the case in earlier levels of development, the real parents become confused with "good" and "bad" introjects. The pattern of adolescent vacillation between rejecting and clinging to parents reflects the influence of these introjective components in the relationships. The introjects were more or less dormant during the latency period but are revivified in the adolescent regression. The attachment to new objects serves a twofold purpose in this regard. It facilitates the decathexis of the old introjects, and at the same time—particularly in regard to the "bad" introjects—it offers the possibility of modifying and neutralizing these potentially toxic introjects by the acquisition of new "good" introjects. Ultimately these inner vicissitudes of the infantile introjects must be resolved through a definitive identification, preferably with the parent of the same sex.

Achieving Identity

The adolescent's capacity to turn to appropriate heterosexual objects and to establish meaningful nonincestuous relations is linked to his emerging sense of sexual identity. The resolution of the oedipal complex carries with it the residues of both positive and negative oedipal strivings. The resulting identifications are composite integrations of identifications with both parents. Little boys carry away with them residues of feminine identification and feminine strivings, and little girls carry away the residues of masculine identification and masculine strivings. The polarity of masculine and feminine roles is fixed, however, in the adolescent synthesis. The adolescent boy experiences an upsurge of homosexual libido and feminine strivings which he must relinquish in order to reach a more definitively masculine position. The girl must relinquish her masculine striving and its underlying component of penis envy in order to achieve her full potential as a woman—and further as a mother. The onset of menarche polarizes and confirms this development. The success of the development to feminine sexual identity depends on the girl's successful renunciation of maternal dependency, but at the same time on her successful identification with the mother as a reproductive and sex role model. These developmental contingencies are in turn dependent on the quality of previous identifications with the mother. If such identifications are contaminated by hostility, the girl will not be able to accept her own heterosexual desires and maternal wishes without anxiety and conflict. The emergence of a healthy and mature sense of identity for both sexes is thus based in part on the establishment of a secure sense of sexual identity and the capacity to accept adult sexual roles without anxiety. Identification with the same-sex parent is a crucial aspect of this process. Obviously, when the parents do not provide the child with adequate models of masculinity or femininity, the child's adjustment in this regard becomes more precarious.

The critical achievement of adolescent development is the sense of identity. The definition of self which emerges in late adolescence is a work of synthetic processes in the ego. Erikson has described the establishment of a sense of identity as a phase-specific achievement which involves the formation of a qualitatively new psychic formation. The formation of a sense of identity is more than a sum of childhood identifications. As Erikson describes it:

> The sense of ego identity, then, is the accrued confidence that one's ability to maintain inner sameness and continuity (one's ego in the psychological sense) is matched by the sameness and continuity of one's meaning for others. Thus, self-esteem, confirmed at the end of each major crisis, grows to be a conviction that one is learning effective steps toward a tangible future, that one is developing a defined personality within a social reality which one understands.[65]

Identity develops out of a gradual integration of identifications, but the resulting whole forms an integrated totality that exceeds the mere sum of its parts. Childhood identifications are subjected to a new integration in the adolescent remodeling which issues in a more final self-definition and to irreversible role patterns which set the young person on his life course.

In the elaboration of these inner processes, it is essential that the emerging adolescent self be recognized and responded to in meaningful ways by the adult community into which he is growing and within which he seeks a place. Such a reciprocal response—an extrapolation of the mutual regulation of earlier phases of development—offers the emergent self of the adolescent a necessary support to enable him to sustain vital defenses in the face of the growing intensity of instinctual impulses, to consolidate areas of growing capacity and achievement with social roles and work opportunities, and finally to reorganize earlier patterns of identification in a consistent fashion, and to integrate the new configuration with the patterns of role and value available within the society. Erikson has stated this complex aspect of adolescent development in lucid terms:

> *Identity formation,* finally, begins where the usefulness of identification ends. It arises from the selective repudiation and mutual assimilation of childhood identifications, and their absorption in a new configuration, which in turn, is dependent on the process by which a *society* (often through subsocieties) *identifies the young* individual, recognizing him as somebody who had to be-

come the way he is, and who, being the way he is, is taken for granted. The community, often not without some initial mistrust, gives such recognition with a (more or less institutionalized) display of surprise and pleasure in making the acquaintance of a newly emerging individual. For the community, in turn, feels "recognized" by the individual who cares to ask for recognition; it can, by the same token, feel deeply—and vengefully—rejected by the individual who does not seem to care.[66]

In summary, adolescent development marks an advance in instinctual drive organization toward a genital heterosexual position. The genital position becomes relatively definitive and irreversible. The libido is directed outward and the ego gains a new investment in objects. The turning to new love objects reactivates oedipal fixations which must be renounced and resolved. The adolescent is thereby enabled to elaborate more mature and adult positions of masculinity and femininity. The ego gains in its capacity to organize more effective defenses and sublimations, to reach restitutive solutions and adaptive accommodations. These become aligned in highly individual and unique patterns which are gradually consolidated into an emerging character structure. Thus adolescent development translates the idiosyncratic constellation of drives and conflicts into more unified and integrated patterns of personality organization. The normal developmental process of adolescence arrives at a final integration in which the emerging pattern is subjectively grasped and more or less accepted as belonging to an inherently identifiable sense of self.

Adolescent Tasks and Maturity

These attainments must be consolidated and integrated in order to achieve adult stability. The emerging patterns must be strengthened and confirmed. Developing ego capacities must be formed into a uniquely individual but stable configuration of ego functions and interests which can be identified and accepted as one's own. Areas of conflict-free and relatively autonomous functioning must be stabilized and reinforced. A sexual position integrated in terms of genital drives and interests must be confirmed and elaborated. The cathexis of both object representations and self-representations must be bound into relatively firm and permanent patterns. Finally, the inner structures which safeguard and foster the integrity of inner psychic processes must be firmly established and confirmed in the face of regressive pulls and disruptive anxieties.

This integration and consolidation leads to further unification of the

247

ego and the preservation of its continuity. The interaction of various processes can be envisioned as a complex system of feedback mechanisms which operate during the period of postadolescent integration to confirm an inner equilibrium and achieve an inner constancy. We have already discussed the developmental role of anxiety. The amount of external stimulation and the degree of internal anxiety which may serve as the optimal stimulus for these growth processes and for their consolidation may vary within wide limits. The integrative processes of ego synthesis, patterning, channeling, and identification require an optimal level of tension and anxiety to elicit their maximal growth potential for these vital consolidations and strengthening of the ego.

It is apparent in all this that the successful resolution of adolescent crises and developmental tasks provides the young individual with the working basis for emotional maturity and psychic health. Blos has designated these developmental tasks as second individuation, achievement of ego continuity, integration of sexual identity, and the mastery of residual traumata. The resolution and definitive achievement of them must be considered in a relative and developmental context. The success of adolescent progression depends upon and derives from earlier developmental levels. The second individuation and the gaining of ego continuity, as we have suggested, depend on the integration of the earlier developmental accomplishments of the first individuation of the child from his mother. Sexual identity and the mastery of residual traumata in turn reflect the resolution of more complex triangular oedipal conflicts. It is the pubescent potential for reopening and renegotiating these crucial developmental issues that gives adolescence its fundamental significance in establishing the character structure and the life pattern of the individual.

We should not forget, however, that the process of individuation—whether in early childhood or in adolescence—implies a capacity to recognize, tolerate, and master painful affects. Individuation cannot succeed without the mastery of ambivalence. The tolerance for and capacity to master both anxiety and depression thus become essential aspects of the developmental process, as well as important strengths of the healthy personality. The rudiments of this capacity are laid down in early relations with the primary objects. Zetzel has suggested that the capacity to establish a successful therapeutic alliance in adult psychoanalysis is determined by the degree to which the second individuation has established a capacity to tolerate anxiety, depression, and intrapsychic conflict. There are many so-called normal individuals who function on an apparently well-adjusted level but whose inner personality structure may be quite defective. Their developmental failure often lies in the area of an incapacity to tolerate those painful affects which reflect preoedipal developmental difficulties. Unless the basis is laid in the preoedipal years, further adaptive steps will rest on omnipotent fantasies, narcissistic goals, and the incapacity to accept the limitations of oneself or of reality.

The process of individuation and achieving ego continuity takes place in the context of one-to-one relationships. The quality of the child's one-to-one relations contributes to the triangular oedipal conflict. The regressive potential of adolescence allows this conflict to be reopened and thus provides a second opportunity for its resolution. A successful resolution establishes a definitive sexual identity which permits satisfactory heterosexual object relations. A successful resolution of this basic conflict requires a tolerance for anxiety in the recognition and dealing with the aspects of the conflict and a tolerance for depression in the giving up and loss of infantile love objects. Thus the tolerance for anxiety and depression which are integral to the emergence of a genuine intrapsychic conflict are essential to the adolescent resolution of the triangular conflict and are thus essential attributes of psychic health and the sustained capacity for emotional growth.

Psychic health, however, requires not merely the capacity for passive toleration of painful affects. It further implies the capacity for active searching and finding of suitable objects and personal goals which allow for not only passive gratification but for active mastery and achievement as well. The resolution of basic conflicts between activity and passivity are fundamental to healthy adjustment and are closely related to the question of sexual roles and functions. The active phallic quality of male sexuality makes the mobilization of active resources and styles of defense more ego-syntonic for men than the relatively passive toleration of anxiety and depression. The characteristic receptivity and passivity of female sexuality makes it more likely, conversely, that women will have difficulty developmentally in achieving modes of active mastery. Thus men who equate masculinity with continued active striving and mastery may run the risk of sacrificing the more passive components of maturity. Likewise women who equate femininity with passivity run the risk of losing the more active components of healthy functioning. Certain women, whose penis envy is relatively intense or unresolved, have difficulty in achieving mature femininity. At the other extreme, however, women who overemphasize passivity can fail to achieve a capacity for active mastery which is essential for psychic health.

Thus, the developmental process which we have been tracing in these pages brings about a differentiation and an integration of the complex aspects of the functioning personality. Optimal development, which lays the foundations for an inner balance and security, achieves an integration of the inner forces and polarities which constitute the basic life conflicts—male as opposed to female, active as opposed to passive, autonomous as opposed to dependent. The developmental process stretches toward an integration of inner structure and capacities which allow for the employment of basic ego strengths in the service of adaptation and—perhaps more significantly—in the service of continuing emotional growth. We have traced this developmental process through the adolescent period. The process does not stop there. But it does reach a more or less definitive reorganization which defines the basic dimensions of individual character. It also sets the fundamental pattern for further adaptive responsiveness in the face of future life crises, losses, disappointments, suffering—and ultimately death. It is this integration of inner structure that allows the individual to face the remainder of his life's experience with a sense of inner confidence and capacity, with a sense of inner value and self-regard, with a capacity for meaningful and trusting relationships to significant others, with a capacity for intimacy and productivity in his life's undertakings, and with the inner strength—based on the capacity achieved through a long course of developmental achievements—to recognize, tolerate, and master the anxiety and depression which will inevitably line his course.

[14]

Neurotic Development and Analyzability

The preceding chapters contain our discussion of normal development. We have discussed some of the more important developmental steps which occur from the beginnings of the child's relationship with the first object in his experience. We have sketched the initial relatedness to the caretaking person, the mother, the establishment of self-object differentiation, the earliest ego identifications, the establishment of meaningful one-to-one relationships, and the emergence and resolution of the triangular oedipal situation and conflict. We have traced the child's development beyond the oedipal resolution into the postoedipal years, into the consolidative accomplishments of the latency years, and further on into the regression and remodeling of the adolescent years, with their definitive reorganization of personality patterns and attainments.

Normal Development

In surveying this complex process, we emphasized particularly the importance of the child's early preoedipal one-to-one relationships with both of its parents. In regard to each of the parents, the child's optimal development depends on the establishment of confident and positive object relationships. It also must achieve the internalization of certain positive and significant ego identifications. During this process, the growing child is constantly confronted by the need to passively tolerate his own limitations. In the course of healthy development the capacity to tolerate limitations is inextricably interwoven with the child's increasing capacity to achieve autonomous functioning in certain specific areas. It is also intimately connected with the child's growing capacity to tolerate the separation from and loss of significant objects. His capacity to separate from and increasingly function autonomously in the absence of the important objects on which he depends so much is correlated with his capacity to internalize and possess as his own the reassurance and reliability of these external objects. We concluded that the more the child is able to attain and integrate the capacity for internalization during the preoedipal years, the more likely will he be to show significant capacities for adaptive mastery during subsequent developmental crises.

Development and Choice of Therapy

In the present chapter we wish to turn our attention to a question which is of major theoretical and practical significance for psychoanalysis. We have been discussing psychoanalysis in these pages primarily as a theory of neurotic functioning and, more broadly, as a general theory of psychological development and functioning. These aspects represent the special and general theories of psychoanalysis which we discussed in Chapter 1. The understanding of human personality and its deviate forms of functioning or maladaptations cannot be left in a theoretical vacuum. Psychoanalysis is first of all a clinical theory. Consequently, psychoanalytic understanding must translate itself into the practical matter of treating emotionally disturbed patients. The practical question, then, which inevitably arises is: For what patients is psychoanalysis the preferred form of clinical treatment? The question we are posing, then, is one that is of central importance for contemporary psychoanalysis and psychiatry. For what patients is psychoanalysis a suitable form of treatment? It is the question of analyzability. We can focus the question more specifically in terms of our preceding discussion. What is the nature of the developmental difficulties that characterize neurotic and potentially analyzable individuals, and how does their development differ from patients who are not suitable for psychoanalysis?

It is a relatively common experience in psychiatry for patients to develop a treatment relationship which provides them with significant relief of symptoms. By retaining their relationship with the therapist such patients are able to avoid serious regression and maintain a fairly good level of adjustment and functioning. The maintenance of mature ego functions, however, requires the continuing availability of the therapist. The patient is unable to take a further step which would enable him to surrender the relationship with the therapist. The patient is unable to tolerate the threatened loss and separation without regression. The course of treatment of such patients is extended and prolonged, often for considerable periods. The crucial question for such patients in determining whether they can complete a course of treatment—whether it be psychoanalysis or psychotherapy—is the extent to which they are capable of internalizing and identifying with the therapist on the basis of a therapeutic relationship. The capacity for internalization depends on the capacity to tolerate both depressive affects and regressive forms of anxiety which might be experienced in the face of threatened loss.

The individual who is a potentially analyzable neurotic, or who is capable of becoming a potentially mature adult—whether or not he or she suffers from neurotic symptoms—has been able to reach a developmental level in which a genuine triangular conflict has been experienced. Such individuals have been able to sustain significant object relations with both parents during their latency years. Despite the regression which inevitably develops during the second individuation period of adolescence, such individuals will be in a much better position to resolve their later identity crisis without having to make a serious or lasting break in their relations to their family. Frequently, however, the post-oedipal relationships between the developing neurotic and his parents are much-less satisfactory and much more ambivalent than the relationships which obtained during the preoedipal period. In many neurotic patients, moreover, psychoanalytic reconstructions in adult life have shown that the relationship with one parent during the preoedipal years was far more ambivalent than the relationship with the other. In general, when the degree of ambivalence in the early mother-child relationship has been excessive, this proves to be a more severe handicap in establishing other secure object relations than an ambivalent preoedipal relationship with the father. This applies equally to both sexes, despite other developmental differences.

Traditional psychoanalysis is thus the treatment of choice for potentially mature adult patients in whom the developmental failure is confined to difficulties in the mastery of genuine internal conflict. This implies that such patients have been able to establish meaningful one-to-one relationships with both parents and have been able to enter into and establish a triangular oedipal conflict. Their neurosis is based in part on the failure to successfully resolve this basic and central conflict. There have been repeated attempts—and attempts will continue to be made—to adapt the technique of psychoanalysis to the treatment of more severe neurotic disorders and to certain forms of more severe character disorder. These attempts, however, can be made with only limited optimism. Patients who have not achieved the level of triangular involvement and conflict are generally unable to benefit from traditional psychoanalysis. The success of any therapeutic intervention with such patients depends largely on their capacity to achieve and sustain a stable one-to-one relationship in the therapeutic situation. We shall consider such personalities and their treatment in Chapter 15.

The use of a therapeutic method—such as psychoanalysis—which fosters regression in the treatment of patients who demonstrate a more severe developmental failure is open to serious question. Experience has shown that patients who are unable to tolerate anxiety or depression will be able to work through a transference neurosis only exceptionally. They are unable to terminate any form of therapy successfully. We must make a clear distinction between the selection of patients for psychoanalysis or similar insight-oriented therapies on one hand, and the use of psychoanalytic understanding in the evaluation of psychiatric patients, no matter how sick. Traditional psychoanalytic technique has only limited application to certain potentially mature individuals. But psychoanalytic understanding can serve as the basis for the development of other treatment techniques suitable for a much broader range of mental disorders, including those which manifest a significant developmental failure.

The Problem of Analyzability

We can best approach the problem of analyzability in terms of analytic experience. Several years ago an extensive evaluation of the criteria for analyzability was made by studying a series of cases accepted for supervised analyses in the Boston Psychoanalytic Institute. A series of one hundred such cases accepted for analysis and subsequently analyzed for several years was examined. The patients who presented themselves as potentially healthy individuals and who seemed to meet the criteria for analyzability seemed to fall into typical patterns of neurotic difficulty. By far the most common difficulty for adult analyzable women was in the area of capacities for heterosexual object relations. This usually reflected the influence of an hysterical personality organization. In contrast, the analyzable men were likely to present with symptoms of a more obsessional nature together with inhibitions in the area of their work. Patients referred to the instutute for therapeutic analysis fell into these two large categories. The women came because of their failure to make a satisfactory heterosexual object choice; the men sought help because of a work problem. This was quite frequently the problem for graduate students who were experiencing difficulties in completing their dissertations.

The majority of the patients in this study, who were accepted for analysis and were given a diagnosis of obsessional neurosis or obsessional character, were relatively well-defended personalities. They presented no unusual difficulties in establishing the analytic situation, but few of them were able to develop an overt and analyzable transference neurosis through the first year of analysis. In considering analyzability we need to distinguish between the patient's capacity to establish and participate in the analytic situation and his capacity to establish a genuine transference neurosis. The hysterical patients presented a different picture. They were either very good or very difficult. Development of an overt transference neurosis was easy and relatively quick. But difficulties arose for these patients in establishing the therapeutic alliance. Hysterics in general were much more capable of the regressive primary process thinking that is required by free association in the analytic process. The success of treatment, however, seemed to hinge on establishing a good analytic situation.

These findings led Zetzel to suggest the importance of considering analyzability in terms of both the analytic *process* and the analytic *situation*. The analytic process refers to the regressive emergence, working through, interpretation and resolution of the transference neurosis. The analytic situation, however, refers to the setting in which the process takes place, specifically the positive relationship between patient and analyst based on the therapeutic alliance (see Chapter 16). Obsessives have difficulty with the former and little difficulty with the latter; hysterics have difficulty with the latter but little difficulty with the former. Further, the analytic progression can be divided into three parts. First, the initiation and consolidation of the analytic situation; second, the emergence and analysis of the transference neurosis; and third, the carrying through of a successful termination. The patient's capacity for succeeding in each phase should be considered in assessing analyzability. The first phase relates to the patient's capacity to enter into, establish, and sustain a therapeutic alliance. The second phase relates to the patient's capacity to develop a genuine transference neurosis, to regress sufficiently to allow that neurosis to emerge and be analyzed, and to work through the elements of it. The third phase relates to the patient's capacity to tolerate separation and loss and to integrate these affects constructively. This is closely related to the patient's capacity for identification. Of Freud's classic cases, the Rat Man stands out as having met these criteria of analyzability. In keeping with his obsessional characteristics, he was able to establish a firm therapeutic alliance from the outset. Despite his obsessive character structure, he was able to develop a highly analyzable transference neurosis. And despite Freud's silence on the matter we know that he was able to terminate.

Hysterical Development

We can look first at the development which seems to be related to the incidence of hysterical symptoms, particularly in adult women. The presence of such symptoms is not a sufficient index that the patient is a potentially analyzable neurotic. Similar hysterical symptoms are often met in women who have failed in the major developmental tasks we have been discussing in previous chapters. Hysterical symptoms often occur in borderline or relatively primitive adult characters. It is important to realize that patients with such character structures desire and seek an excessive one-to-one relationship with the father or with a father surrogate without maintaining any meaningful relationship with the mother. This is one of the factors which contributes to the relatively high incidence of intense and highly sexualized transference reactions in women treated by male therapists. Freud's original observations of transference phenomena, as you recall, were made in patients suffering from major hysterical symptoms. Most contemporary analysts, however, would not regard these patients as meeting the criteria for analyzability. The case of Dora is a case in point.[67]

The factors which might contribute to making the little girl's preoedipal relationship with her mother more ambivalent than that with her father are multiple. Any unresolved ambivalence in the mother's relationship with her own mother is likely to be reflected in her relationship to her daughter. We can also anticipate that many fathers will be less demanding and more openly affectionate toward their daughters than they would be toward their sons. There is an optimal degree of affection in the father-daughter relationship which makes the libidinal investment necessary for the development of the oedipal relationship possible. Helene Deutsch has pointed out that some degree of seduction is required from parents to make this involvement meaningful and to elicit adequate oedipal attachments. If this has played an excessive role in the child's preoedipal development, it can contribute to the impairment of full genital development and the creation of a genuine triangular relationship. Furthermore, it is significant that for the little girl the development of an oedipal conflict entails a specific shift of libidinal object choice. Her first libidinal object is the mother. In entering the triangular situation, however, the mother becomes her rival. Her libidinal choice is then shifted to the father. Earlier failures in the mother-child relation will tend to impair the maintenance of a good object relationship between mother and daughter during the infantile neurosis. The failure of this relationship may contribute to her failure to achieve a positive feminine identification and the internalization of a positive ego ideal. In addition, insofar as the little girl's early internalizations have been marked by a significant degree of identification with the aggressor, she will be more likely to have internalized a harsh, punitive superego. There will consequently be a larger tendency to masochism in her character as well as a tendency to low self-esteem.

The little girl's libidinal shift to the father is preceded by the recognition of sexual differences during the period of phallic narcissism. Where earlier failures, in terms of ambivalent preoedipal relationships to the parents, particularly the mother, have occurred and impaired the child's growing sense of feminine identification, the little girl's penis envy will be intensified and compounded and thus interfere with the development of a more feminine approach to her father. In other cases the little girl may experience an increase of ambivalence and respond by a regressive return to an earlier and more passive position. Instead of tolerating her disappointment in the oedipal relation to her father and mobilizing her adaptive capacities, she may turn to a reliance on others for the maintenance of her fragile self-esteem. This is a common finding in the treatment of many adult women who reveal an underlying depressive character structure behind their hysterical facade.

Analyzability of Hysterics

Zetzel has described a series of four subgroups of women who present with hysterical symptoms. The first group, the "true good hysterics," are young women who are capable of meeting the criteria for analyzability in all three phases of analysis. The second group, the "potential good hysterics," are young women whose development, symptoms, and character structure indicate an analyzable hysterical disorder, but who are less prepared and ready for the commitment to establishing a viable analytic situation. The third group comprises women who present with manifest hysterical symptoms which mask an underlying depressive character structure. The fourth group consists of women whose hysterical facade masks pregenital and preoedipal developmental failures. These last patients seldom meet the criteria for analyzability. These are the "so-called good hysterics."

Truly good hysterics—whether they be male or female—have experienced a genuine triangular conflict. The hysteric has also been able to maintain significant object relations with both parents. Often the postoedipal relations are more ambivalent than the preoedipal relations. Hysterics generally pay a price for the attempted resolution of the oedipal situation. But we must distinguish between instinctual progression and regression on one hand, and the ego achievements which allow one to recognize and master internal danger and conflict on the other. Good hysterics retain a capacity to recognize and tolerate internal reality and internal conflicts. They are also able to distinguish internal reality from external reality. This is a major criterion of analyzability and is directly related to the patient's capacity to distinguish between the therapeutic alliance and the transference neurosis. The therapeutic alliance is based on external reality; the transference neurosis is based on internal reality.

Successfully analyzed patients, despite their characteristic sexual differences, share certain major developmental accomplishments. The ability to establish and maintain a positive therapeutic alliance and to work through the terminal phase of analysis seems best in those patients in whom there has developed a substantial mastery of ambivalence in the early relationship with the mother. This seems to entail certain defensive reaction formations which serve as a buffer against significant ego regression during the phase of establishing the analytic situation. This is most prominent in more obsessive patients, but also is a factor in hysterical ones who succeed in this initial phase of analysis. These patients had also consolidated genuine one-to-one relationships with both parents before the emergence of oedipal conflicts. They maintain the capacity to distinguish between external and internal reality in their response to the analytic situation and the transference neurosis. They demonstrate a sustained capacity for tolerating anxiety and depression through the whole of the analytic process. Many of the most analyzable patients reveal a combination of obsessive and hysterical characteristics and can thus be described as "mixed neuroses."

The group of ideally analyzable hysterics differs from the potentially good hysterics in a number of aspects. The second group usually presents with a wider range of symptoms. They are generally younger, less mature, often youngest or only children. They often fail to demonstrate the development of relatively stable and ego-syntonic obsessional defenses as are seen in the more analyzable hysterics. Good hysterics usually manifest consistent achievement in their work and in the maintenance of friendships. The second group is less successful in both these areas. They are less consistent and more passive, often fearful of their dependent wishes, which usually lie closer to the surface than is typical in good hysterics. The major problem for these patients comes in the first phase of analysis. They have difficulty in establishing a stable analytic situation which would allow an analyzable transference neurosis to emerge. They may respond with a flight into health or by plunging into a regressive transference neurosis before a therapeutic alliance can be established. If these pitfalls can be avoided, however, these patients have little difficulty in the emergence and analysis of the transference neurosis or the working through of the terminal phase. They can achieve a genuine therapeutic and analytic result.

Hysterical women with underlying depressive character structures have generally failed to mobilize their active resources during important developmental crises. Some of them may be analyzable, but a long and difficult analysis must be expected. Their self-esteem is low and they tend to devalue their own femininity. They may have experienced some genuine triangular conflict, often with an excessive idealization of the father. They may be able to recognize and tolerate considerable depression, but they have failed significantly in the area of positive mastery. They tend to be passive and to feel helpless and vulnerable. The depressive aspect is difficult to recognize in the initial evaluation, but feelings of helplessness and depression are usually verbalized early in treatment. Such women develop passive and dependent transference reactions which interferes with their capacity to distinguish between therapeutic alliance and transference neurosis. All of these patients present serious problems in the terminal phases of analysis. They present the serious risk of drifting into a relatively interminable analytic situation. They should not be referred for traditional analysis without careful assessment and evaluation of their capacity for progressive alteration and active mastery.

The last group of hysterics, Zetzel's "so-called good hysterics," usually have a floridly hysterical symptomatic picture. In treatment they prove incapable of tolerating a genuine triangular conflict. They express intense sexualized transference fantasies and tend to regard such fantasies as areas of potential real gratification. They are incapable of distinguishing between internal and external reality, and consequently have considerable difficulty in establishing the therapeutic alliance and in distinguishing it from the transference neurosis. These patients do not meet the criteria for analyzability. The major pathology reflects a significant developmental failure in basic ego functions. The difficulty in evaluation is in distinguishing between more analyzable patients in regression and the developmental failure in these patients. More analyzable patients will reconstitute more rapidly, while the so-called good hysteric will tend to develop an intense sexualized transference even in the structured face-to-face situation. They have usually been through a previous unsuccessful course of treatment—analysis or therapy—and usually have few areas of conflict-free or autonomous functioning in their lives. These patients should not be taken into traditional psychoanalysis. They meet none of the criteria for analyzability. They may profit, however, from more structured and less regression-inducing forms of therapy.

Obsessional Development and Analyzability

The developmental circumstances that lead to obsessive symptoms and character structure are somewhat different. We have already noted that the obsessive configuration is more frequently seen in analyzable men, although the presence of obsessive mechanisms seems to facilitate the engagement of hysterics in the analytic situation as well. We can link our consideration of obsessive structure to the developmental tasks of the young boy during the emergence of triangular relationships. Unlike the little girl, he does not need to shift his libidinal attachment in progressing from pregenital to oedipal relationships. His libidinal attachment remains fixed on the same object—the mother. While the object of his libidinal attachment does not change, the quality of it does. He must shift from the predominance of his earlier passive and receptive oral wishes to the increasing emergence of more active phallic striving.

During the closing phases of the preoedipal period, he has already begun to integrate some degree of identification with his father. This emerging identification fosters and reinforces his reaction formations against this underlying passivity and dependence. A similar pattern is also seen in the development of the more analyzable neurotic women. Many of these women defend themselves against underlying feelings of passivity, dependence, and vulnerability by a reinforcement of penis envy and an intensified ambition for active achievement and mastery. For them too, this reflects in part an identification with the father. But it also frequently reflects a wish to please the father, who is not merely an oedipal object but the parent with whom the child had the more stable and less ambivalent preoedipal relationship. Such obsessively tinged women have frequently tried to become the boy that they believe father really wanted. In any case, the relatively healthy and analyzable man who has failed to adequately resolve his oedipal conflicts is much more likely to present obsessional symptoms and/or character structure than is the correspondingly analyzable woman.

The criteria for analyzability in obsessional patients do not depend on the content or the severity of the presenting symptoms. It is well known that obsessional defenses may be masking or containing an underlying psychotic process. What is crucial in determining the analyzability of obsessive patients is the degree to which they are able to tolerate the instinctual regression which is necessary for an analyzable transference neurosis to emerge, without losing the capacity for the essential therapeutic split between fantasy and reality, i.e., between transference and therapeutic alliance. Freud had noted in his clinical studies of obsessional patients their tendency to develop conflicts over a number of important dichotomies—love vs. hate, activity vs. passivity, omnipotence vs. helplessness. These polarities were generally experienced as exclusive and more or less total. Today we can recognize that the resolution and substantial mastery of such conflicts are crucial developmental tasks. The resolution of the conflict of love and hate—the tolerance for ambivalence—is one of the crucial developmental tasks involved in the achievement of healthy self-object differentiation and early identifications. This determines one of the basic criteria for analyzability. The individual who can maintain a real object relationship in the face of conflicting negative feelings must have gained the capacity to tolerate simultaneous feelings of love and hate toward the same object. The obsessional patient's symptoms reflect his difficulties in resolving these basic conflicts, especially in connection with his inhibitions, doubts, and compulsions. The successfully analyzable obsessional patient, however, must have a sufficient tolerance for conflicting emotions to allow him to endure the alternation between love and hate that emerges in the transference neurosis. Beyond tolerating his ambivalence in the analytic situation, the patient must be capable of distinguishing such transference feelings from the analytic relationship. He must be able to sufficiently tolerate his ambivalence to allow himself to maintain the real therapeutic relationship.

We must distinguish carefully in these cases between substantial developmental failure to integrate emotions and perceptions, which are experienced as mutually exclusive, and the regressive impairment of a previously established integration during neurotic symptom formation. The exclusive quality of the obsessional treatment of dichotomies and its associated intolerance for inner conflict and ambivalence may reflect either developmental course. The early development of individuals who are psychologically healthy or analyzable adults shows a genuine achievement of one-to-one relationships with both parents. This allows the oedipal conflict to emerge without jeopardizing these important object relations. Such a developmental failure in pregenital object relations usually involves an all-or-nothing aspect to establishing relationships which can decidedly impair the patient's capacity for a positive therapeutic alliance. This must be distinguished from a regressive response to trauma which may lead to deceptively similar symptoms.

Nonetheless, it is quite clear that the major unresolved conflict in analyzable and relatively obsessional men is derived from the triangular conflict at a genuinely oedipal level. There is a deceptive element, however. Just as a picture of hysterical symptoms does not constitute evidence of an analyzable neurosis, so the presence of obsessional symptoms calls for careful evaluation. As we have suggested, reaction formations can be established in obsessional development before the onset of the genital oedipal situation. Where reaction formations and related obsessional defenses have been prematurely integrated and consolidated, this too-early crystallization of the personality may form an impediment to the emergence of a genuine triangular conflict. Whether or not the presenting symptoms are primarily hysterical or obsessional is less important in evaluating the patient's potential for psychoanalysis than the degree to which certain major developmental steps have been accomplished and integrated.

Where such premature defenses have been installed in an obsessional character it may be impossible to develop a sufficiently secure therapeutic alliance which would facilitate the undoing of the relatively rigid defenses that are maintained with such intense investment. Such patients may go through the motions of analytic work, but they are so heavily defended that the emergence of an analyzable transference is impossible. Where the intensity of defenses and their relative rigidity is due to the developmental failure in establishing positive one-to-one relations and in an inability to tolerate and resolve ambivalence, we can expect a failure to achieve genuine triangular oedipal involvement. Consequently, such patients do not meet some of the basic criteria for analyzability.

Criteria for Analyzability

The analyses of individuals who fulfill the criteria of analyzability amply confirm the importance of the infantile oedipal situation both as a prerequisite for mental health as well as the significant unresolved conflict in potentially analyzable neurotics. The patient's achievement of the oedipal conflict represents certain developmental accomplishments which are reflected in the analytic process. The ability to achieve and maintain a positive therapeutic alliance, as well as the capacity to work through the terminal phase of analysis, has been optimal in those patients whose analytic material reveals substantial mastery of ambivalence in the early mother-child relationship. This usually entails the development of certain defenses which prove to be prophylactic against undue regression during the analytic process. Their response in treatment demonstrates the capacity to distinguish between internal and external reality as well as considerable capacity to tolerate anxiety and depression.

In many of these patients, however, the analysis reveals difficulties or adverse experiences either during the period of the infantile neurosis itself or in the early postoedipal years. Such adverse experiences cover a wide range of problems and losses. At one extreme, these patients may have suffered the loss of one or the other parent through death during this crucial time. Or the child may have experienced some disturbance of the relationship to the mother as a result of the birth of a younger sibling. Such experiences and others tend to undermine the one-to-one relation with one or the other of the parents. This complicates the emergence of the oedipal conflict and thus impairs the child's growing capacity to tolerate and master the internal conflicts involved in it.

The capacity to tolerate anxiety and depression is one of the central concerns in evaluating analyzability. It is a frequent clinical finding that men who have relatively obsessional character structures are vulnerable to involutional depressions toward the end of their active careers. In general, however, depression—like hysteria—is more commonly observed in women than in men. The tolerance and mastery of depression involves a dual developmental task. It involves the passive toleration of a painful reality which cannot be immediately modified. It also involves

a subsequent mobilization of resources in the available areas of achievement and gratification. The masculine ideal of striving and mastery
reinforces the second phase of this developmental task throughout the
oedipal period. It is hardly surprising, therefore, that analyzable men
who tend to rely on obsessional defenses should have a relative intolerance for passivity and depression, or that this should be compatible
with an analyzable transference neurosis.

For women, however, the situation is quite different. Passivity rather
than activity is central to the image of femininity. Women may have
difficulty in dealing with the second phase of this important developmental task, whereas men are more likely to have difficulty with the
first phase. This can lead to the exaggerated sense of passivity, helplessness, and vulnerability which is so prominent in the feminine depressive
character structure. It is often linked with hysterical symptoms. Such
women are often capable of tolerating a considerable degree of passivity
and depression. But their inability to mobilize active ego resources for
mastery and growth leaves them vulnerable to regression and/or narcissistic injury. Thus the basic conflicts for men tend to cluster around
problems related to recognizing, tolerating, and integrating passivity,
dependence, and depression. Much of the male insistence on striving
and activity serves a defensive function in avoiding and countering the
underlying difficult and conflict-laden feelings. The development of the
transference neurosis can unmask such feelings and thereby severely
threaten the patient. The basic conflicts for women, conversely, tend to
cluster around problems related to mastery, activity, and self-assertion.
The feminine recourse to a more passive, dependent, depressed—and
often masochistic—position serves as a defense against and avoidance
of more conflicted areas of aggressive activity.

The evaluation of depression and the patient's capacity to bear and
master it are crucial aspects of the evaluation for psychoanalysis. Depression is often a major presenting symptom in patients who are suffering from hysterical and obsessional neuroses. Such patients often turn
out to be potentially analyzable neurotics and meet the criteria for analyzability. The evaluation of the depression is difficult, however, as well
as important for assessing the patient's potential for analysis. Often
such patients require a preliminary course of psychotherapy aimed at
re-establishing a sufficient level of self-esteem and a mobilizing of the
patient's more active coping resources to facilitate development of a
positive therapeutic alliance. The patient's therapeutic response allows
the therapist to more extensively evaluate the patient's capacity to toler-

ate the depressive affects without significant regression, and his capacity to respond by mobilizing resources for mastery and active coping.

The patients who are relatively healthy and potentially analyzable, therefore, do not form a large percentage of those with emotional difficulties who present themselves at our outpatient clinics or in the emergency wards of general hospitals. Few of the patients who fulfill the criteria for analyzability ever present themselves as psychiatric emergencies. They usually carry on their lives rather effectively and are able to function quite adequately in many areas of conflict-free activity. When they do present themselves in a psychiatric clinic, it is not altogether unlikely that they will be either overestimated or underestimated. They may be told that there is nothing very much the matter with them or be offered quite inadequate treatment which accomplishes little more than producing unfortunate and unnecessary regressive responses. This tendency is readily understandable in terms of the magnitude and treatment difficulty of other more disturbed patients who flood outpatient facilities. It is also understandable in terms of the usual clinic philosophy. As Winnicott has described it, the treatment attitude in an outpatient setting is usually to try to get away with as little treatment as is necessary. In considering patients for analysis, however, we are adopting a quite different attitude—instead of asking how little we can get away with, we are asking how much can we hope to accomplish with and for the patient.

We are emphasizing the importance of the problem of analyzability and the pragmatic clinical aspects of determining analyzability because there is a definite body of patients for whom analysis is the treatment of choice. Without analysis it is unlikely that a woman who has failed to renounce her oedipal attachment to her father will ever be able to achieve satisfactory heterosexual object relations and to form a satisfactory marriage relationship. Without analysis it is quite unlikely that the man who is inhibited and conflicted over his work can reach his full potential and allow himself to reach the degree of professional success for which he is otherwise fully equipped.

But the point we are emphasizing is that psychoanalysis is a highly specific and limited method of clinical treatment. It can only be expected to succeed in the precise area of its proper application. Much of the disenchantment with and devaluation of psychoanalysis in recent years has stemmed from attempts to apply psychoanalytic techniques inappropriately to patients who did not meet the criteria for analyzability. Therapeutic success with such patients is predictably foredoomed. Thus the selection of patients who will be suitable for this sort of therapeutic intervention is crucial—as it is for any form of therapy. It is also clear, however, that psychoanalysis has provided a body of information and understanding that can serve as the basis for the understanding not only of certain forms of neurotic disturbance but of the broad range of human psychopathology. It can thus provide the conceptual basis for forms of treatment more applicable to other types of emotional dysfunction, even those based on relatively severe forms of developmental failure. And beyond that—in terms of the general theory of psychoanalysis—it provides the meaningful and scientific basis for the understanding of all human development and functioning—pathological as well as normal.

[15]

An Approach to the Borderline Patient

Up to this point in our discussion we have concerned ourselves primarily with the historical and conceptual underpinnings of the basic psychoanalytic formulations. We have tried to elaborate these basic notions in terms of the development of the psychologically healthy and normal personality. We have discussed the deviations from normal development which offer the possibility of therapeutic correction through the psychoanalytic technique. In the present chapter, however, we are shifting our interest somewhat to focus on a form of psychopathology which represents a more radical departure from normal development and which does not lend itself to psychoanalytic intervention—at least in the classic manner.

The Borderline Problem

The reasons for focusing on the borderline conditions are multiple. The definition and clarification of borderline states is a matter of recent concern among psychoanalysts and among psychiatrists in general. In our clinics and practices we are seeing—or perhaps with increasing awareness, we are recognizing—more and more cases of this sort. In addition these patients typically form a most difficult problem in therapeutic management for the psychiatrist. There is an additional interest for the psychoanalyst. There seems to be good reason to believe that some of the cases that Freud dealt with in his early studies were not simply neurotics as he might have thought. Their personality structures seem to be considerably more primitive than the kind of personality organization that we have described as neurotic. These patients, viewing them from the historical perspective of our greater awareness of borderline forms of pathology, seem to manifest many borderline characteristics. Furthermore, it is a not infrequent experience for patients to present themselves in the evaluation for psychoanalysis as apparently reasonably well-put-together neurotics, but when they are put on the couch and begin to regress, their personality structure seems to be somewhat less than neurotic. The induced regression of the analytic couch makes it clear that many of these patients are more borderline than neurotic, and therefore must be considered less suitable for psychoanalytic treatment. This is one of the basic questions in the assessment of the patient's suitability for analysis, and one for which the answers are neither easy nor readily available.

It can be readily seen that the diagnostic considerations are of primary importance in dealing with borderline problems. The classic British psychiatric text of Mayer-Gross, Slater, and Roth made the observation some years ago that "diagnosis has never been only naming and labelling. Ideally it implies judgement of causation and even if this is impossible for lack of knowledge it always includes a plan of action, i.e., treatment." [68] The treatment appropriate for a certain group of patients, like the borderline group, may depend on a specific diagnostic formulation. Diagnostic considerations in regard to the borderline are noteworthy in that they refer directly to the patient and his personality structure. They do not refer to the presenting symptoms or mental status.

Diagnostically the borderline conditions have presented a consistently difficult problem for psychiatrists. Apart from a passing reference to borderline schizophrenia under the description of latent schizophrenia, the *Diagnostic and Statistical Manual of Mental Disorders* (DSM II) does not mention borderline states as a diagnostic category.[69] Similarly, the term does not occur in a recent cross-cultural national study of the diagnosis of mental disorders. More than a third of the patients included in this study, however, were lumped together into a heterogeneous category labeled "all other disorders." It would not be difficult to guess that a significant percentage of the patients in this leftover group would be described as "psychopathic personalities" or "character disorders" by British-trained diagnosticians, and that the same patients would just as readily be described as "borderline" by their American colleagues.

The relatively widespread use of the terms "borderline" and "borderline states" in American circles highlights a problem that is quite peculiar to psychiatric diagnosis. Psychiatric diagnoses are often made not on positive grounds, using positively identifiable signs and symptoms, but rather on negative grounds. For example, conversion hysteria, which was one of the first conditions investigated by Freud, has often been diagnosed only after the examining physicians satisfy themselves that they are unable to identify any organic condition or disease which might account for the patient's physical symptoms or disability. Something similar happens often in the case of the borderline patient. The *Glossary of Psychoanalytic Terms and Concepts,* for example, does not describe the borderline patient, but it does refer to borderline states and defines them negatively: ". . . a group of conditions which manifest both neurotic and psychotic phenomena *without* fitting unequivocally into either diagnostic category." [70] In contemporary American psychiatry the diagnosis of borderline personality is often made on a relative and generally negative basis. The patient does not seem to be suffering from an overt psychotic disturbance; he does not seem to fit any of the generally accepted personality disorders. There is no organic component identifiable. Both the symptoms and the character structure, however, seem to preclude a diagnosis of either a symptom neurosis or a straightforward neurotic character structure. They are consequently lumped into the borderline category.

The Borderline Personality

The diagnosis and definition of borderline states have become gradually clarified in recent years. Early studies described the borderline phenomena, but tended to regard these patients as fundamentally schizophrenic; they were labeled preschizophrenic, psychotic characters, ambulatory schizophrenia, pseudoneurotic schizophrenia. They were viewed as well-compensated schizophrenics who regressed to psychotic levels as a transitory reaction to stress or in response to toxic effects. Gradually, however, the view emerged that these individuals were not schizophrenic, but represented a stable form of personality structure which was somewhat less mature than neurotic and somewhat more developed than psychotic personality organizations. They are now seen as having a fairly typical constellation of symptoms and defenses, a typical pattern of defect in object relations, and a characteristic developmental course.

Descriptively borderline patients present with a variety of neurotic symptoms and character defects. Their anxiety is usually chronic and diffuse. They often present a variety of neurotic symptoms—multiple phobias, obsessive-compulsive thoughts and behaviors, conversion symptoms, dissociative reactions, as well as hypochondriacal complaints or paranoid traits. Sexuality tends to be promiscuous and often perverse. The personality organization tends to be impulsive and infantile. The need to gratify impulses breaks through repetitively, giving the borderline's life style an acting-out quality. Such personalities frequently turn to alcohol or drugs for relief of tension and gratification. Addictive personalities often have a borderline structure. Borderlines often tend to show an emotional lability and a tendency for emotional overinvolvement and overidentification which reflects a more hysterical element. Narcissism is often a predominant element in their character structure —needing and demanding attention and adulation from others. This behavior often serves to cover a deep distrust and helps to defend against underlying paranoid traits which are based on the projection of a rather primitive oral rage. The underlying character structure may also take the form of a severe depressive-masochistic pathology. Paranoid and depressive-masochistic traits are often closely related in these patients.

These features of the borderline personality organization make it very difficult for such patients to enter into a productive therapeutic relationship. Instead of forming and being able to sustain a therapeutic alliance with the therapist and being able to mobilize resources in the service of therapeutic work, the borderline patient can only expect to be given in therapy. Tolerance for frustration and delay is low. Narcissistic expectations and entitlements are large. The interaction is often highly contaminated with attempts to manipulate the therapist in order to gain needed gratifications. Not infrequently such patients will pull away from treatment enraged at the therapist's refusal to gratify their wishes, only to return in an emotional crisis which is generated in highly manipulative fashion. This often takes the form of a manipulative suicidal gesture aimed at the therapist or other significant figures in the patient's environment who are denying the patient's wishes. Therapy with such patients can often be very trying and difficult.

From the point of view of the inner organization of the borderline personality, these patients reveal an underlying weakness in the structure and organization of the ego. These patients show a marked lack of tolerance for even low degrees of anxiety. They have a poor capacity for impulse control and a lack of available channels for sublimation. The ego's overall capacity for neutralization of instinctual drive derivatives is poor. The cognitive organization shows a generalized shift toward primary process organization. This is hardly ever manifested in a formal thought disorder in the mental status examination, but it often shows up on projective test data and in relatively unstructured and stressful situations. The difficulty in eliciting this aspect of borderline functioning in the usual interview setting makes projective test evaluation a useful aspect of the diagnostic evaluation of these patients. We can add, by way of footnote, that this is an important aspect of the evaluation of patients for psychoanalysis. In view of the relatively frequent experience of neurotic-looking patients revealing more borderline forms of personality organization once an analysis is undertaken, more extensive use of projective evaluations in assessing analyzability should be recommended.

Splitting

One of the predominant—if not characteristic—defenses of the borderline patient is "splitting." Under the influence of drive derivatives, the ego early in development builds up "good" and "bad" introjects. The good introjects are derived from libidinal drives and the bad ones are derived from aggressive drives. The separation of good and bad objects and the correlative separation of good and bad introjects (internal objects) stems from a preambivalent level of development before the child is capable of integrating good and bad part objects into a whole good-and-bad object. The emerging ego can resort to this mechanism as a defense against anxiety flooding it and thus protecting the positive ego core which is centered around positive introjects. The defensive process of internal splitting of the ego into good and bad parts is supported and engineered through the interplay of introjection and projection. The operation of these primitive mechanisms prevents the ego from achieving any meaningful integration of both self and object images, which have been built up out of libidinal derivatives, with the self and object images which have been built up out of aggressive derivatives. Thus the ego is prevented from developing a tolerance for ambivalence, either internally or externally, and from increasing its tolerance for anxiety. The progression of cycles of the projection of aggression and the subsequent reintrojection of hostile and destructive object and self images are central to the development of psychotic as well as borderline personality organization. In psychotic development, this process produces a regressive refusion of self and object images with the loss of ego boundaries and self-object differentiation. In the borderline, however, the process does not reach that level of regression, but rather brings about an intensification and fixation of splitting processes.

Thus splitting achieves an active separation of introjects of opposite

quality—good as opposed to bad. The integration of such object derivatives is one of the major ways in which aggression is neutralized and de-
toxified. In this respect Freud spoke of the fusion of libidinal with aggressive instincts. Splitting, therefore, results in inadequate neutralization of instinctual energies and thus the ego loses an essential source of
growth potential. Splitting is consequently a basic dimension of the
borderline patient's ego weakness.

The effects of splitting are reflected in certain other aspects of the patient's functioning. There is a tendency to idealization. This works in
both directions. The patient may idealize external objects, viewing them
as totally good and powerful, thus assuring him that the external object
can protect him from the bad objects and also that the external object
will not be destroyed or contaminated by the patient's own aggressive
and destructive wishes. One such patient described her therapist as a
powerful sponge which soaked up all her poison and made it harmless.
The idealization may work in the reverse fashion as well. The patient
may feel omnipotent in an attempt to deny any threat from the bad introjects. The patient may shift back and forth between idealization and
devaluation of the therapist, or between overvaluation and devaluation
of the self. These feelings frequently have a magical quality which reflects the operation of mechanisms of projection and introjection—at
once expelling evil aspects out of the self and putting them in objects,
leaving the self good and strong, or again taking them in again thus
making the self weak, helpless, and evil.

The Diagnostic Problem

The importance of accurate diagnosis is thus essential in determining
the appropriate treatment of these patients. The diagnosis of a personality disorder of this type, however, is extremely difficult. We cannot rely
on the information supplied by the case history to enable us to make the
diagnosis convincingly. Nor can we rely on the data derived from a
brief diagnostic interview or an examination of the patient's mental status to provide sufficient evidence to permit us to make the diagnosis. To
begin with, as the *Diagnostic and Statistical Manual* implies, many patients who are initially evaluated as borderline because their mental status examination does not reveal any signs of frank psychosis later
prove, after further investigation or therapeutic intervention, to be actually schizophrenic. But on the other hand, we frequently see in the
clinic a number of patients, particularly late adolescents and young

adults, whose presentation and mental status could easily be described as borderline, but whom we are seeing in the midst of an acute developmental or situational crisis. Thus patients who clinically look borderline may in fact turn out to be either a good deal sicker or a good deal healthier.

The recognition or description of a borderline state, therefore, does not justify our making a diagnosis of borderline personality organization. The subsequent history of such patients, including their response to appropriate therapeutic intervention over a sufficient period of time, often demonstrates that a diagnosis of borderline personality would have been premature and misguided. The converse of the diagnostic dilemma, as we have already indicated, also caused difficulties. Borderline patients do not always present initially with symptoms which might suggest a borderline state or an underlying borderline personality. Often truly borderline personalities will present as apparently normal, or their symptomatology will amply justify a diagnosis of neurotic personality structure. The borderline features reveal themselves only after psychoanalysis or another related therapeutic approach has been undertaken. Even then the borderline characteristics may not reveal themselves for some months.

Thus it seems that the definitive diagnosis of certain forms of schizophrenia and the differentiation of these forms from a transient regression due to a developmental crisis will often require a more or less extended evaluation of the patient's response to therapeutic intervention. To put the matter briefly and succinctly, the nature of the doctor-patient relationship which the patient is able to establish may prove to be the crucial factor in making a definitive diagnostic evaluation. In the diagnosis of the borderline personality this factor has special application and relevance. Unlike the potentially healthy or neurotic patient who may be seen during an acute crisis, the borderline personality is unable to readily establish a confident and trusting doctor-patient relationship. In the therapeutic relationship, magical expectations, impairment of the distinction between fantasy and reality, episodes of anger, suspicion, and excessive fears of rejection are to be anticipated over a relatively extended period.

The therapy with borderline patients, however, does not show the level of impairment of object relations or of ego functioning that one sees in schizophrenic patients. In a favorable treatment situation—which we will discuss later in this chapter—the borderline patient becomes gradually and increasingly able to acknowledge and at least partially relinquish unrealistic magical expectations and ultimately to surrender his equally unrealistic fears and suspicions. He can accomplish this without the help of antipsychotic medications. Such patients can gradually establish areas of relatively autonomous functioning which are more or less freed of the toxic effects of evil and destructive introjects. Schizophrenic patients are rarely if ever capable of this amount of more integrated functioning. As we shall see, the borderline integration is precarious, often subject to regressive pulls, and dependent on certain external supports for its stabilization. We believe that the elements of such a therapeutically benign and favorable treatment situation can be understood optimally within the context of contemporary psychoanalytic theory, particularly with reference to psychoanalysis as a comprehensive developmental psychology.

The Developmental Failure

A number of contemporary psychoanalysts have reached the conclusion independently that certain crucial aspects of definitive psychic structure and functioning are initiated in and derived from the early mother-child relationship. We have discussed these developmental achievements of the earliest stages of life in preceding chapters. The developmental accomplishments of the primary mother-child relationship include the achievement of definitive self-object differentiation; the development of the capacity to recognize, tolerate, and master frustration, delay, separation, loss, and narcissistic injury; and finally—and this aspect is probably the most important for the understanding of borderline pathology and treatment—the internalization of a positive ego identification which serves as the basis for a basic self-esteem and a relatively substantial sense of autonomy. The elements of autonomy and self-esteem are essential for the capacity to elaborate stable one-to-one relations. Briefly, the potentially healthy individual has acquired and taken away from the earliest mother-child relation these crucial attributes of ego functioning. The psychotic individual has either failed to acquire these attributes or has become significantly impaired in respect to all three. The psychotic process reflects a decathexis of ego boundaries and an impaired sense of differentiation between the self and objects. The psychotic displays minimal capacity to tolerate or master separation or loss. And his capacity for identification and the development of inner ego structure is severely impaired.

The picture presented by the borderline personality, however, is somewhat different. These patients reveal a relative, although not necessarily equal, failure in respect to each of these developmental tasks. Their ego functioning may present a rather heterogeneous picture at any given point in their treatment. The self-object differentiation of the borderline patient is rather vulnerable. This is illustrated by their difficulties in distinguishing fantasy and reality. This lack of differentiation can most easily be seen either under conditions of stress or when the patient is in a therapeutic situation which fosters the emergence of a regressive transference reaction. Such is frequently the case in borderline patients who find their way to the analytic couch. In the borderline, however, the impairment is more readily and completely reversible than it is in less healthy, psychotic patients.

Such regressive responses may be largely determined by the borderline patient's limited capacity to tolerate painful affects. Borderline patients typically manifest an intolerance of aggressive impulses—whether they be their own or those of other people. The pain of loss and separation is closely linked with vicissitudes of aggressive and hateful feelings toward the lost object. The capacity to tolerate and bear such losses becomes a function of the individual's capacity to sustain and master ambivalence. Borderline patients are peculiarly impaired in this aspect of internal functioning, since their pathology is so closely linked to the separation of good and bad introjects. This makes them particularly susceptible to the toxic effects of destructive and hateful impulses and impairs their capacity to master ambivalance. This capacity may show a gradual increase during the course of successful treatment. Often it is linked in treatment with an idealization of the therapist which prevents a true internalization of this capacity. Consequently, the patient's need for the therapist as an external regulator of his own inner impulses does not meaningfully diminish. Termination of therapy is thus nearly impossible.

Perhaps the most telling impairment of the borderline patient is his limited and vulnerable capacity to internalize a sufficiently stable ego identification and thus gain some level of stable and genuinely autonomous functioning. It is this limitation and basic impairment in the capacity of the ego that sets a limit on the effectiveness of therapeutic efforts. Such patients may continue through a long and apparently successful course of treatment with considerable development of insight and modification of self-defeating and self-destructive behaviors, but show a capacity to regress with surprising rapidity to pretreatment levels of functioning under stress or significant losses. These are the patients—or at least some of the patients—whose analyses seem to drag on interminably. The benefit they derive from insight and the therapeutic relationship never seems to produce any persistent effect or any increase in the capacity to cope effectively and to master painful affects. The reason is that these patients can do everything that is required for successful therapy except effectively internalize whatever strength is to be had from the therapist. The capacity for identification is defective.

We are proposing, therefore, that the diagnosis of the borderline patient involves a distinction among three very different developmental difficulties. We must distinguish (1) problems determined by unresolved intrapsychic conflict, (2) regressive changes which are attributable to transient, although serious, developmental or situational stress, and finally (3) a significant failure to initiate and develop certain basic ego functions. The differentiation among these developmental patterns is based on complex and interrelated problems in both instinctual and ego development. Freud himself was clearly aware of the crucial importance of these factors when he wrote the *Formulations on the Two Principles of Mental Functioning* in 1911. He observed then:

While the ego goes through its transformation from a pleasure ego into a reality ego the sexual instincts undergo the changes that lead them from their original auto-erotism through various intermediate phases to object love in the service of procreation. If . . . each step in these two courses of development may become the site of a disposition to later illness, it is plausible to suppose that the form taken by the subsequent illness will depend on the particular phase of the development of the ego and of the libido in which the dispositional inhibition of development has occurred. Thus unexpected significance attaches to the chronological features of the two developments (which has not yet been studied) and to possible variations in their synchronization.[71]

This statement illustrates in the first place the depth and scope of Freud's approach to and understanding of mental life. Further, although it antedates the formulation of the structural theory by a dozen years, its emphasis on the importance of the reality principle is specifically relevant to the discussion of the treatment of borderline personalities. The borderline patient's perception of reality and his capacity for reality testing are generally accepted as characteristic. The basis of their pathology does not lie in this area of ego functioning. The reality principle and this aspect of borderline functioning may point a way to effective treatment of these cases. Finally, although Freud himself never discussed therapeutic techniques other than those of traditional psychoanalysis, this statement is entirely compatible with the contemporary view of psychoanalysis as a comprehensive developmental theory. We can suggest, therefore, that the techniques appropriate to the treatment of patients suffering from developmental failure may differ considerably from the techniques applicable to the much healthier patients treated with traditional psychoanalytic techniques. The techniques which are appropriate for the resolution of intrapsychic (neurotic) conflict may be totally inappropriate for the treatment of failures to develop certain basic ego functions, and vice versa.

Regressive Potential

Contemporary viewpoints within psychoanalysis demonstrate considerable divergence as to how patients with borderline personalities should be treated. The question is put in terms of the extent to which such patients can benefit from the application of techniques closely allied to the technique of clinical psychoanalysis. Some authors would hold that classical psychoanalytic technique, without any significant parameters, is the treatment of choice for such disorders. It has been our experience, however, that relatively intensive or unstructured therapeutic situations present significant dangers to patients who suffer from the sort of developmental failure that is found in borderline personalities.

In fact, it has been shown that a somewhat more intensive and caring hospital atmosphere has a rather paradoxical effect on such patients. Borderline patients for whom hospitalization is necessary often regress dramatically in such an atmosphere. The attempts of the hospital staff to be supportive and caring, to relate more intensely and therapeutically with the patient, result only in outbursts of disruptive behavior and the development of angry, recriminatory struggles. The patient's wish for immediate gratification and narcissistic satisfaction are not adequately confronted in such an atmosphere, so that the borderline patient's tendency to react to frustration with rage and intolerant demanding is given broader scope for its exercise. Borderline patients, for whom the pattern of dealing with frustration has usually been rage and manipulation of the environment, easily fall into acting out their rage in disruptive or destructive ways. Such behavior—including breaking windows and slashing wrists—mobilizes responses of caring and attention giving from the hospital staff which serve as substitute gratifications for such patients. Thus the failure of the hospital environment to set adequate limits on such patients and to confront their narcissism and demands for gratification can actually induce a regression in their capacity to function.

Borderline patients who show less disruption in their functioning, and thus avoid hospitalization, often become involved in a treatment situation which offers them many gratifications and supports their regressive needs, so that the therapy is excessively prolonged and seems to achieve little in the way of therapeutic results. Patients are often seen who come after years of intensive but unsuccessful treatment which has been characterized by highly regressive transference responses. Zetzel's experience of supervising the treatment of borderline patients also emphasizes the dangers which are involved in the treatment of them in a relatively unstructured treatment situation with a nonparticipating and silent therapist. Such a treatment situation serves only to induce regression and deprive the patient of the growth-stimulating experiences he needs in order to compensate for the developmental failure from which he suffers.

Treatment Rationale

We are aware of the pressing need to find appropriate and more available methods and techniques of treating this very difficult group of patients. We would like to shift the emphasis in the treatment rationale of these patients toward the importance of developing and formulating techniques which demand a minimum of psychiatric attention rather than a maximum. It is our position that the classic psychoanalytic technique is not indicated for these patients and, in fact, that it is not at all suited to the treatment of the type of developmental defect that we must deal with in them. This is a specific application of the basic principle that therapy must be designed to deal with the patient's difficulties in terms of accurate diagnostic evaluation and the nature of the patient's developmental accomplishments and deficits.

The technique we are recommending is based primarily on the experience of the senior author (Zetzel), who has had long and broad experience both in the treatment and the supervision of treatment of borderline patients. It is also based on the premise that the basic pathology of the borderline personality lies in the relative developmental failure of certain basic ego functions. The developmental failure could be expressed in terms of instinctual vicissitudes as well, but this might be deceptive. The defect can best be understood in relation to those ego attributes which are initially established in the child's one-to-one relationships. In the therapeutic context, these attributes are focused primarily in the achievement of a stable, realistic, and consistent doctor-patient relationship. The ego capacities and attributes which were initially developed in the one-to-one relationship with the parents serve as the basis and essential core of this important therapeutic one-to-one relationship. This aspect of the relationship, it should be noted, is over and above the transference issues that are also operative. The patient brings not only libidinal and aggressive components from his relationship to his parents and transfers them to the therapist, but also brings to bear certain ego capacities and functions which were originally developed in the relation to each of his parents. This is not so much a matter of transference as it is the availability of acquired ego functions.

The recognition of the primary core of this relationship, which Zetzel has defined elsewhere as the "therapeutic alliance," was originally derived from experience with patients in the traditional psychoanalytic setting. Even relatively healthy neurotic patients may experience a regression in the analytic situation which impairs certain basic ego functions. However, the regression is usually not severe and does not generally interfere with the patient's capacity to form a reasonable and therapeutically productive alliance with the analyst. Thus, as a rule, the establishment of a good doctor-patient relationship does not present any serious difficulties in the treatment of neurotic patients. In the technique of psychoanalysis, therefore, while it is of considerable importance in the working of the analytic process, it does not become a focal problem in the analysis.

As we have already indicated, however, borderline patients, particularly during the opening stages of treatment, have serious difficulties in relating to the therapist in a confident or consistent manner. Often when borderline patients are seen in the midst of a regressive crisis they adopt an appealing, distressed, demanding, and highly manipulative posture. For the therapist at such times to accede to the borderline patient's excessive demands—even reluctantly as sometimes happens—is to frustrate the goals of therapy and defeat his own therapeutic intentions. Like psychotic patients, borderline patients are unusually sensitive to any inconsistency or affective responsiveness in the therapist. Such responses in the therapist can be grouped under the heading of countertransference reactions, and the course of the therapy is particularly affected by any negative countertransference reactions on the part of the therapist. It is thus essential that the therapist structure the treatment setting and course so that he is able to consistently fulfill his initial goals and objectives. Any decision to embark on intensive therapy should be carefully and slowly considered and planned. It should be put into effect only through a mutual decision process between the therapist and the patient. It should only be initiated with full realization of the risks and by a therapist who is fully prepared and resigned to a long, demanding, and difficult course of treatment.

In actual practice it has been our experience that the establishment of a satisfactory therapeutic relationship has seldom been significantly furthered by frequent appointments. The more important element in the treatment program is that the therapist be able to maintain a certain stability, consistency, and the ability to set realistic and appropriate limits in the therapy setting. These elements are of primary importance in the treatment of the borderline patient. It should be emphasized that such treatment is far from being merely supportive. The borderline patient will test the therapist in innumerable ways. The treatment is difficult and trying. One successful interview with a difficult borderline patient may be far more demanding and stressful than four or five sessions with an analyzable neurotic. The demanding and manipulative propensity of the borderline can be extremely subtle and can severely test the therapist's mettle. Borderline patients also know instinctively how to elicit untherapeutic feelings in the therapist and are often quite adept at generating negative countertransference attitudes. All of these aspects present special difficulties to the therapist's efforts to work therapeutically with the patient.

It is essential that the therapist should not present himself as an omnipotent figure with inexhaustible resources. This is particularly important in view of the borderline patient's propensity for the use of splitting and idealization as defensive maneuvers. The patient may try to move the therapist into the position of being the all-powerful, protecting, and caring external object. The failure of the therapist to satisfy these needs and demands of the patient can lead to an infantile rage and bitter recriminations on the part of the patient. The therapist's inability to meet such excessive demands and expectations and to satisfy the narcissistic entitlement that lies behind them is an aspect of reality. The therapist must undercut the patient's attempts to put him in that position, as an unconscious means of justifying the patient's rage and sense of frustrated entitlement. By undercutting this aspect of the patient's defense, the therapist also sets the conditions in which the patient must deal with him in realistic terms and without magical expectations. The patient is thereby in a better position to tolerate and master his own ambivalence, without resorting to splitting as a way of avoiding ambivalence. In this context it is vital for the therapist to make the important distinction for himself and for the patient between the clarification of regressive transference distortions, which are impairing a more realistic and therapeutic doctor-patient relationship on the one hand, and a transference interpretation which is directed toward achieving intrapsychic insight. The former has to do with the relationship between doctor and patient, while the latter depends on the patient's capacity to differentiate fantasy from reality.

In view of these considerations, regular but limited contact—not more and often less than once a week—is thus often an optimal spacing of treatment sessions for the patient and the therapist. Under these circumstances the therapist is less likely to develop the ambivalent countertransference reactions which may contribute to a more regressive therapeutic relationship. The setting of careful structure, once accepted by the patient, often leads to a greater acceptance of the limitations of reality. It often has the added benefit that the patient begins to use each session in a more productive and therapeutic manner. Under favorable circumstances this can have the effect of facilitating an increased mobilization of the patient's own resources.

The situation for the neurotic patient and the borderline patient differ radically. The former can profit from the limited regression which is induced by the analytic situation and which is characteristic of the transference neurosis. Such a regression is a disservice to the borderline patient. The latter on the contrary needs help to develop his capacities in the areas of progression and mastery. Since the developmental failure for these patients lies in the inability to develop positive and meaningful one-to-one relationships, the path to improvement and growth is best approached through the establishment and working through of a new and better one-to-one relationship than the patient had been able to achieve in the earlier periods of developmental crisis. This is a new and real relationship which cannot be subsumed under the heading of transference. Once it is established it can be maintained by relatively infrequent therapeutic interviews. Since it is a relationship based on real factors, it does not depend on frequency or intensity of contact in order for it to maintain its therapeutic effectiveness. In this respect it differs from the transference neurosis, which is fostered and maintained by frequent contacts and the intimacy of the situation of the analytic setting. For many borderline patients, however, even if the contacts with the therapist be few and far between, it may be necessary for the therapist to remain at least potentially available over an indefinitely extended period. This continuing need for the therapist as a stabilizing object reflects the basic incapacity for internalization that is so characteristic of borderlines. While such patients remain dependent on the external object, they are often capable of functioning quite adequately for extended periods of time with the assurance that the therapist is still available to them. They return only occasionally to reassure themselves of the persisting real relationship and to renew and confirm that relationship.

The Developmental Perspective

To summarize our consideration of the development and treatment of the borderline personality organization in this chapter, we can say that psychoanalysis is a comprehensive developmental psychology. As such it includes an understanding of the developmental achievements which are required for attaining psychological maturity and psychic health. The borderline patient reveals a developmental failure in respect to crucial ego capacities and attributes which are contingent on the establishment of stable one-to-one relationships. The treatment rationale of these is therefore based on the establishment and carrying through of a stable and meaningful one-to-one relationship with the therapist.

The therapeutic process with these patients calls for a considerable degree of activity and definite structuring of the situation on the part of the therapist. This activity and structuring is primarily directed toward helping the patient to achieve further progress and growth through the experience of a realistic and productive doctor-patient relationship. Borderline patients are seldom, if ever, capable of tolerating the painful affect which is involved in the emergency of regressive transference reactions. A further difficulty is that they readily lose the capacity to maintain the crucial distinction between transference and reality. That capacity is one of the necessary prerequisites for undertaking psychoanalysis successfully—the capacity for an observant ego to differentiate and compare the experience of transference effects with the reality of the situation and the relationship. This capacity is essential to any insight-oriented form of therapy. Despite these limitations, many borderline patients prove capable of maintaining a high degree of effective functioning and adaptation—providing the therapist remains available to them in a limited manner for an indefinite period of time.

Although such a treatment rationale and technical approach differs radically from the technique of traditional psychoanalysis, it is nonetheless based on our contemporary understanding of early psychic growth and development. Further it is a treatment rationale which is rooted in a specifically psychoanalytic understanding of developmental process and psychic functioning. To look at it from the reverse perspective—from that of diagnosis rather than from the perspective of treatment—we can begin to hope that the diagnosis of the "borderline personality" can begin to meet the criteria of diagnosis which we cited in the beginning of this chapter. It becomes not merely a labeling or naming, but it implies a judgment about causation—a specific form of developmental failure. It also includes a plan of therapeutic action—treatment directed to developmental progress in a one-to-one relationship—where the developmental failure is to be located.

[16]

Psychoanalysis As Therapy

In the preceding chapters our emphasis has been on the historical and conceptual aspects of psychoanalysis. In tracing Freud's ideas about instinctual life and its vicissitudes and his progressive formulation of a concept of the ego and the structural theory, we have indicated that this conceptual development was closely related to his clinical work and experience. We have not, however, focused specifically on the analytic process itself in a clinical sense. The dominating fact about psychoanalysis is that it is basically and primarily a clinical theory. It has its roots and its application in the clinical approach to patients and in the treatment of their neurotic disorders.

Psychoanalysis As a Theory of Therapy

More particularly, then, psychoanalysis in a basic sense is a theory of therapy. We have considered other aspects of the general and special theories in psychoanalysis. Here we are turning to the essential link between psychoanalytic theory and psychoanalytic therapy. We have taken up some of the related considerations in the chapters immediately preceding the present one, on the determination of analyzability and on the rationale for treatment of borderline personalities. We would like to turn now to the treatment process of psychoanalysis itself. Our approach, however, is not technical in the sense that we might focus our attention on how analysis is carried out. Rather our consideration will be an attempt to integrate the consideration of psychoanalysis as therapy with the considerations that have been advanced in the preceding pages of this book. We wish to emphasize that the theoretical understanding, as presented, serves as the basis for a theory of therapy. It is particularly the developmental understanding that serves us most directly in developing a rationale for treatment, although the other metapsychological assumptions play their essential roles.

It should also be noted that the theory of psychoanalysis provides a much broader basis for the understanding of disturbed behavior and for the development of treatment rationales than is brought to bear in the practice of psychoanalysis itself. We have already suggested this in the discussion of the treatment of borderline patients. Thus, while our attention is directed here to psychoanalytic therapy as such, it must be remembered that the theory of therapy has much broader application. One of the basic tenets of the theory is that the treatment process must be adapted to the developmental level of the patient and his pathology. The psychoanalytic technique is appropriate for patients who have reached a level of development consistent with a genuine triangular conflict. The discussion of analyzability was based essentially on developmental considerations. Patients who have not achieved a comparable developmental level must be approached with techniques which are proportioned to their developmental achievements and level. This is one of the most challenging areas of contemporary psychiatric thinking.

The theory of therapy which we are proposing rests on several basic assumptions which have been developed in the preceding sections of this book but which can be restated here. The patient's early experience, as well as the quality and stability of the object relations he has been able to achieve—particularly the early relationship with the mother—play a central role in the development of early ego identifications. These early identifications play a part in determining the individual's developmental progression to a level of maturation which involves the achievement of a capacity for tolerating frustration, delay, and separation. Between this early period of self-object differentiation and the onset of the oedipal situation there is a period of psychological development which determines the individual's capacity to enter and genuinely experience the oedipal conflict. The quality and stability of the individual's one-to-one relationships with both parents influences both the formation of the oedipal situation and the nature of its resolution. This in turn establishes the individual's predisposition to different types of regression in adult life. It also determines the individual's capacity in terms of therapy to develop, work through, and resolve an analyzable transference neurosis.

Any treatment process—restricting our discussion to individual treatment based on the relationship between the patient and a therapist—is based on and takes place in the setting of a one-to-one relationship. The relationship between therapist and patient both draws on the strengths of and reveals the underlying weaknesses in the patient's capacity to enter and maintain a meaningful and stable one-to-one relationship. These attributes are acquired early in life. Even in relatively healthy or stable individuals, however, they can be undermined by stress. One of the characteristic features of psychoanalysis is the limited regression which fosters and is part of the transference neurosis. The patient must be able to regress in ways which allow the development of further mastery and adaptation. But he must be protected from the forms of regression which can undermine previously acquired ego functions and attributes. Thus the analytic regression requires a certain stability of ego functions and capacities which can permit limited regression without loss of function. Patients who have not reached that developmental level can be harmed by analytic regression rather than helped. Patients who have not developed the capacity for meaningful one-to-one relationships consequently are poor risks for individual treatment. The development of other group- or family-based treatments may provide more useful approaches to the treatment and management of such patients.

Unless certain crucial capacities and ego functions are initiated in the original one-to-one parent-child relationships, we must seriously question to what degree psychotherapy can help the individual in adolescent or adult life to acquire the capacities he has failed to develop in the appropriate stage of development. One of the essential capacities for treatment success is the patient's capacity to internalize and identify with the therapist. This requires a capacity for tolerating frustration, separation, and loss. Individuals who suffer from serious developmental defects are significantly handicapped in their capacity for emotional growth. They are also quite vulnerable to regression in the face of developmental or situational stress. In predisposed patients such regression may result in relatively irreversible impairment. Thus forms of treatment which are based on induction of regression are contraindicated in such patients. The therapy of such seriously impaired patients focuses on the establishing of a one-to-one relationship. Such patients find it difficult to relinquish their magical expectations and to accept the limitations of reality. Some treatment goals can be realized, but only at the cost of a long-term, often indefinite, investment—and even then the goals can only be envisioned in terms of remission and possible rehabilitation.

One of the basic distinctions, then, in approaching a theory of therapy is that between developmental failure and functional regression. The limitations of analysis as well as therapy in the face of developmental failures must be recognized. We can also suggest that the analysis and undoing of precarious or seriously pathological defenses may not only be ineffective in promoting the patient's growth, but may in fact be quite dangerous. This is particularly true of defenses against primitive aggression. The relative failure of ego development precludes or raises massive difficulties for the establishing of a positive and stable one-to-one relationship. It also presents the risk that the patient might regress seriously into an infantile, often predominantly hostile, transference situation.

We want to turn our attention, however, at this point, to the consideration of traditional psychoanalytic therapy. In approaching this discussion we are presuming and recalling the considerations of the nature of the specific developmental failures which characterize neurotic and analyzable patients. We are also presuming the points made in the discussion of analyzability (Chapter 14). We will focus on the aspects of psychoanalytic treatment that are most characteristic and distinguishing of traditional psychoanalysis. Such elements also come into play in other forms of therapy, particularly forms of insight-oriented therapy which have been developed on the basis of a psychoanalytic rationale. But it should be understood that the following discussion has specific reference to the psychoanalytic process in a narrow sense, and as applied specifically to patients who meet the criteria for analyzability.

The Psychoanalytic Process

The psychoanalytic process is based on and includes several elements that serve to distinguish it from related forms of therapy. The patient and the therapist meet on a regular and rather intense basis, usually four or five times a week, each time for a full therapeutic hour. The patient lies on a couch and the therapist sits out of the patient's line of vision, usually behind the head of the couch. The patient is asked to free associate, to let his thoughts and feelings flow freely and to communicate these thoughts and feelings to the therapist without any of the selection or censoring that are usually employed in interpersonal communication. The treatment is carried on in an atmosphere of deprivation, which is created by the patient's not being able to see the analyst and by the analyst's relative silence. The treatment setting induces the conditions which provide the basis for therapy. The patient undergoes a regression in the analytic situation which allows for the re-emergence of infantile conflicts and which induces the formation of a transference neurosis. In the transference neurosis the original infantile conflicts and wishes become focused on the person of the analyst and are thus re-experienced and relived. The analyst's therapeutic interventions are based primarily on interpretations of these experiences with the objective of helping the patient to develop insight into the infantile sources of the neurosis. Interpretation is a matter of technique and consequently we shall consider it only in passing. The basic elements in the psychoanalytic rationale of therapy are regression and transference. Our discussion, therefore, will focus on these aspects.

The regression that is induced by the analytic situation serves to revive earlier infantile conflicts. As such it can be seen as a manifestation of the repetition compulsion. Regression, like the repetition compulsion, can be viewed in a twofold light—either as an attempt to return to an earlier state of real or fantasied gratification, or as an attempt to master a previously traumatic experience. One can think of an inherent need of the organism to return to a previously unsolved or unresolved problem to try to master it. From this point of view one could regard the regressive aspects of the analytic situation and the transference as preliminary conditions for the mastery of unresolved conflicts. But these regressive aspects may also reflect the unconscious wish to return to an earlier state of rest or narcissistic gratification. Both aspects of regression and the repetition compulsion can be found in the course of any analysis. The analytic process, in a sense, must work itself out in the face of this dual potentiality. The analytic regression has a destructive potentiality which must be recognized and guarded against. It also has a progressive potentiality for reopening and reworking of infantile conflicts and a reorganization and consolidation of the personality on a more mature and healthier level. As in any developmental crisis, the risk of regressive deterioration must be balanced against the promise of progressive growth and mastery. The crucial determining element, against which the regression must be balanced, and in terms of which the destructive or constructive potential of the regression can be measured, is the therapeutic alliance. A firm and stable alliance offers a buffer against excessive regression and a basis for positive growth.

Analytic Regression

In the face of the analytic regression, it is necessary to emphasize the importance of the continuing influence of the quality and stability of early object relations. This developmental accomplishment is an essential guarantee against the dangers of regression. During the course of analysis, a secure one-to-one relationship must be established, maintained, and continuously integrated. The basic conflicts which underlie the pathology of analyzable neurotic patients, however, are not primarily in the area of one-to-one relationships. These patients were able to reach a level developmentally in which a genuine triangular conflict had at least begun to emerge. The resolution of this conflict at the close of the oedipal period had resulted in the establishment of a relatively closed personality system. The analytic regression serves to reopen this basic conflict and thus offers the possibility for reworking and resolving these conflicts in the service of progressive mastery.

Classical analysis thus involves a reopening of basic conflicts which had been dealt with in the course of development by neurotic, inadequate, or excessive defenses. A more adaptive resolution of these conflicts is possible, however, only if and insofar as the ego functions which depend on secure object relations are not only maintained in the face of regression but also strengthened. Psychoanalysis can be compared—for both analyst and patient—to the situation for both parent and child in working through the infantile neurosis. The analyst must not only interpret the manifestations of the transference neurosis, but he must maintain an objectivity and distance in dealing with repressed instinctual derivatives. He becomes like the parent who can recognize the child's incestuous fantasies without gratifying them.

It is generally agreed among analysts that regression is a necessary preliminary to a new and better resolution of intrapsychic conflicts. The need to revive and work through conflicts derived from early levels of development is central to the analytic process. Nonetheless certain forms of regression may lead to interminable or unsuccessful analyses. The differentiation between different types and degrees of regression can be approached in terms of psychoanalysis as a general developmental psychology. Just as psychic development presents regressive hazards, so there are dangers in psychoanalytic regression as well. We can relate the theory of psychoanalytic therapy to the developmental process. A crucial differentiation that needs to be made is between those ego capacities which are needed for progressive maturational and developmental achievement and those ego defenses which must be renounced during the course of transference analysis. These aspects of ego functioning represent different developmental levels and different developmental accomplishments.

The theory of psychoanalytic therapy is based on Freud's dynamic hypothesis and the notion of intrapsychic conflict. Repression and the related dynamic defenses tend to close off and render relatively inaccessible certain fantasies, wishes, and memories. The emergence or return to consciousness of these repressed contents would produce a situation of internal danger. The repressive forces of the mental apparatus tend to contain these elements in a relatively closed system. Signal anxiety serves as the motive for repression, but we now recognize that the development of signal anxiety and its related defenses requires a certain level of the organization of psychic structure and functioning. The analytic process, therefore, requires the capacity to recognize, tolerate and master the anxiety which is mobilized by the analytic regression and which represents a specific internal danger. This is only possible if previously maintained neurotic defenses are gradually undermined and thus become less effective in maintaining the closed repressive system.

The analytic process, therefore, requires that the patient have the capacity to regress to a sufficient degree to allow the reopening of conflicts which had been previously closed off by defenses which were the ego's response to signal anxiety. Regression leads to a diminution of unconscious defenses and a re-emergence of unconscious conflicts. The regression need not undermine the patient's capacity for reality testing nor his capacity for sustained object relations. The regression can affect the defensive ego and its related instinctual derivatives without affecting basic ego capacities. Successful analysis requires a capacity to relinquish neurotic defenses in the interest of further growth. It also requires the mastery of developmental tasks which concern the stabilization of early object relations and ego identifications which set a limit to and minimize the possibility of serious ego regression. We must distinguish, therefore, between instinctual regression and ego regression in the analytic process. Instinctual regression results from an increase of instinctual energy in the relatively closed system. This brings about a mobilization of anxiety as a signal of internal danger and a partial reopening of the closed system. The amount of instinctual energy thus exceeds the specific defensive capacity of the ego to contain it. This regressive release of energy is consistent with the maintenance of considerable secondary autonomy, as long as the basic ego functions remain intact. The stability and security of these basic ego capacities, developed in the patient's early object relations, sets a limit to the severity of the regression. If such ego functions are undermined, the regression can be more damaging than adaptive. Thus instinctual regression is essential to the analytic process and can be regarded as potentially adaptive. Ego regression impedes the analytic process and must be regarded as ominous.

Transference

The notion of transference was originally conceived in terms of the displacement of the repressed wishes and fantasies derived from childhood onto the person of the analyst. The formation of the transference neurosis was regarded as another form of compromise between repressed content and repressing forces, like dreams and neurotic symptoms. Transference resistance was regarded as due to the threat involved in the emergence of unconscious material. After Freud's proposing of the structural theory, the superego elements of the transference came into prominence. The superego was the heir to the oedipal situation, and the analyst thus came to serve not merely as an object for displaced incestuous oedipal wishes and fantasies but also as the projected representative of parental prohibitions that had been internalized in the superego. The shift in emphasis gave the analysis of superego elements and the mitigation of the patient's superego severity a prominent position in the rationale of psychoanalytic treatment and technique for many years.

The role of early object relations in the development of both the ego and the superego has been increasingly acknowledged and has played an increasingly important role in the understanding of transference phenomena. Some authors have emphasized the recapitulation in the transference of crucial aspects of the mother-child relationship. The analyst's role in this context has been described as like that of the gratifying parent. In these terms it is perhaps useful to distinguish between elements in the transference relationship which are derived from the earliest object relations—and thus are essentially dyadic—and elements which are derived from the oedipal situation, which is essentially triadic or triangular. Successful analysis not only requires resolution of the oedipal conflicts but also involves the revival and reworking of earlier pregenital conflicts. The transference neurosis can be expected to embrace both types of elements and both levels of development.

It should be noted that not all the distortions or misperceptions that the patient brings to the relationship with the analyst—particularly in his initial perception of the analyst—can be attributed to transference. Seen in the broader context of the patient's ego development and capacity for object relations, other elements of his personality may interfere with his capacity to relate to the analyst. Such distortions may be determined by relatively stable aspects of the patient's personality structure which relate to his capacity to achieve and maintain a stable object relationship. In the initial interaction between analyst and patient, transference elements may play a role, but the patient's responses probably reflect more of his own personality organization than the regressive emergence of previously unconscious infantile fantasies and wishes. Patients often bring a variety of pretreatment fantasies which also influence their perception of and relationship to the psychiatrist. The clarification of the patient's anxiety, suspicions, fears, and unrealistic hopes and expectations are not to be regarded as transference interpretations. The objective of such interventions on the part of the analyst is to support and reinforce the patient's capacities to enter and establish a meaningful therapeutic relationship.

The Therapeutic Alliance

The establishment of the therapeutic relationship is one of the most important aspects of the treatment process, and it is one of the major objectives of the early phases of treatment—whether analysis or psychotherapy. The analyst must somehow ally himself with the patient and the patient with himself in the work of the analysis. The "therapeutic alliance" can be described as a stable and positive relationship between the analyst and the patient which enables them to productively engage in the work of analysis. This allows a split to take place in the patient's ego. The observing part of the patient's ego allies itself with the analyst in a working relationship. It gradually identifies with the analyst in analyzing and modifying the pathological defenses which the defensive ego has put up against internal danger situations. The relationship between the patient's observant ego and the analyst is based on an object relation and depends on the patient's capacity to form and sustain a meaningful one-to-one relationship.

In terms of the maturity and stability of the patient's ego functions, his ability to maintain a real relationship to the analyst as a separate individual seems to be closely related to his capacity for therapeutic alliance. This requires the maintenance of self-object differentiation, tolerance and mastery of ambivalence, and the capacity to distinguish fantasy from reality in the transference. From the other side, it is also recognized that the analyst contributes to the relationship. The latter's personality and his own individual characteristics have an important influence on the establishment of the therapeutic alliance and the analytic situation. The analyst, therefore, enters the analytic process as a real person, not merely as a transference object. The recognition and the understanding of this aspect of the analytic situation should be clearly differentiated from any excessive activity or inappropriate participation in the analytic relationship by the analyst. It should be recognized, however, that the analyst's real characteristics can interfere with the achieving of a basic working relationship between him and the patient. This impediment to establishing the therapeutic alliance can interfere with a satisfactory working through and resolution of the transference neurosis.

The analytic situation can thus be regarded as a situation of therapeutically induced and controlled conflict. The capacity to bear and resolve this induced conflict is contingent on the individual's success at a preoedipal level in establishing and maintaining a secure and trusting relationship which recognizes the separateness and integrity of the participating individuals. The therapeutic alliance, therefore, requires as its basis the capacity to tolerate anxiety and depression, to accept reality limitations, and to differentiate between the mature and infantile aspects of experience. The therapeutic alliance serves a double function. It acts on the one hand as a significant barrier to regression of the ego in the analytic process. It serves, on the other hand, as a fundamental aspect of the analytic situation against which the wishes, feelings and fantasies stirred up and evoked by the transference neurosis can be measured and evaluated. The achievement and maintenance of this relationship can often be very difficult, since they depend in part on the patient's psychopathology and in part on the stage of analysis. In many pathological conditions—some character neuroses, borderline personalities, and severe neurotic disorders—it may be impossible to maintain any distinction clinically between the therapeutic alliance as a real object relationship and the emergence of the transference neurosis. Moreover, during the course of every successful analysis, the therapeutic alliance must evolve into transference analysis if the patient is to be able to work through the impediments to his optimal maturity and capacity for object relations.

The therapeutic alliance, then, depends on the mobilization of ego resources on which the capacity for object relations and reality testing rest. The analyst's technique must be directed toward eliciting the patient's capacities to establish a relationship that must be able to withstand the inevitable distortions and regressive aspects of the transference. Since the ego capacities involved are so closely related to the resolution of pregenital conflicts experienced in the context of one-to-one relationships, it is not surprising that, when the analysis begins to reach the level of pregenital conflicts, the relationship which forms the basis of the therapeutic alliance must itself be included in the transference analysis. It is inevitable ultimately that certain fundamental features of the therapeutic alliance become integral to the analysis of the transference neurosis.

Therapeutic Alliance vs. Transference Neurosis

It is important, therefore, at least clinically in the analysis of patients who meet the criteria for analyzability, to distinguish between the therapeutic alliance, defined as a real object relation which fosters the mobilization of the patient's relatively autonomous ego resources, and the transference neurosis, in which the analyst serves as the object for displaced and unresolved infantile wishes and fantasies. The differentiation between the establishing and maintenance of the therapeutic alliance in the early stages of analysis and the fact that this relationship must ultimately involve transference interpretation if the analysis is to be successfully terminated, is particularly relevant to the analyses of neurotic patients for whom the problem of reality testing is not significant. The analysis of hysterical patients is interesting in this regard. The initial transference neurosis of such patients tends to present unmistakably oedipal material. But we have learned to recognize and appreciate the importance of underlying oral factors in the genesis of hysterical disorders. This makes it necessary to emphasize the establishment in the early stages of analysis of a meaningful therapeutic alliance. This simultaneously elicits the patient's more mature ego resources and limits the premature early development of a regressive transference. In the terminal stages of analysis of these patients, however, it becomes increasingly clear that the resolution of conflicts initially presented at an oedipal level depends on the successful analysis of conflicts from a much earlier level of development. This involves conflicts related to achieving early object relations and the acceptance of reality and its limitations. These are the elements which form the basis of the therapeutic alliance.

This raises the question of the analyst's role in helping to establish the therapeutic alliance—especially in the early stages of analysis. The nature and degree of the analyst's active intervention in the opening hours of analysis are matters of considerable discussion and controversy. The transference neurosis usually develops only slowly and gradually, so that premature interpretations may not be productive in the early hours. This has tended to foster the excessive use of prolonged silence, lack of participation, rigidity—as if any reference to the analytic situation or the person of the analyst was substantially a transference interpretation and thus to be avoided. It is our opinion, however, that serious problems in subsequent analysis of the transference are due to the failure to achieve a meaningful alliance in the initial stages of the treatment. Suitable verbal interventions by the analyst help to establish the alliance.

The position of the analyst in the early stages of treatment can be compared to the position of a mother adapting to the innate dispositions of her child. From the beginning, the analytic situation requires mobilization of those resources of the patient which derive from developmental attainments at a very early level. Such a mobilization can be fostered by the analyst's intuitive adaptive responses which are comparable to the adaptive responses of the successful parent. The analyst responds to the anxiety aroused by the regressive impairment of the patient's previously established defensive achievements. The regression is inevitable and a necessary part of the analytic process, but it must be contained. It is a regression in the service of the ego, and therefore must retain and strengthen the patient's capacity for basic trust and positive identification in order that the analytic process may work to the patient's advantage.

To summarize the significant points regarding the therapeutic alliance, we can say that in the analytic situation a relationship must exist over and above the transference neurosis which enables the patient to differentiate between objective reality and the distortions and projections of the transference. The relationship is influenced by current external reality and is modified by the real personality characteristics of the analyst—as opposed to transference elements. The capacities which enable the patient to form the therapeutic alliance derive from early pregenital levels. As the transference analysis begins to touch on these levels of pregenital conflicts, transference neurosis and therapeutic alliance tend to merge, often to a degree that they become indistinguishable. The elements of the therapeutic alliance merge as specifically dyadic elements with the previously apparent triadic elements of the transference.

The therapeutic alliance derives from early stages in the development of object relations and reality testing. This is a period in which the child has made decisive steps toward achieving a separate identity. Encouragement of the child's efforts for independence are as important in later stages of infancy as are security and gratification in the early phases. The capacity for mutual trust and understanding, in terms of which the inevitability of limitations, frustrations, and disappointments can be accepted and understood, derives from the earliest mother-child relationship. Developmental failure at this level predisposes the child to a seriously regressive transference neurosis in adult treatment. Successful treatment must involve revival of these basic conflicts over object relations, but it is essential in the process that a relatively mature and stable object relationship should be established in order to avoid harmful regression to a level at which reality testing might be seriously impaired.

The therapeutic process in psychoanalysis, therefore, involves a dual approach. The analyst must respond to the patient both in terms of the transference material and in terms of the therapeutic alliance. He must continue to respond intuitively to the patient's affect, particularly the patient's basic need to feel accepted and understood as a real person. He must also, at the same time, objectively recognize and interpret for the patient material—in the forms of verbalizations, dreams, fantasies, actions, and other nonverbal communications—which reveals the wishes and fantasies derived from the transference neurosis. Successful analysis requires the continual recognition of the difference between the transference neurosis, which is changing and variable during the course of the analysis, and the therapeutic alliance, which remains as a continuing and stable nucleus of the treatment.

It should be added that no patient will be capable of tolerating the stress and anxiety aroused by the emergence of the transference neurosis unless the therapeutic alliance is established and maintained throughout the course of the analysis. The analogy to the developmental process is useful here. Only the child who has been able to establish an early positive ego identification and capacity for object relations can maintain positive object relations and attain further ego identifications during the subsequent periods of development which culminate in the oedipal situation. Similarly, only the patient who has established a positive and secure therapeutic alliance can tolerate the reopening of neurotic conflicts which had previously been closed off by neurotic or excessive defenses. The analyst remains objective in his interpretation of fantasies and wishes derived from the repressed past. Thus he resembles the parent who can recognize without gratifying the child's oedipal fantasies. He must also continue to present himself to the patient as an object for continuing positive ego identification through the therapeutic alliance.

The Analytic Situation

It is useful in considering clinical aspects of psychoanalysis to think in terms of aspects of the analytic relationship. We can focus first on the analytic situation. The latter is the setting within which the analytic process takes place, specifically a one-to-one relationship between the analyst and the patient which imposes certain demands and exacts certain frustrations from the patient. The structure of the analytic situation is such that even the most mature and stable patients experience significant objective anxiety. The degree and quality of the anxiety are obviously subject to considerable variation and reflect the patient's previous life experience, including the events leading immediately to undertaking the analysis. The successful negotiation of the initial stage of the analysis, however, involves the establishing of the analytic situation—the achievement of a special object relation which determines the nature and quality of the therapeutic alliance. The therapeutic alliance, therefore, involves both an object relationship and ultimately an ego identification. It should be noted that our description and understanding of the analytic situation cannot adequately be formulated in terms of intrapsychic dynamics. We are dealing with a relationship in which both analyst and patient are actively involved. The nature and meaning of this central relationship constitute the essence of the analytic situation.

The analytic situation, therefore, depends on and requires certain basic qualities or capacities in the patient. He must have a capacity to maintain basic trust in the absence of immediate gratification. He must be able to maintain self-object differentiation in the absence of the object. He must retain a potential capacity to accept the limitations of reality. The patient must be able to acknowledge his own limitations and lack of omnipotence, and at the same time must be able to appreciate that the failure of the object to gratify wishes and demands may not be due to hostility or rejection, but may reflect realistic limitations that have to be accepted. These capacities represent a mobilization of preanalytic ego resources and they are essential to establishing the analytic situation.

These characteristics are an integral part of a meaningful doctor-patient relationship in any form of therapy. They are a major goal in the treatment of maturational or situational crises or in the treatment of seriously disturbed patients on a long-term basis. But the specific features of the analytic situation set it apart from other forms of therapy which rely on a central relationship. The analytic situation requires that the patient place himself in a passive and recumbent position. It requires that he abandon certain cognitive and verbal controls and that he deprive himself of certain forms of perceptual and verbal feedback. He must tolerate the anxiety, helplessness, and dependence that this situation arouses. He is required to place his confidence in an unseen and largely silent object in this new and strange setting. Finally he is asked to establish a new and special relationship and to accept a new identification which will change his own inner attitudes.

Phases of the Analytic Process

The establishing of the analytic situation and the therapeutic alliance sets the stage on which the analytic process can begin to work. The analytic process can be roughly divided into three phases. The initial phase is concerned with the establishment of the analytic situation. We have been discussing this phase in the immediately preceding pages. The second phase is concerned with the emergence and interpretation of the transference neurosis. The last phase involves a working through of transference elements and the problems of separation and termination of the analysis.

The development of the transference neurosis involves a reopening and reworking of oedipal conflicts. These basic conflicts are relived and re-experienced in the transference and thus become available to the patient for interpretation and understanding. The emergence, reworking, and resolution of these conflicts involve a number of therapeutic attainments. The therapeutic attainments are paralleled by the developmental attainments in the resolution of the original conflicts. This involves the development of a capacity to initiate and sustain intrapsychic defenses against instinctual wishes. It involves an integration of both the autonomous ego and the ego ideal in a positive identification with the parent of the same sex. It involves the renunciation of sexualized goals in regard to the parent of the opposite sex in favor of a strengthening of a positive object relationship with that parent. It involves a successful neutralization or sublimation of the aggressive energy mobilized in the rivalry with the parent of the same sex. Thus the working through of the transference aims at a resolution of these basic conflicts in order to attain in some fashion the capacity for meaningful growth inherent in the resolution of oedipal issues.

The terminal phase of a successful analysis concerns itself in more specific and direct ways with the issues of autonomy and independence. These issues have been operative through the whole of the analysis but become particularly relevant in the final phase. As the end approaches, however, the patient's passive and dependent wishes are inevitably revived. The analyst's position in this final phase is considerably different from his position in the initial phase of the analysis. In the initial phase his position was comparable to that of a parent who was responding to the regressive passive and dependent aspects of the infantile neurosis. In the terminal phase of the analysis, however, he functions more like the parent of a late adolescent who is willing to foster and support the maturation and autonomy of the child. The passivity and dependence which are essential to the analytic process become increasingly ego-alien as the process continues and are regarded as alien infantile wishes in the terminal phase. The patient tends instead to work toward a mature acceptance of realistic limits and begins to mobilize his resources in the direction of more secure autonomy and independence. The analyst is retained as an object for continuing positive identification. He also remains a potentially available object in case of future need. In these regards he is again like a good parent who remains available and supportive to the child even after the separation involved in growth has been accomplished. The ultimate achievement of maturity—whether for the child or for the patient—involves the recognition that he is neither so independent nor so invulnerable that he can do without the help and support of meaningful objects.

The reappearance of primitive fantasies and separation anxiety represents the regressive concomitant that we have learned to recognize in any maturational crisis. Although the analyst may interpret dependent wishes as they turn up, the analyst is no longer responding to dependent needs. The patient must achieve more active motivation for autonomy while the analyst is realistically retained as the object for identification within the area of autonomous ego functioning. It is hardly surprising that this complex task should be accompanied by anxiety, depression and regressive wishes. The work of termination involves the interpretation and ultimate integration of those relatively passive components of the therapeutic alliance which will facilitate the patient's future capacity for regression in the service of the ego. The patient must surrender his passive and dependent wishes. The analyst must be renounced. The patient must mobilize those basic resources which allow him to tolerate and master the anxiety and depression involved in such a renunciation. Termination is thus a form of mourning in which the analyst as a parent surrogate is renounced. The mourning process leads to mastery of the mobilized affects, which substantially increases the patient's future autonomy and freedom.

The Developmental Analogue

Thus we can re-emphasize the central proposition of this chapter. The psychoanalytic process presents many significant analogies to the developmental process. Successful development in the later stages of infancy depends on the quality of object relations established in earlier interactions between the child and its parents—particularly the mother. Similarly, successful emergence and resolution of the transference neurosis in the analytic process is contingent on the establishment of the therapeutic alliance in the initial phase of treatment and its maintenance throughout the course of the analysis. The qualities in the analyst which best foster the therapeutic alliance correspond to the qualities of the successful parent who responds intuitively and adaptively to the child in ways which facilitate the latter's early ego development.

Psychic development—whether in the maturational process or in the analytic process—implies both regressive and progressive potentialities at all levels. Progression cannot take place without a regressive component. Such regression offers the potentiality for further mastery and adaptation only if the basic functions of the ego are maintained intact. This applies in any developmental context or crisis—in the infantile neurosis, in the reworking and resolution of the adolescent crisis, or in the working through and resolution of the analytic process. The essence of the analytic process, therefore, lies in controlled regression in the service of further mastery and growth.

The successful completion of the developmental process in childhood and adolescence leads to the independence, maturity, and significant autonomy and capacity for mastery in the young adult. Normal development leads to the achievement of a sense of identity. Similarly, the analytic process reaches its satisfactory termination in the patient's achievement of autonomy and independence. Clinical psychoanalysis and normal development require a process of separation which includes a process of grief and mourning, which leads ultimately to the reintegration of successful, positive, and stable ego identifications. The achievements of the developmental process and the achievements of the analytic process, however, are neither final nor absolute. The process of growth and acquisition of strengths continues through the course of life. It requires in progressive ways the capacity to accept the limitations of reality as one advances in age, in weakness, in countless disappointments, to face the ultimate reality of death. It requires the renunciation of fantasies of omnipotence. It requires an ability to seek and accept help when help is needed. Just as this willingness and capacity to accept help is an essential part of personal development in life, so it is in a similar sense an essential part of and a crucial acquisition of a successful analysis.

NOTES

1. S. Freud, *The Origins of Psychoanalysis*, ed. M. Bonaparte et al. (Garden City: Doubleday, 1957), letter 24.

2. E. R. Zetzel, "Concept and Content in Psychoanalytic Theory," in *The Capacity for Emotional Growth* (New York: International Universities Press, 1970), pp. 115–116.

3. H. Werner, *Comparative Psychology of Mental Development*, rev. ed. (New York: International Universities Press, 1957), cited in *The Collected Papers of David Rapaport*, ed. M. M. Gill (New York: Basic Books, 1967), pp. 821–822.

4. E. R. Zetzel, "Symptom Formation and Character Formation," *International Journal of Psychoanalysis* 45 (1965), p. 153.

5. Freud, *Origins of Psychoanalysis*, letter 96.

6. Freud, *Standard Edition of the Complete Psychological Works of Sigmund Freud*, ed. James Strachey et al., 23 vols. (London: Hogarth Press, 1953–1966), vol. 14, p. 16.

7. Freud, *Standard Edition*, vol. 4, p. 101.

8. Ibid., p. 137.

9. Freud, *Origins of Psychoanalysis*, letter 96.

10. Freud, *Standard Edition*, vol. 18, p. 253.

11. Ibid., vol. 11, p. 38.

12. Ibid., vol. 18, p. 9.

13. Ibid., vol. 2, p. 12.

14. Ibid., p. 7.

15. Freud, *Origins of Psychoanalysis*, letter 69.

16. Ibid., letter 71.

17. D. Rapaport, "A Historical Survey of Psychoanalytic Ego Psychology," in *Collected Papers*, pp. 745–757.

18. Freud, *Standard Edition*, vol. 20, p. 162.

19. Ibid., p. 110.

20. H. Hartmann and E. Kris, "The Genetic Approach in Psychoanalysis," *The Psychoanalytic Study of the Child* 1 (1945), p. 11.

21. Freud, *Standard Edition*, vol. 16, pp. 340–341.

22. Rapaport, "A Historical Survey of Psychoanalytic Ego Psychology," in *Collected Papers*, pp. 745–757.

23. Freud, *Standard Edition*, vol. 12, pp. 224–225.

24. Rapaport, "Psychoanalysis As a Developmental Psychology," in *Collected Papers*, pp. 820–852.

25. Freud, *Standard Edition*, vol. 7, p. 201.

26. Ibid., pp. 239–240.

27. Ibid., vol. 16, p. 347.

28. J. D. Benjamin, "The Innate and the Experiential in Child Development," in *Lectures in Experimental Psychiatry*, ed. H. Brosin (Pittsburgh: University of Pittsburgh Press, 1961), p. 34.

29. E. H. Erikson, "Observations on Sioux Education," *Journal of Psychology* 7 (1939), pp. 131–132.

30. Freud, *Standard Edition*, vol. 5, p. 595.

31. Ibid., vol. 4, pp. 307–308.

32. Ibid., vol. 5, p. 507.

33. Ibid., p. 597.

34. Ibid.

35. Ibid., pp. 599–600.

36. Ibid., pp. 607–608.

37. D. Rapaport, *Organization and Pathology of Thought* (New York: Columbia University Press, 1951), pp. 693–694.

38. Freud, *Standard Edition*, vol. 12, p. 219.

39. Ibid., vol. 5, p. 604.

40. Ibid., p. 542.

41. Ibid., p. 543.

42. Ibid., p. 548.

43. Ibid.

44. Ibid., vol. 13, p. 161.

45. Ibid., p. 95.

46. Ibid., vol. 12, pp. 219–220.

47. H. Hartmann, *Ego Psychology and the Problem of Adaptation* (New York: International Universities Press, 1939).

48. Freud, *Standard Edition*, vol. 12, p. 221.

49. Ibid., vol. 14, p. 94.

50. Ibid., p. 249.

51. Ibid., p. 247.

52. Ibid., vol. 16, p. 427.

53. Ibid., vol. 19, p. 56.

54. Ibid., vol. 23, pp. 145–146.

55. Dora's case is presented and discussed in Freud's "Fragment of an Analysis of a Case of Hysteria" (1905), in *Standard Edition*, vol. 7, pp. 3–122.

56. Freud, *Standard Edition*, vol. 19, pp. 28–29.

57. Ibid., vol. 20, pp. 154–156.

58. E. H. Erikson, *Childhood and Society*, 2d ed. (New York: Norton, 1963).

59. Ibid., p. 247.

60. Ibid., p. 249.

61. E. H. Erikson, *Identity and the Life Cycle* (New York: International Universities Press, 1959), pp. 56–57. In *Psychological Issues* 1 (1959).

62. Ibid., p. 68.

63. Ibid., p. 76.

64. Ibid.; see also, Erikson, *Childhood and Society*.

65. Erikson, *Identity and the Life Cycle*, p. 89.

66. Ibid., p. 113.

67. Freud, "Fragment of an Analysis of a Case of Hysteria," *Standard Edition*, vol. 7, pp. 3–122.

68. W. Mayer-Gross, W. Slater, and M. Roth, *Clinical Psychiatry*, 2d ed. (Baltimore: Williams and Wilkins, 1960), p. 6.

69. *Diagnostic and Statistical Manual of Mental Disorders,* 2d ed. (Washington, D.C., American Psychiatric Association, 1968).

70. B. E. Moore and B. D. Fine, eds., *A Glossary of Psychoanalytic Terms and Concepts* (New York: American Psychoanalytic Association, 1967), p. 19.

71. Freud, *Standard Edition,* vol. 12, pp. 224–225.

INDEX